QUALITATIVE RESEARCH IN SOCIAL WORK

INTRODUCING QUALITATIVE METHODS provides a series of volumes which introduce qualitative research to the student and beginning researcher. The approach is interdisciplinary and international.

One stream of the series provides texts on the key methodologies used in qualitative research. The other stream contains books on qualitative research for different disciplines or occupations. Both streams cover the basic literature in a clear and accessible style, but also cover the 'cutting edge' issues in the area.

SERIES EDITOR
David Silverman (Goldsmiths College)

EDITORIAL BOARD
Michael Bloor (University of Wales, Cardiff)
Barbara Czarniawska-Joerges (University of Gothenburg)
Norman Denzin (University of Illinois, Champagne)
Barry Glassner (University of Southern California)
Jaber Gubrium (University of Florida, Gainesville)
Anne Murcott (South Bank University)
Jonathan Potter (Loughborough University)

TITLES IN THE SERIES
Doing Conversational Analysis: A Practical Guide
Paul ten Have

Using Foucault's Methods
Gavin Kendall and Gary Wickham

The Quality of Qualitative Research
Clive Seale

Qualitative Evaluation
Ian Shaw

Researching Life Stories and Family Histories
Robert L. Miller

Categories in Text and Talk: A Practical Introduction to Categorization Analysis
Georiga Lepper

Focus Groups in Social Research
Michael Bloor, Jane Frankland, Michelle Thomas, Kate Robson

Qualitative Research Through Case Studies
Max Travers

Qualitative Research in Social Work
Ian Shaw and Nick Gould

QUALITATIVE RESEARCH IN SOCIAL WORK

Ian Shaw and Nick Gould

SAGE Publications
London · Thousand Oaks · New Delhi

H
62
S44

First published 2001

SAGE Publications Ltd
6 Bonhill Street
London EC2A 4PU

SAGE Publications Inc
2455 Teller Road
Thousand Oaks, California 91320

SAGE Publications India Pvt Ltd
32, M-Block Market
Greater Kailash – I
New Delhi 110 048

British Library Cataloguing in Publication data

A catalogue record for this book is available from the
British Library

ISBN 0 7619 6181 X
ISBN 0 7619 6182 8 (pbk)

Library of Congress Control Number available

Typeset by Type Study, Scarborough, North Yorkshire
Printed in Great Britain by Biddles Ltd, Guildford, Surrey

Contents

Acknowledgements   vii
Notes on Contributors   ix

**PART 1   THE SOCIAL WORK AGENDA FOR   1
QUALITATIVE RESEARCH**

  Introduction   3

1 The Social Work Context for Qualitative Research   14

2 A Review of Qualitative Research in Social Work   32

**PART 2   EXEMPLIFYING QUALITATIVE SOCIAL   47
WORK RESEARCH**

3 Caught Not Taught: Ethnographic Research at a Young   49
   People's Accommodation Project
   Tom Hall

4 Interviewing Interviewers and Knowing about Knowledge   60
   Jonathan Scourfield

5 Personal Troubles as Social Issues: A Narrative of Infertility   73
   in Context
   Catherine Kohler Riessman

6 'People Listened to What We Had to Say': Reflections on   83
   an Emancipatory Qualitative Evaluation
   Elizabeth Whitmore

7 Auto-Ethnography as Reflexive Inquiry: The Research Act   100
   as Self-Surveillance
   Sue White

8 Identifying Expert Social Work: Qualitative Practitioner   116
   Research
   Jan Fook

PART 3   QUALITATIVE WORK IN SOCIAL WORK   133

  9   Fieldwork Choices in Context   135

10   Inquiry and Action: Qualitative Research and Professional   157
     Practice

11   The Consequences of Qualitative Social Work Research   179

References   203
Index   225

Acknowledgements

IS and NG would like to thank Christine Morley of Deakin University, Australia for her invaluable help with library research.

Notes on Authors and Contributors

Jan Fook is currently professor of social work at Deakin University, Australia where she has been involved in establishing a new social work programme. She has practised as a social worker in the areas of intellectual disability and with overseas students, and has been a social work academic for approximately 20 years at several universities. Her teaching and research span the areas of critical practice, critical reflection, practice research and professional expertise. She has authored or co-authored 30 book chapters and articles. Her books include *Radical Casework* and *The Reflective Researcher*. She has recently co-edited two books on postmodernism and social work practice. Her most recent books include (with Martin Ryan and Linette Hawkins) *Professional Expertise: Practice, Theory and Education for Working in Uncertainty* and *Breakthroughs in Practice: Social Workers Theorise Critical Moments* (edited with Lindsey Napier). She is currently working on a book on critical practice (forthcoming with Sage).

Nick Gould is reader in social work, and currently head of the department of social and policy sciences at the University of Bath, UK. He has been a social work practitioner in local authority and forensic settings, and maintains an involvement in mental health practice. He has published widely in the social work field, including *Reflective Learning For Social Work*, co-edited with Imogen Taylor, and *Information Management in Social Services*, Volumes 1 and 2. His current research interests include professional learning, new technology and social work, and the development of qualitative methodologies.

Tom Hall is an anthropologist and a lecturer in the school of social sciences at Cardiff University. His research interests include: youth and inequality, homelessness, and 'street' life. He is the author of *No Place Like Home* (2001), an ethnography of youth homelessness, published by Pluto Press.

Catherine Kohler Riessman is professor of social work and sociology at Boston University, USA. Her publications are in women's health/medical sociology, gender and divorce, qualitative methods, and the narrative study of lives. Using narrative methods of interviewing and analysis, she has examined accounts of a variety of life events that disrupt individuals' assumptions about biographical order, specifically divorce, chronic illness, and infertility. Her books include *Divorce Talk* (Rutgers University Press, 1990), and *Narrative Analysis* (Sage, 1993). She is currently comparing narratives of childless women from South India to analyse the performance of identity in research interviews.

Jonathan Scourfield job-shares a lectureship in the Cardiff University school of social sciences, UK, and is a former practitioner in the fields of HIV, drug and alcohol rehabilitation, and probation. Most of his published research has focused on gender in social welfare, and the sociology of men. His doctoral research, which he draws on in his chapter for this book, is an ethnographic study of the construction of gender in child protection social work. He has also researched the provision of programmes in the UK for men who are violent towards women, probation officers' views on working with men, and the experiences of black and minority ethnic children living in the South Wales valleys. He is currently engaged in two funded research projects which use solely qualitative methods. These are a study of the formation of national identity in children aged from 8 to 11, and a study of outcomes for children in family group conferences.

Ian Shaw is a reader in Cardiff University school of social sciences. His work combines aspects of the social science of welfare practice, the development of qualitative and evaluation methodology, research on several aspects of social exclusion, and innovative learning methods linked to the development of computer-assisted learning software. He is co-editor of the journal *Qualitative Social Work*, launched from 2002 (Sage). His recent books include *Qualitative Evaluation* (1999, Sage) and *Evaluation and Social Work Practice* (with Joyce Lishman, 1999, Sage). He is presently co-editing with Jennifer Greene and Mel Mark a *Handbook of Evaluation* for Sage, and facilitating a user-led evaluation of an advocacy scheme for older people.

Sue White is a lecturer in the department of applied social science at the University of Manchester. Her principal research interests are in the discursive construction of child health and welfare and the practical-moral dimensions of professional practice. She has recently completed an ethnographic study of clinical judgement, institutional discourse and inter-professional relations in a child health setting. She is the co-author (with Carolyn Taylor) of *Practising Reflexivity in Health and Welfare: Making Knowledge* (2000, Open University Press) and is currently writing a book on clinical judgement. Prior to her academic career, she was the manager of a hospital based social work service for children and families.

Elizabeth Whitmore, known to most as Bessa, has been a social work educator and practitioner for 30 years. Her focus on participatory and emancipatory approaches to evaluation and research came as a logical extension to her practice in working with grassroots and marginalized groups. Bessa is currently an associate professor at the Carleton University School of Social Work in Ottawa, Canada. Her publications include *Understanding and Practicing Participatory Evaluation* (1998, New Directions for Evaluation, Volume 80, Jossey-Bass) and *Seeds of Fire: Social Development in an Era of Globalism* (2000), co-authored with M.W. Wilson (Fernwood, CCISD and Apex Press).

Part 1

THE SOCIAL WORK AGENDA FOR
QUALITATIVE RESEARCH

Introduction

It would not be unreasonable to expect a book such as this to fit into some bigger picture, and for its value to be assessed in the context of that picture. What is that larger context? The several writers of this book share, with some variation, expectations that research in social work should:

- contribute to the development and evaluation of social work practice and services
- enhance social work's moral purpose
- strengthen social work's disciplinary character and location
- promote social work inquiry marked by rigour, range, variety, depth and progression.

Social work practice and services may gain in three broad ways from research. First, research may shed light on the processes and outcomes of practice, thus assisting in building knowledge and skills for practice. American research has contributed relatively strongly to outcomes research, through, for example, the sustained development of task-centred intervention. More recent work on reflective practice, stimulated by Donald Schon and others, is also a form of intervention research. Second, social work has also gained from the wider range of knowledge-questioning research that seeks to describe or explain social problems encountered by human services practitioners. The phrase 'knowledge-questioning' serves partly to ensure we keep open the question whether social work research is progressive and beneficial.

Third, practice and research may mutually benefit from considering how far the perspectives and methods of one provide a template for the other. For example, is social work akin to research, in the sense that it is marked by 'the systematic collection of data, the cautious use of inference and the consideration of alternative explanations, the application where possible of research based knowledge, and the discriminating evaluation of the outcomes of one's efforts' (Reid, 1995: 2040)? The question is far from straightforward, and it surfaces several times in the subsequent chapters of this book.

The expectation that social work research should be assessed by the extent to which it enhances the strength with which the moral purpose of social work is promoted, is both substantial and complex. The infusion of practice, methodology and research utilization with criteria of justice is one of the most contested and central issues facing social work. The problem is tackled in two main ways in this book. First, we wish to reflect on the different moral and political positions that share a common commitment to justice-led research and practice. It would be premature to rally round one particular flag, just as it would be inconceivable to evacuate social work research of a justice agenda. Second, we will give space to addressing the question whether there is a direct connection between methodology and justice. More particularly, we will consider whether qualitative methodologies are especially congenial to the promotion of justice in social work services and practice. These discussions surface in several of the contributors' chapters and in Chapters 1, 2 and 10.

Research will also be judged according to its contribution to strengthening social work's disciplinary character and location. We do not think social work researchers and academics need be too preoccupied with the more arcane reaches of debates as to whether social work is a distinct discipline. But we do believe that disciplinary issues such as theorizing, conceptualization, doctoral level work, practice/higher education interfaces, and research ethics are ignored at our peril.

Finally, we suggested that social work research, and books thereon, should be judged by the extent to which they promote social work inquiry marked by rigour, range, variety, depth and progression. This is more likely to be achieved if we

1. Avoid ethnocentrism. Social work and its research enterprise are not hermetically sealed from cognate enterprises in the fields of education, health, criminal justice, and evaluation. Social work research has special characteristics. It is a large part of our hope to demonstrate this in the chapters that follow. But social work research, though difficult, is not more difficult or demanding than research in education or health. We have no reason to be precious regarding our professional enterprise.
2. Remember – but are not stifled by the realization – that regimes of truth are regimes of power.
3. Eschew sentimentalism of the kind that refuses to question dearly held positions, or launches attacks on straw figures. Naïve constructionism and relativism, attacks on so-called positivism, and uncritical adoption of the latest research vogue, whether it be of methods (e.g. focus groups) or methodology (e.g. critical realism), are among the less than helpful trends that leave us feeling intellectually and occasionally morally queasy.

Doubts have sometimes been raised as to whether qualitative research is adequately equipped to deliver these gains for social work and social science. There have been a number of such doubts, the focus of which varies according to the direction from which they come. For example, adherents of conventional research strategies have been heard to argue for the greater benefits of tightly designed evaluative research on the grounds that such research is more adapted to the needs of social work. Qualitative research, so it is thought, is ill-adapted to shed light on social work outcomes, is sometimes lacking in rigour, is not susceptible to enabling generalization to other contexts, and, more generally, is less likely to yield findings that are useful in a clear, instrumental form (e.g. Macdonald, 1999; Thyer, 1989, 2000). We will have a good deal to say about these issues of rigour, outcomes, generalization and research uses through this book – both by way of illustration in the core contributed chapters, and by further reflection in the early and final chapters.

Qualitative research within social work and related professions has also come under 'friendly fire' from some quarters within mainstream ethnographic research. The origins of this, especially in Britain, can be found in the development of social science disciplines, and the divergent paths of sociology and social policy. This can be put, admittedly over simply, as aiming to achieve discipline development in the case of sociology, and applied relevance in the case of social policy (Atkinson et al., 1988; Finch, 1986; Jacob, 1987). Qualitative research, particularly when it has a strong applied agenda, has been criticized for being atheoretical or lacking rigour, for promoting a diluted, token form of ethnography, and for being generally methodologically weak.

We will resist any knee-jerk 'not guilty' pleas to these charges. It does neither social work nor qualitative research a service to either caricature or unquestioningly dismiss criticisms from conventional or qualitative methodologists. Social work research too often lacks methodological imagination. Decisions about methods seem to be treated as technical matters, to be taken with naïve pragmatism. This unnecessarily strengthens the arms of critics, insofar as pragmatists 'exist in splendid isolation from developments and debates in research methodology outside of social work' (Trinder, 2000: 43). The response in the following chapters is to seek to exemplify imaginative and uncompromising qualitative methodology in the contributed chapters, and to reflect further on methodological issues, for example in Chapters 2 and 9. We take a similar stance regarding theorizing. Several of the contributors write explicitly regarding theorizing within their research, and we subsequently reflect in a sustained way on the place of theorizing within qualitative social work research in the final chapter.

Criticisms of qualitative social work research have also come from within social work. For example, some research funders, especially within government departments in Western countries, too often mistrust qualitative research as anecdotal on the one hand or guilty of mystification on the other. The first of these criticisms may be based on a misreading of the logics of qualitative research. If so, then mutual conversations are called for, and the underlying issue of the bases for generalization brought to the foreground. We do this in Chapter 11. The second charge of mystification has been conceded by some qualitative researchers. For example,

Janesick aspires to an accessible language, and concludes that students 'are more excited about theory, practice and praxis when they are not excluded from the conversation' (Janesick, 1998: 3). Her hopes for qualitative research – with which we entirely concur – are that it will disrupt, educate and engage, inspire, demystify and democratize.

Qualitative research has also been criticized for being methodology-led, for example by feminist practitioners and researchers, and by activists in the disability movement. Linked to this have been criticisms that it does not go far enough in its engagement with participatory methods and practices (e.g. Heron, 1996). Issues of justice, empowerment and user-led inquiry recur constantly through the following pages. Yet, we are left with an unresolved question.

> There is a central and perhaps inescapable paradox in social research. The need to know is based on the one hand on a wish to make a social problem visible and to empower people to combat that problem. Yet knowledge of a problem may lead to growth in social control, and efforts to make a problem visible may make people more likely to live for the record and to avoid visibility. The social worker and the researcher have to work with the paradox that they seek to be empowering and yet in so doing risk increasing people's marginality – the wish to understand in itself increases the risk of greater social exclusion. (Shaw, 1998: 35)

We say towards the end of this Introduction that the contributors were asked to write without compromising strong allegiances, yet with critical awareness of the contradictions and lacunæ associated with their position. If these twin commitments mark the whole book we will not be disappointed.

Qualitative research

We have taken for granted so far that we can refer to qualitative research without undue ambiguity. However, any attempt to list the shared characteristics of qualitative research will fall short of universal agreement, and some think the effort itself is misguided. Nonetheless, many qualitative researchers would identify with the majority of these descriptors.

- It involves immersion in situations of *everyday life*. 'These situations are typically "banal" or normal ones, reflective of the everyday life of individuals, groups, societies and organizations' (Miles and Huberman, 1994: 6). It involves 'looking at the ordinary in places where it takes unaccustomed forms', so that 'understanding a people's culture exposes their normalness without reducing their particularity' (Geertz, 1973: 14). Geertz introduced the phrase 'thick description' to describe what goes on in such research. Traditionally, qualitative research is conducted

th?h long-term contact with the field. Hall and Whitmore raise
iss of enduring contact in their contributed research accounts.

- Th searcher's role is to gain an overview of the *whole* of the culture
  an ntext under study. The word 'holistic' is often used.
- Ho om is pursued through inquiry into the *particular*. 'The anthropologist characteristically approaches . . . broader interpretations . . . from
  the direction of exceedingly extended acquaintance with extremely
  small matters.' Grand realities of Power, Faith, Prestige, Love, etc. are
  confronted 'in contexts obscure enough . . . to take the capital letters
  off' (Geertz, 1973: 21). Qualitative researchers 'make the case palpable'
  (Eisner, 1991: 39).
- The whole and the particular are held in tension. 'Small facts speak to
  large issues' (Geertz, 1973: 23), and 'in the particular is located a general
  theme' (Eisner, 1991: 39). This process is anything but obvious or simple
  – what we understand about individual service users, particular social
  workers, local clinics, and so on, may not be transferable in a straightforward way to understanding other service users, social workers or
  clinics.
- 'The researcher attempts to capture data on the perceptions of local
  actors "from the inside", through a process of deep attentiveness, of
  empathic understanding (*verstehen*), and of suspending or "bracketing"
  preconceptions about the topics under discussion' (Miles and Huberman, 1994: 6). Michael Agar[1] talks in this context about the need for
  us to have 'a theory of noticing', and to look for 'rich points'.
- A caveat is in order. This stance is sometimes referred to as one of
  'ethnomethodological indifference' (after Garfinkel). However, it need
  not preclude a normative position. Indeed, qualitative approaches 'can
  effectively give voice to the normally silenced and can poignantly illuminate what is typically masked' (Greene, 1994: 541).
- Respondent or *member categories* are kept to the foreground throughout
  the research. This is linked to the strong inductive tradition in qualitative research – a commitment to the imaginative production of new
  concepts, through the cultivation of openness on the part of the
  researcher.
- Qualitative research is *interpretive*. 'A main task is to explicate the ways
  people in particular settings come to understand, account for, take
  action, and otherwise manage their day-to-day situations' (Miles and
  Huberman, 1994: 7). Hence, 'qualitative data are not so much about
  "behaviour" as they are about *actions* which carry with them intentions
  and meanings, and lead to consequences' (p. 10). This is partly what is
  meant when the word 'constructivist' is used.
- Relatively little standardized instrumentation is used, especially at the
  outset. The researcher is essentially the main instrument in the study.
  It is here that the important word 'reflexive' often occurs – referring
  to the central part played by the subjectivities of the researcher and of
  those being studied. Qualitative fieldwork is not straightforward. 'The

features that count in a setting do not wear their labels on theireve' (Eisner, 1991: 33). The part played by the self in qualitative resezalso raises the special significance of questions of ethics in qutive research, and renders the relationship between researcl and researched central to the activity.

- Finally, 'most analysis is done in words' (Miles and Huberman, 1994: 7). This is true – perhaps even more so – with the advent of increasingly sophisticated software for analysing qualitative data. There are frequent references in this connection to 'texts'. Judgement and persuasion by reason are deeply involved, and in qualitative research the facts never speak for themselves.

Is there a central organizing idea behind this characterization of qualitative research? Maybe not, and anyway the question is not very interesting. But we like, for example, Elliot Eisner's comment that qualitative research slows down the perception and invites exploration, and releases us from the stupor of the familiar, thus contributing to a state of 'wide-awakeness'. He compares this to what happens when we look at a painting. If there is a core – a qualitative eye – it has been expressed in different ways. For Riessman, it is 'Scepticism about universalising generalisations; respect for particularity and context; appreciation of reflexivity and standpoint; and the need for empirical evidence' (Riessman, 1994a: xv).

Qualitative research is not a unified tradition. The term qualitative 'refers to a family of approaches with a very loose and extended kinship, even divorces'. 'Beyond focus on text . . . it is sometimes hard to see the relation-ship between what various qualitative scholars do. They use very different kinds of texts . . . They also treat texts in radically different ways' (Riessman, 1994a: xii). These differences of research *practice* stem from diverse *theoretical* positions. For example, *symbolic interactionism* is concerned with studying subjective meanings and individual ascriptions of meaning. Symbolic interactionist research is founded on the premises that

- people act towards things on the basis of the meanings such things have for them
- the meaning is derived from interactions one has with one's fellows
- meanings are handled in, and modified through, an interpretive process used by the person in dealing with the things encountered (Flick, 1998).

These processes form the starting point for empirical work. 'The reconstruc-tion of such subjective viewpoints becomes the instrument for analysing social worlds' (Flick, 1998: 17). There has been a major research interest in the forms such viewpoints take. These include subjective theories about things (e.g. lay theories of health, education, counselling, or social work), and narratives such as life histories, autobiographies, and deviant careers.

Ethnomethodology addresses how people produce social reality through interactive processes. 'The focus is not the subjective meaning for the participants of an interaction and its contents but how this interaction is organised. The research topic becomes the study of the routines of everyday life' (Flick, 1998: 20). Interaction is assumed by ethnomethodologists to be structurally organized, and to be both shaped by and in turn shape the context. Hence, interaction repays detailed attention, because it is never disorderly, accidental or irrelevant.

We avoid a partisan position on traditions and schools within qualitative social science. Nonetheless, we believe that social work researchers have been unduly selective in their awareness of developments in qualitative methodology. For example, in Chapter 1 we argue that qualitative social work research should be more strongly grounded in an understanding of and puzzling about issues of context. We also think that the concentration of qualitative research on the local, the small scale and the immediate has sometimes mistakenly been taken to justify an individualizing approach to practice and research. This may follow from a misreading of what is entailed in a commitment to understanding matters from the actor's perspective. Wolcott tells the story of 'Brad', a 'sneaky kid' who lived on his land and with whom he came to have a relationship. Brad had a breakdown, and came to get Wolcott with the intent to kill him. His discharge from a penal institution was pending at the time of Wolcott's writing. Here was a situation with multiple meanings for every actor. In reflecting on this chain of experiences Wolcott concludes 'I personalize the world I research, and intellectualize the world of my experience' and believes 'you do not have to be neutral to try to be objective' (Wolcott, 1990: 144, 145). He is cautious about saying he wants to understand things from the actor's perspective. 'It is system qualities I seek to describe and understand. To attempt to understand a social system is not to claim to understand or be able to predict the actions of particular individuals within it, oneself included' (p. 146).

Reading this book

In recent years, social work has made strenuous efforts to increase its standing and authority by establishing an empirical base. The proliferation of public domain performance measures and rankings has stimulated these efforts. Similarly, public inquiries into the 'failures' of social work frequently cite lack of a research-related culture in the field.

Debate regarding appropriate research paradigms and strategies within social work increasingly has addressed issues of objectivity, validity, process, power and activism in social research, all of which are given additional purchase within a framework of qualitative methodology. While these issues are not all new to social research, their contextualization within social work is still relatively recent. Characteristically, social work research

seeks to increase understanding of processes, meanings and actors' definitions within complex, open-ended domains, and this is often more naturally suited to fine-grained qualitative inquiry. Although there have been
milestone qualitative social work studies by 'outsiders', there has until
recently been limited systematic treatment of qualitative inquiry within
the social work literature. Mainstream social work research books typically
treat qualitative research as a minority interest. Those volumes that do consider qualitative approaches more sympathetically often have as their focus
either practitioner research (e.g. Fuller and Petch, 1995), evaluation (Shaw,
1996) or the development of arguments for a particular stance undergirded
by qualitative methodology (e.g. Fook, 1996).

   Among the main exceptions are the books by Sherman and Reid (1994b),
Riessman (1994c), Padgett (1998b) and Jokinen, Juhila and Pösö (1999). All
but Padgett are edited books. They are important collections. Sherman and
Reid still stands as the most comprehensive organization of material. Riessman's own work has received notice beyond the immediate confines of
social work. Jokinen, Juhila and Pösö bring together interesting recent
work, mainly from the Nordic countries. Padgett's book is a basic introduction to qualitative methods. The main thrust of all four is to take problems
as arising from methodology, rather than problems and practices distinct to
social work. There is a clear place for a book that treats qualitative research
in social work as a substantive theme, setting epistemological and methodological issues in a context whose agenda is set by and is relevant to social
work. We do not think this can easily be done either in the format of a conventional edited book, nor in a single authored text. We have aimed to give
the present book both coherence and diversity. The coherence stems from
the introductory chapters by the main authors, which set the book within a
context of social work developments and issues, and the final three chapters
in which we review qualitative research in social work, and aim to exemplify
ways in which the four anchoring expectations of social work research can
be advanced through qualitative inquiry. The diversity is incorporated
through the six core contributed chapters that form the centre of this
book – both organizationally and substantively.

   It will illustrate the focus of the book if we mention the brief that was
given to the contributors. The six contributors have developed their work
in countries as diverse in character, history and size as Australia, the
USA, England, Wales and Canada. Some of their work is regarded as
part of the benchmark against which good qualitative inquiry can be
assessed. All contributors address an agreed methodological theme
through the presentation and discussion of qualitative research for which
they have been responsible. Hence, the writers were asked to write in a
methodologically focused way, rather than simply illuminate the range of
issues that their research had raised. The chapters fall into two sections.
The chapters by Scourfield, Hall and Riessman each take as their starting
point a relatively mainstream methodological focus. Scourfield explores
interviewing in a team of professional social work interviewers, while

Hall describes ethnographic research in a homelessness project, and writes as a social anthropologist. Riessman's chapter illustrates the expanding influence of narrative methodology, in which field she has been one of the main contributors within social work. But in every case the focus is firmly on the data from the reported research.

The next three chapters each start from a wider methodological issue within qualitative social work research. Whitmore has exemplified and written extensively about emancipatory research. In her chapter she explores emancipatory and advocacy research issues from her work with Canadian street youth. White picks up in her chapter the issues of reflection and reflexivity from her research as an 'insider' in a British social services department. Fook's chapter on qualitative practitioner research extends the discussion of the issues raised by White. She draws on her previous and current work on feminist and postmodern research perspectives. Once again the methodological foci are anchored in substantive accounts of the contributors' research.

The structure of the book in part models the inductive process that typifies much qualitative research, in the sense that the discussion of methodological choices, contextualization and strategy in the chapters by the main authors emerge from the commissioned chapters. We were aware that the research in the chapters by the contributors would not always be drawn from a conventional social work setting. However, because the theme of the book (and of other titles in the series) is the interaction between professional contexts and qualitative research, the contributors were asked to recount the implications of their research for social work.

We asked contributors to include critical, reflexive assessments of the positions with which they are associated. Our aspiration is that this book will be judged to constitute an authoritative and relatively comprehensive statement of the contribution of qualitative research to social work in the early years of the new century. To help achieve this we asked contributors to identify those issues within their remit that they judged to require further development and understanding.

The third section of the book is linked closely to the issues addressed in the central section. In Chapter 9 the issues of methodology introduced by Scourfield, Hall and Riessman are set in the context of a wider case for qualitative methods. In Chapter 10 we reflect on the questions posed by Whitmore, White and Fook. In the final chapter we consider a cluster of remaining questions about the consequences of qualitative research in social work which will recur through the contributors' chapters. Does qualitative research have anything useful to say about the outcomes of social work? More generally, how might such research prove useful within social work and the wider human services? Do such uses include contributions to developments in theory, practice and method in social work?

But the argument needs some important preliminaries, and these are the focus of the next two chapters. This first section of the book sets out the social work agenda for qualitative research. We express the relationship in this direction quite deliberately. Contextual issues, whether relating to the settings in which social work occurs, the policy, professional and managerial thought forms which shape social work, or the audiences to which social work and social work research is addressed, are central to understanding and developing the distinctiveness of qualitative social work research. In Chapter 1 we discuss how roles within social work, policy relationships, organizational developments and professional practice, vocabulary and discourse, shape the purpose and form of qualitative research. We reflect on how the strategic interests of qualitative social work researchers influence research, and how researchers contextualize their choices regarding methodologies. Our central concern in this opening chapter is to demonstrate how social work poses an agenda for qualitative research – to commence from the problems and practices of social work rather than those of methodology. In so doing we lay the foundations for subsequent chapters that demonstrate ways in which theory and method mutually permeate.

In Chapter 2 we trace the development of qualitative research in social work. We review the contribution that qualitative social work research has made to the larger picture with which we commenced this Introduction. This review is based on a commissioned audit of qualitative social work research undertaken for this book. Several of the issues that recur elsewhere in the book come to the surface in this chapter. In that respect, the chapter is one possible way of getting into the book.

This book can be read in different ways. First, it stands as an illustration of diversity in qualitative research, yet diversity combined with depth. The contributors are unsympathetic to lowest common denominator varieties of qualitative social work research. Second, the book provides examples of research practice that we hope will stimulate awareness of the possibilities for substantive and methodological imagination in social work research. Third, the book is up front regarding a wide range of deliberated and partly resolved issues, whether these be the relationship of emancipatory agenda to research, reflective practice, the relationship of qualitative and quantitative methodology, outcomes research, trends and directions in qualitative social work research, theorizing, practitioner research, the uses of research, or a range of associated questions. Finally, the general question of the relationship between practice and inquiry lies only just beneath the surface throughout the book. This reflects our conviction that committed rigour and unflinching relevance should be the twin hallmarks of qualitative research in social work.

The book has been a rewarding exercise in collaboration between the main authors and with the contributors. The chapters by the main authors have been divided between us, but we jointly 'sign up' to the whole, in the hope that it delivers on the coherence as well as diversity that we claim. Ian Shaw was primarily responsible for Chapters 1, most of 10, 11 and the

Introduction. Nick Gould was primarily responsible for Chapters 2, 9, part of 10, and for the audit of qualitative research sources.

Note

1. A remark made during a presentation to the International Institute of Qualitative Methods conference in Alberta, Canada, February 1999.

Recommended reading

We started the Introduction by referring to the place of qualitative social work research within the wider research enterprise. William Reid's essay (Reid, 1995) provides a succinct and thought-provoking account of research in social work written from an American perspective. A briefer assessment written from a British starting point has been written by Shaw (2000b).

We assume that readers will have a basic understanding of qualitative research methodology. There is no shortage of good texts on the market, and the Sage catalogue is as good a place as any to start. But for a more original – and certainly accessible – approach, we recommend reading Janesick's exercise-based book of 'stretching exercises' (Janesick, 1998). She offers an introduction that is unusual but attractive to practitioners for its unashamed commitment to being useful. More demanding and wide-ranging books are available, and Denzin and Lincoln (1994b) is a leading collection, and probably more helpful methodologically than its year 2000 successor handbook.

The short essays by Reid and Shaw carry implications for how we should approach research. We strongly recommend that social work researchers pay greater attention to this issue, although we do not believe that there is a final answer. Much can be gained by reading interventions that are more polemical. For example, Martyn Hammersley (1992) has raised a good number of hackles through his claims about the present and future place of ethnography within social research.

Finally, time spent reading good qualitative studies is well repaid. The best collection of research papers is still the fat volume of American contributions, edited by Sherman and Reid (1994b). However, short accounts end up tantalizing as much as satisfying. One of the most engaging studies of social work, from the title onwards, is Andrew Pithouse's symbolic interactionist study of social work teams, *Social Work as an Invisible Trade* (1987).

1

The Social Work Context for Qualitative Research

CONTENTS

Context and method   17
Choices for qualitative research and social work practice   23
Paradigms or pragmatism?   23
Qualities and process or numbers and outcomes?   26
Recommended reading   31

We usually think of research and practice in precisely that order. Social workers and those with and for whom they work are regarded as the beneficiaries, perhaps reluctant, of the outcomes of research. Researchers are taken to be the experts, while social workers are expected to dutifully 'apply' the results of expert inquiry to their practice. 'Findings' – data, practice prescriptions, evidence-based outcomes, assessment and prediction tools, generalizations and occasionally theories – are presented for implementation, often in the form of 'key lessons from research'. It is small wonder if practitioners quail at the very thought of swallowing the latest dose of expert knowledge.

The writers of this book share a very different starting point. They are persuaded that social work practice, human services, service users and social work management, create and sustain a rich and diverse agenda for the practice of qualitative research. They commence from the problems and practices of social work rather than those of research methodology. In turn, the diverse, inter-related cluster of methodologies that makes up qualitative research challenges and recasts the conventional image of the relationship between knowledge, skills and values in social work.

The dilemmas and puzzles that surface in everyday practice are variations of preoccupations shared with social researchers. Did my practice, in this instance, stem from an underlying and unified worldview, or was it a more or less appropriate and pragmatic case of opportunism in the face of human need? Is what seems to work in my practice unique to me, or can I generalize it to my immediate or even more distant colleagues?

Is social work practice to be assessed by 'what works', or according to moral or political principles? Is my practice lacking integrity if I find myself implementing common-sense versions of formal models of intervention? What matters more – the evidence-based outcomes of practice or the quality of service delivery? Are social workers agents of change or constrained by deterministic structures?

The terminology may occasionally differ, but researchers share corresponding puzzles. The following quandaries are almost the mirror image of the practice preoccupations in the previous paragraph. Should research methodology be founded on a paradigm or on pragmatic choices? Are research results locally, and only locally, relevant or can we safely generalize? What quality criteria should be used to assess research – moral authenticity or canons of validity? What is the relationship between common-sense, everyday explanations and scientific theorizing? Is quantitative research best for measuring service outcomes and qualitative research better for understanding social work process? If some research methods are strong on analysing constraining structures and others are strong on understanding action and intentions, does my methodological choice inevitably presume something about human nature? Indeed, there are some social scientists that make a career out of such problems by specializing in what Becker engagingly calls 'philosophical and methodological worry as a profession' (Becker, 1993: 226).

The chapters that form the central core of this book illustrate the ways – often unanticipated – in which qualitative research stems from and in turn addresses issues of social work values, knowledge and skills. Riessman demonstrates through a narrative account of infertility how qualitative research can support values of decreasing inequalities and increasing life chances of all citizens by documenting inequalities in lives and analysing precisely how social structures and social policies enhance and restrict opportunities for individuals and groups. Whitmore's account of emancipatory research with street-involved youth reflects a form of participatory, egalitarian qualitative research that is honoured more in the breach than in the observance, while avoiding romanticizing those who are marginalized. Fook and Hall write in different ways about knowledge issues in social work. Hall's chapter echoes closely the emphasis later in this chapter on the significance of context for understanding the arena in which social work produces and reproduces its activities. Fook has much to say regarding what is involved in theorizing in social work. Issues of social work knowledge are also evident in White's account of being an inside 'out' researcher in a social work team. Yet her chapter is of equal interest for the implications of her reflections on reflexivity for social work practice skills. Social work skills also are close to the surface in Scourfield's absorbing consideration of interviewing those who are professional interviewers.

We will briefly develop the idea in Scourfield's chapter that social work practice and research practice may in some ways be methodological mirrors of one another, as an apt illustration of how the research–practice relationship repays attention.

Are research and practice rather similar enterprises? This is an issue more about the character of practice than the character of research. Not, of course, that this need inherently be so. For example, the methodology of the early Chicago School focused on case studies with a strong emphasis on the kind of life histories and personal documents collected by caseworkers in the course of social work with the marginal groups of the metropolis (Platt, cited in Dingwall, 1997a: 54).

The idea that research is just like practice in its methodology is in many ways an enticing one, which, in the naïve form we have stated it, promises more than it will yield. We are reminded of the story of Pinocchio, and the occasion when the fox and the cat persuade Pinocchio that if he would only bury his four gold coins in a field they know in a nearby town they would overnight produce a tree with gold coin leaves. We do not wish to leave the impression that the question is a recipe for sadness and intellectual poverty. Indeed, we have elsewhere explored how methodology and professional practice may coincide to promote a critical, participatory practice (Gould, 1999a; Shaw, 1996, 1997, 2000a). The dangers lie in drawing a too simple conclusion that the two either *are* or are *not* much the same – and in the risk of pushing normative positions about how professional practice (or research) ought to alter its ways.

Two illustrations may help. At one extreme, Fortune has claimed that social work and research (in particular, standard ethnographic studies) are fundamentally different (Fortune, 1994; cf Padgett, 1998b[1]). She argues that the differences between ethnography and social work practice include the following.

1. 'Practice is action-focused, while qualitative methods, including ethnography, intend only to describe' (Fortune, 1994: 64).
2. The practitioner needs additional skills in deductive and inductive logic 'as well as a fine sense of timing about when to stop data gathering' (p. 65).
3. Ethnographers seek to generalize, whereas in social work practice 'there is no inherent need to communicate that reality to other persons or to generalize beyond the experience of that individual' (p. 65).

An almost opposite claim is Goldstein's belief in a natural affinity of ethnography and practice when he says 'the language of ethnography is the language of practice', and that 'both the qualitative researcher and the practitioner depend on similar talents' (Goldstein, 1994: 46, 48). McIvor advances a more general argument of that kind. She pleads for practitioner evaluation in the British probation service from 'the twofold belief that practitioners should be encouraged to engage in the evaluation of their own practice and that they possess many of the skills which are necessary to undertake the evaluative task' (McIvor, 1995: 210). The skills she has in mind include problem solving, effective interviewing and planning, 'which can, with a little advice and support, be readily applied in assessing the effectiveness of their work' (p. 217).

Our own view is that these arguments about shared skills and purposes are unduly simple. A determined process of translation is needed if the potential for mutual dialogue is to be realized. A good example is developed by Lang, who explores the differences between the data-gathering and data-processing strategies of social work and qualitative methodology, and recommends the integration of the latter within social work practice, not only for knowledge-building purposes, but also for 'action-deriving purposes' (Lang, 1994: 277). She compares the data processing of qualitative researchers and practitioners, and suggests that 'The practitioner "names" the data through reference to theory; the researcher "names" the data through a conceptualising process that derives from the features of the data' (p. 271).

She believes that several problems follow for social work because, 'The press to know what to do, what action to take, may close the avenue of knowledge development from practice for many practitioners' (p. 271). She invites an inductive, theory-building approach to practice, with the paradox that 'existing theory must have a more provisional status, a less central locus in our practice teaching, in order to open the possibility of theory-building' (p. 276). Social workers should pull action out of the features of the data rather than turn to existing theory as a first resort. Ruckdeschel has begun to develop comparable methods for qualitative case study. He follows Denzin's idea of 'behavioural specimens' as nearly complete descriptions of interactions between individuals within particular time frames (Denzin, 1989c), and also accepts that the case study's task is 'to give the poor a voice' (Ruckdeschel et al., 1994: 255).

Context and method

When risking a brief overview of the hallmarks of qualitative research in the Introduction, we emphasized holism, everyday life, the particularities of culture, and a strategy of immersion. We deliberately stressed these aspects as a corrective to two features of qualitative inquiry in North American and British social work. First, what often goes under the name of qualitative research in social work is a diluted version of what might be. We have speculated on the possible reasons for this state of affairs in the Introduction; stated in this bald manner, it perhaps sounds too dismissive. There has been some excellent social work research influenced by symbolic interactionist theorizing, and by more recent efforts to integrate this with postmodernism and analyses of power relations in social work (e.g. Fawcett et al., 2000; Jokinen et al., 1999; Pithouse, 1987). The edited collection by Sherman and Reid is still unsurpassed in its success in assembling a range of papers from across the spectrum of qualitative research (Sherman and Reid, 1994b). The emergence of journals such as *Qualitative Inquiry* and *Qualitative Social Work* also promises to provide outlets for the dissemination of quality research. In addition, there has been new attention to the contribution of qualitative evaluation methodology to social work (Shaw, 1999a; Shaw and Lishman, 1999). But the concern still lingers, the more so because it may be part of a wider problem. Dingwall is lamenting a perceived trend in qualitative sociology when he complains that

> The dominant kind of qualitative study appears to be one in which the investigator carries out a bunch of semi-structured interviews which are then taped and transcribed. The results are thrown into a qualitative data management package and a few themes dragged out in a way that seems rather like what we used to call 'data dredging'. (Dingwall, 1997a: 52)

We could add 'focus groups' alongside semi-structured interviews, but the broad conclusion still holds – too much qualitative research is minimalist in nature.

Second, stronger qualitative research in social work often can be described as 'constructivist' in orientation. There is far less research that carries the imprint of ethnography and traditional aspects of social anthropology. This is not an 'anorak' preoccupation with intellectual bypaths of methodology. On the contrary, thoroughgoing ethnography sets in the foreground the liberating or constraining features of everyday life, the particularities of culture, and above all an emphasis on context – and these are all central to understanding and good practice in social work. The methodologically self-conscious research accounts in the core of this book aim to exemplify strong ethnographies that are context-sensitive.

'Context' should not be treated as a taken-for-granted feature of social work. Make a mental note of what you assume 'social work context' means. Possible roughly the same as 'setting' or 'agency', and as something that is a 'given' of social work practice. Perhaps you distinguished the local from the extended setting. This extended setting may be spatial, or defined by membership. Did service users appear in your image of the social work context? Possibly you envisaged the extended context as including policy and managerial contexts. But what about the time dimension? Contexts are retrospective as well as prospective. Strong constructivist explanations notwithstanding, social work contexts cannot be understood apart from mutual knowledge that constrains and enables. And context cannot be restricted to spatial models. Professional and organizational discourses, and the almost endless deposit of written texts also form core elements of social work contexts.

It will be clear from this that the frameworks of meaning within which social workers practice are not fixed and given. They are the result of mutual 'labour' on the part of actors. Such labour encompasses the methods members engage in, for making their activities 'accountable' – visible, rational, and reportable (Pithouse, 1987; Bull and Shaw, 1992).

But contexts are more – much more – than the collaborative endeavour of peers. One weakness of some interpretive sociology has been 'a failure to examine social norms in relation to the asymmetries of power and divisions of interest in society' (Giddens 1993: 164). Giddens argues 'that the creation of frames of meaning occurs . . . in terms of the differentials of power which actors are able to bring to bear . . . *The reflexive elaboration of frames of meaning is characteristically imbalanced in relation to the possession of power . . .* What passes for social reality stands in immediate relation to the distribution of power' (Giddens, 1993: 120 emphasis in original). This underlines the central importance of both language and structure in grasping the significance of social work contexts.

Giddens summarizes his argument as follows. Language is a *condition* of the generation of speech acts, and also the unintended *consequence* of speech and dialogue. Language is *changed* by speech and dialogue. He sees this as being at the heart of the process of what he calls 'structuration' and as reflecting the 'duality of structure' – 'as both condition and consequence of the production of interaction' (p. 165). Hence, 'structure must not be conceptualized as simply placing constraints upon human agency but as enabling' (p. 169).

'All interaction involves (attempted) communication, the operation of power, and moral relations.' So structures are constituted and reconstituted and 'exist only as the reproduced conduct of situated actors with definite intentions and interests' (pp. 133, 134). Hence structures are neither stable nor changing. 'Every act which contributes to the reproduction of structure is also an act of production, a novel enterprise' (p. 134). The work of Foucault has also been influential in dissecting the intimate relationships between language, knowledge and power, and in showing that power can be productive as well as disciplinary (Stenson, 1993). Recent developments in conversation analysis applied to social work illustrate the significance of language, speech intentions and structures (e.g. Hall et al., 1999; Housley, 1999, 2000; Silverman, 1997). The general area of conversation analysis is large and diverse and includes those approaches such as conversation analysis, membership categorization analysis and applied discourse analysis, that are interested in the analysis of 'talk-in-interaction' within formal and informal settings.[2]

Corresponding arguments apply to the importance of *written texts* in social work contexts. Texts can only be understood in context (Scheff, 1997, 4.4). As with settings and structures they are not fixed entities. Miller provides a persuasive argument along these lines in his discussion of how organizational texts are 'inextricably linked to the contexts in which they are produced' (Miller, 1997: 77). Conventional assumptions about social work contexts pose the problem that texts become crystallized 'when we treat them as authoritative representations of stable, objective realities'. 'The words, numbers and images "freeze" the ongoing events of life . . . We crystallize institutional texts by glossing over the various contingencies and other contextual factors associated with the texts' production and use in institutional settings' (Miller, 1997: 78).

Qualitative research and analysis can counter these tendencies by emphasizing the spatial, temporal and practical contingencies associated with the texts. These contingencies entail the same interplay of intention and structure that we have already noted. Hence, 'While the interpretive resources provided by institutional settings do not *determine* the meanings assigned to aspects of everyday life by setting members, the settings might be described as "encouraging", "privileging" or "preferring" some interpretations over others.' This can happen, for example, through the use of standardized forms for assessment, thus providing actors with pre-set categories of meaning and interpretation. However, because this is not a deterministic model, it is true that meanings are sometimes contested, and it is possible for institutional actors 'to construct and justify meanings that might be called "dis-preferred"' (pp. 79, 80).

In order to uncover and understand the operation of these processes, observational methods and constructionist strategies are necessary. This is because 'texts have local histories that are unlikely to be evident from a typical reading of their contexts' and 'institutional texts constructed to explain past decisions inevitably [gloss] over the openness and complexity of the decision-making process' (pp. 84, 91). We return to this point in our later comments on process and outcomes.

If the centrality of context pushes us uncompromisingly to explore intentions, structures, language, power and written texts, it also presents us with the problem of what we mean when we talk about 'cases'. The term 'case' is still part and parcel of the everyday language of social workers when talking about those who willingly or reluctantly use their services. Practitioner researchers also commonly use it if they describe their research as a 'case study'. In both instances an awareness of 'context' is vital. Suppose a social worker is asked to describe what makes a 'good client'. In the following extracts two social workers are identifying the grounds they draw on when supporting their belief that work had gone well in particular 'cases'.

> The client was positive and wanted to find other things to do instead of offending, so there was more of a rapport . . . There were goals that were set by both of us . . . he was the one who was coming up with them . . . He was motivated to improve . . . he was part of the working agreement . . . he was the one who was keen to assess what was happening.

> She was coping with the bereavement, trying to contemplate being a single parent . . . She was able to talk about the kind of support she would have . . . she was beginning to plan . . . she was talking about her deceased husband in quite a healthy way. She was clearly projecting into the future rather than dwelling in the past. So really she was measuring herself in a way which I would have looked at as well.

'Measuring herself in a way which I would have looked at as well' seems to be the key phrase. Here is someone who in effect approaches problem solving with the same set of assumptions as the professional – where partnership is possible, but perhaps on the social worker's terms (Shaw, 1996: Ch. 6).

We should not assume that practitioners always view 'good clients' in this way. It is possible, for example, that good clients will be seen as those who clearly fit the 'gate-keeping' criteria for an agency as a clear-cut child protection case, for example. They may also be 'good clients' in the sense of 'presenting' an interesting problem that matches the professional interests and agenda of the practitioner, in similar ways to Wieviorka's brief description of a good hospital patient (Wieviorka, in Ragin, 1992). In every instance the definition of a 'case' is context-dependent. Once again, the inference emerges. Cases are not fixed empirical entities of a general category – objects waiting to be found. It is more often true that they are waiting to be 'made' (Atkinson and Delamont, 1993; Ragin, 1992).

It is precisely at this point that qualitative inquiry has something to offer to both practice and research. It is *contextualized* usefulness that social workers and managers need, and not 'decontextualized statistical power' (Braithwaite, quoted in Smith, 2000: 3). This is because it is context that provides meaning rather than the 'universalised generalizations' that Riessman eschews. Smith concludes that context matters, and 'it makes little sense to try to understand a special project without reference to the local environment which sustains it (or fails to do so)' (Smith, 2000: 6). The centrality of context also reminds us of the value of observation as a means of immersion – both for research (Dingwall, 1997a; McKeganey et al., 1988) and social work practice (Tanner and Le Riche, 1999; Shaw, 1996).

Context is also important when we consider *ethics* in qualitative research. Developments in technology, genetics, and private sector services are currently posing fresh questions for research ethics in the fields of health and human services. The exponential growth in the possibilities for data linking and secondary analysis, the emergence of major banks of private sector data, the challenges posed by cybersecurity, and the problems of genetic privacy triggered by developments in applied genetics, all pose new ethical questions of considerable scale and complexity. Yet within the human services there has been relatively slight attention to ethical issues. Within this neglect, the ethical questions posed by qualitative research have been still more disregarded. This is due in part to the divergent ethical focus of models of research ethics based on the custom and practice of medical research, and those posed by qualitative research. There is a range of areas where attention needs to be given, and for most of these qualitative research imparts a distinct twist to the direction in which solutions may be sought. We have suggested key sources where more detailed discussions of the issues can be pursued (Box 1.1).

What are the ethical issues distinctive to a particular research *paradigm*?	Johnson, 1995; Lincoln and Guba, 1989; Shaw, 1999a
How can the principle of *informed consent* be adequately stated and protected in qualitative research?	Eisner, 1991; Kayser–Jones and Koenig, 1994
What are the central elements of an ethical *research agreement*?	House, 1980
How can the principles of *confidentiality and privacy* be adequately stated and protected in qualitative research?	Eisner, 1991
What are the particular ethical questions posed by qualitative *practitioner* research?	Archbold, 1986; Kayser–Jones and Koenig, 1994
Are there special ethical questions posed by different qualitative *fieldwork methods*?	Harrison and Lyon, 1993
Are there special ethical questions posed by qualitative research with different *service user groups*?	Kayser–Jones and Koenig, 1994; Shaw, 1999a: 167–9
How can ethical decisions in qualitative research be *locally contextualized*?	Altheide and Johnson, 1997; Johnson, 1995
How should relations of *power* be handled ethically in qualitative social work research?	Acker et al., 1983; Stacey, 1988
What ethical issues are posed when a qualitative researcher adopts an advocacy role?	Archbold, 1986
What ethical questions are posed by the analysis, reporting and uses of qualitative research?	Finch, 1985, 1986

BOX 1.1   Ethical issues in qualitative social work research

The solutions will not be easy. Ethical issues are dealt with implicitly or explicitly in the core chapters of this book. For example, Hall's ethnographic account of a homelessness project and Whitmore's collaborative work with young people, both posed ethical issues for the participants. Reflecting on his own experience of ethical mistakes, Eisner concludes,

> We might like to secure consent that is informed, but we know we can't always inform because we don't always know. We would like to protect personal privacy and guarantee confidentiality, but we know we can't always fulfil such guarantees. We would like to be candid but sometimes candour is inappropriate. We do

not like to think of ourselves as using others as a means to our own professional ends, but if we embark upon a research study that we conceptualize, direct, and write, we virtually assure that we will use others for our purposes. (Eisner, 1991: 225–6)

Choices for qualitative research and social work practice

We have tried so far to develop two related points. First, we believe that social work practice poses its own agenda for qualitative research. Second, we believe that such research needs to make contextual issues central to an appropriate research strategy. They can be presented as a series of somewhat synthetic choices:

- paradigms or pragmatism?
- numbers or qualities?
- process or outcomes?
- unique or shared?
- values or validity?
- motives or structures?
- practical or theoretical?

These issues recur throughout this book. Theory and practice relationships are discussed in Chapter 11; values and validity issues are dealt with extensively during this book, for example in the contributed chapters by Whitmore, Riessman and Fook, and the editors' Chapters 2 and 11. Questions about generalization are discussed in Chapter 11. Matters of motives and structures have been referred to already in this chapter. In addition, they come to the fore in several of the contributed chapters, for example those by Fook and White. For the moment we will outline where we stand on the first three of these questions, and also pick up the question of process and outcomes once more in Chapter 11.

The paradigm question in many ways foreshadows the subsequent questions. The choices about numbers and qualities, and process or outcomes, are significant because they enable us to place qualitative research and practice in relation to different inquiry and practice frames of meaning. The underlying philosophical questions have been discussed at length elsewhere (e.g. Guba, 1990; May and Williams, 1998; Phillips, 1987; Seale, 1999), and also in relation to professional practice and research (Shaw, 1999a; Shaw and Lishman, 1999; Witkin and Gottschalk, 1988).

Paradigms or pragmatism?

It is necessary to break down this deliberately polarized choice into its key elements. We believe it makes sense to understand the issues in terms of the seven following questions.

First, are there paradigms, in the sense of 'a basic set of beliefs that guides action' (Guba, 1990: 17)? The question is about whether meaning is relative, and if 'the meanings of terms . . . have to be grasped hermeneutically, that is in relation to . . . *frames of meaning'* (Giddens, 1993: 149). We can answer in the affirmative without sounding at all controversial – except perhaps to those few researchers who hold a strong belief that research is able to yield an exact or close correspondence to reality, or to extreme pragmatists who believe that the issue is irrelevant.

Second, are such paradigms characterized by internal unity? Are there taken-for-granted assumptions shared by communities of scientists, where rivalries within the paradigm are on relatively secondary matters, and the activity of researchers can be described in Kuhn's terms as puzzle-solving 'normal science'? We think the answer to this question is 'probably no'. Active debates between rival schools of thought, and 'a potential scepticism regarding the claims of science' (Giddens, 1993: 150) are both part and parcel of 'normal' research activity.

Third, are paradigms 'closed systems', such that it is logically impossible simultaneously to hold aspects of more than one paradigm position, or to stand outside a paradigm and assess it? The very fact that we can have this discussion suggests that the answer must be in the negative. For example, how does someone find his or her way around in a new paradigm? By learning what it is and what it is not – i.e. by drawing on some external reference point. Hence, almost all the debate about whether one should hold a particular paradigm position in social work research is conducted in terms of the alleged superiority of one paradigm over another.

Fourth, are there recognizable paradigms within social work research? In a general sense the answer is clearly 'yes'. If there are paradigms in the first place then social work – practice as well as research – must be understood in the light of them. The tricky part of the answer lies in saying just what those 'basic sets of beliefs' are. Perhaps there are two – quantitative and qualitative, or realist and idealist, or positivist and postpositivist? Maybe there are three – realist, constructivist and critical theory? Or should we elaborate by splitting realist into positivist and critical realist?

Fifth and sixth, do paradigms guide the action of 'science' or research in more or less direct ways? Do we need to conduct our research within one paradigm only? It is here that much of the recent debate has centred. The following statements lucidly state the positive answer to this question:

> The adoption of a paradigm literally permeates every act even tangentially associated with inquiry, such that any consideration even remotely attached to inquiry processes demands rethinking to bring decisions into line with the worldview embedded in the paradigm itself. (Lincoln, 1990: 81)

> The arguments for mixing and matching, for blending and combining, for accommodating or compromising, lose all validity. Paradigms do imply methodologies, and methodologies are simply mindless choices and procedures unless they are rooted in the paradigms. (Guba and Lincoln, 1988: 114)

Within social work and related professions there have been corresponding arguments for some versions of feminist methodology (usually those known as 'standpoint theories', e.g. Swigonski, 1993), for critical theory-based research on racism, and for some research within the disability movement in Britain.

There are two kinds of *negative* answers. The first is to claim that the relationship between philosophy and methodology is relatively insignificant, or that the real differences between researchers only exist at the level of methods. We regard both of these assertions as untenable. They are reductionist and result in a naïve pragmatism that is indifferent to methodological purpose.

The second response is to acknowledge that there are real philosophical differences between paradigms, but that the relationship between paradigm and methodology is less direct. Seale, for example, says

> I regard research as a craft skill, relatively autonomous from the requirement that some people seem to want to impose that it reflect some thoroughly consistent relationship with a philosophical or methodological position. (Seale, 1999: 17)

He suggests that relativism may helpfully be adopted as an interesting way of thinking if one is trying to understand a person or another culture. This does not require one to accept relativism as a foundational basis, but as an attitude of mind. We should regard philosophical positions 'as resources for thinking, rather than . . . problems to be solved before research can proceed', and hence see these debates as 'conversations stimulating methodological awareness among researchers, rather than laying foundations for truth' (pp. 25, 26). Reid has taken a similar position within social work. 'Irreconcilable conflicts may indeed exist in the discourse of philosophers, but their perspectives are not essential to the task of resolving differences and building consensus in the practical worlds of social work' (Reid, 1994: 478).

Seale's position is influenced by writers such as Hammersley (e.g. Atkinson et al., 1988; Hammersley, 1992). Our own view is that Hammersley and Seale overstate the weakness of the relationship between philosophy, values and methods. We think there is a real if imperfect linkage between paradigm and method and concur with Greene when she concludes that 'epistemological integrity does get meaningful research done right' (Greene, 1990: 229).

However, we are unhappy with some strong defences of paradigm-like positions in social work, because they lead to a tendentious and ill-grounded tendency to caricature opposing positions and treat one's own position with undue sentimentality. This is true whether the position being defended is evidence-based practice, scientific practice, 'gold standard' randomized control trials, qualitative methodology, feminist standpoints, or postmodern iconography (Shaw, 1999b; see corresponding criticisms of Romanticism in research in Hammersley, 1992, 1995; McLennan, 1995; Strong and Dingwall, 1989; Woolgar and Pawluch, 1985).

Seventh, what is entailed in research pragmatism? We have warned above about the dangers of naïve pragmatism that proceeds on the principle that what works is what's right. But there are more serious defences of pragmatism, that fall into two overlapping versions – methodological pragmatism and philosophical pragmatism (Shaw, 1999a: 50–3). Social work research is gradually being influenced by the writing of the American pragmatist philosopher, Richard Rorty (see Rorty, 1991 for a brief defence of the radical potential of pragmatism). Reasoned defences of pragmatic stances also can be seen in the work of Becker, Howe, Patton and Schwandt (Becker, 1993; Howe, 1988; Patton, 1990; Schwandt, 1993).

A standpoint such as this clearly combines elements of relativity of meaning, realism, and power. Paradigms are best seen as including 'regulative ideals' (Phillips, 1990: 43), entailing normative rather than always-achievable standards (McKay, 1988), and as more akin to ideal types, where we should expect few to reflect 'pure' versions of paradigm-led research. We should take an empirical interest in paradigms as much as a philosophical interest. For example, 'study of notions of bias, error, mistakes and truth as used in ordinary practice might be a profitable way to gain a sense of the actual epistemologies used by social workers' (Reid, 1994: 469). We should also note the relevance of these debates for social work practice. Debates surrounding values and philosophical positions in social work are often conducted in similar ways to debates about paradigms and pragmatism in research. This should not be surprising. At their philosophical and moral roots they are more or less the same problems.

The stance we have taken parallels much current dialogue and debate about research strategies in social work research, which is about the relative weight that should be given to aspects of power, rigour and relativity of meaning, and just how allegiances to more than one of these can be consistently held. For example, how can we hold to both *constructed* realities and some version of *realist* positions regarding the existence and nature of reality? Is it possible to hold simultaneously to postmodern *relativism* and an *empowerment* vision for research? Can we defend both *rigour* and some version of *advocacy* research? (Fawcett et al., 2000; Fisher, unpublished; Oliver, 1999; Popkewitz, 1990; Schwandt, 1997).

Qualities and process or numbers and outcomes?

'These two purposes of evaluation research, process versus outcome studies, may be best respectively addressed by qualitative versus quantitative methodologies' (Thyer, 2000: 401). Thyer captures in this single sentence the most common image of the relationship between quantitative and qualitative research in human services research, and links it to the related question of how such research should address issues of process and outcomes. The two sets of relationships have often been expressed either in terms of a functional division of labour – what may be described as a *horses for courses* approach – or in terms of a relationship of hierarchy, where aspects of one methodology are alleged to be intrinsically superior to the other. Macdonald advocates the latter position in a contribution to a book that claims to seek a rapprochement between quantitative and qualitative approaches. In discussing the case for randomized control trials (RCTs), she concludes that it is 'essential that *all* research designs deployed in outcomes research pay heed to the sources of internal validity that RCTs are best able to control' (Macdonald, 1999: 101). Commentators who adopt the horses for courses position also occasionally slip into a hierarchical mode. For example, Chelimsky refers to the randomized control trial as the 'gold standard, the Rolls Royce of evaluation approaches' (Chelimsky, 1997: 101).

Fortunately there have been more constructive, if more cautious, dialogues regarding the relative merits and characteristics of quantitative and qualitative methodologies. From the quantitative side of the case, Reid in the USA and Sinclair in Britain have developed mediating positions. Reid seeks to 'redefine the nature of the mainstream so that qualitative methodology is a part of it not apart from it'. He regards quantitative research as strong when dealing with linkages, control, precision, and larger data sets, while qualitative research is able to depict system workings, contextual factors, and elusive phenomena, and provide thorough description. 'Neither method is superior to the other, but each provides the researcher with different tools of inquiry' that can be set against a single set of standards (Reid, 1994: 477).

Sinclair adds significant additional points when he says that qualitative methods are in many ways 'more adapted to the complexity of the practitioner's world than the blockbuster RCT'.

> Qualitative research draws attention to features of a situation that others may have missed but which once seen have major implications for practice. It counteracts a tendency to treat the powerless as creatures with something less than normal human feelings. It contributes to an ethically defensible selection of outcome measures. And, in combination with simple statistical description, it can lead to an informed and incisive evaluation of programmes in social services. (Sinclair, 2000: 8)

He turns common assumptions on their head when he concludes that,

> Quantitative social work research does face peculiarly acute difficulties arising from the intangible nature of its variables, the fluid, probabilistic way in which these variables are connected, and the degree to which outcome criteria are subject to dispute. (pp. 9–10)

Qualitative researchers have also addressed the relationship between different methodologies in ways that fruitfully extend the debate (e.g. Bryman, 1988; Greene and Caracelli, 1997), and have explored the relative contributions different methodologies make to evaluation studies of process and outcomes. For example, we noted earlier Miller's discussion of ways that institutional texts constructed to explain past decisions inevitably gloss over the openness and complexity of the decision-making process. He gives the example of evaluation research on a bowel-training programme in a nursing home. The evaluation consisted of counting when and how patients had bowel movements. The programme was judged to have a successful outcome if patients used a toilet or bedpan and ineffective for those who continued soiling beds. One patient had soiled her bed. However, observation methods enabled the researcher to view a nursing aide contesting the definition of this as 'failure' on the grounds that the patient knew what she was doing and had soiled her bed as a protest act against staff favouring another patient. This illustrates how mundane, everyday life is illuminated by observing the context of text construction. This would not have found a way into the formal outcome record. Text production in institutions is 'micro-politically organized', and this includes textual outcome records.

The roots of these debates go back at least to the work of Campbell and Cronbach from the 1960s onwards in America (Shaw, 1999a). Their work, and the debates between them on issues of internal and external validity, process and outcomes, and rationality, has not been sufficiently taken into account by the current generation of evidence-based evaluators and supporters of scientific practice. In some cases, they have not even been acknowledged.

It would be highly premature, however, to conclude that the debates should now be closed. For example, it is sometimes tacitly assumed that using multiple methods will lead to sounder consensual conclusions in an additive fashion – rather like realist versions of the logic of triangulation. One of the most insightful discussions of the problems raised by this assumption is Trend's early classic account of an evaluation of a US programme designed to test the effectiveness of direct payment of housing allowances to low income families (Trend, 1979). In one case study the *quantitative* data suggested that the programme was producing major improvements in housing quality. Yet all the *qualitative* data indicated the programme would fail. The major part of Trend's paper records his assiduous sifting of the data in an attempt to discover a plausible explanation that did not simplistically cut the Gordian knot, either by prioritizing one kind of data above the other through paradigm arguments, or by premature syntheses. His conclusion still stands as a warning against such easy solutions:

> The complementarity is not always apparent. Simply using different perspectives, with the expectation that they will validate each other, does not tell us what to do if the pieces do not fit. (1979: 83)

His advice is:

That we give the different viewpoints the chance to arise, and postpone the immediate rejection of information or hypotheses that seem out of joint with the majority viewpoint. (p. 84)

He quotes approvingly Paul Feyerabend as saying 'It seems that it is not the puzzle solving activity that is responsible for the growth of knowledge, but the active interplay of various tenaciously held views' (p. 84).

The inter-relationship of qualitative and quantitative methods is not only, nor even primarily, about choice of methods. It is about the questions shown in Box 1.2.

Single cases or comparison

Cause and meaning

Context as against distance

Homogeneity and heterogeneity

Validity and the criteria of quality in social work research

The relationship of researcher and researched

Measurement

BOX 1.2   Qualitative and quantitative methodology

It is also inextricably relevant to issues of the politics and purposes of social work research, values, participatory forms of research, interdisciplinary research, and the uses of research.

How we understand the relationship between different methodologies will, of course, be closely linked to the position taken on paradigms. Hence we have already anticipated our likely direction. There are three broad positions (the terminology is that used by Greene and Caracelli, 1997). The *purist* position argues that different frameworks of inquiry embody fundamentally different and incompatible assumptions about the nature of social reality, claims to knowledge, and what it is possible to know. Multi-methods at the paradigm level are not an option. The *pragmatic* position is best represented by what we have described as a functional division of research labour. The position that is likely to prove most creative for social work research is that described by Greene and Caracelli as *dialectical*. This position accepts that philosophical differences are real and cannot be ignored or easily reconciled. We should work for a principled synthesis where feasible, but should not assume that a synthesis will be possible in any given instance. This represents,

a balanced, reciprocal relationship between the philosophy and methodology, between paradigms and practice. This . . . honours both the integrity of the paradigm construct and the legitimacy of contextual demands, and seeks a respectful, dialogical interaction between the two in guiding and shaping evaluation decisions in the field. (Greene and Caracelli, 1997: 12)

Giddens's exposition of the 'double hermeneutic' in social science research has often been appealed to in support of this kind of approach. Giddens is developing the basic logic of social science when he argues that,

> Sociology, unlike natural science, stands in a subject–subject relation to its 'field of study'; not a subject–object relation; it deals with a pre-interpreted world, in which the meanings developed by active subjects actually enter into the constitution or production of that world; the construction of social theory thus involves a double hermeneutic that has no parallel elsewhere. (Giddens, 1993: 154)

This 'double hermeneutic' relates both to 'entering and grasping the frames of meaning involved in the production of social life by lay actors, and to reconstituting these within the new frames of meaning involved in technical conceptual schemes' (p. 86).

His exposition of the double hermeneutic includes the fact that scientific concepts filter back to influence lay understandings (in both natural and social sciences). The difference is that in the social sciences these then become 'constituting elements of that very "subject matter" they were coined to characterize, and by that token alter the context of their application'. Hence there is a 'relation of reciprocity between common sense and technical theory' (p. 86). The double hermeneutic, and also his exposition of the process of structuration, outlined earlier in this chapter, together provide grounds for circumspect dialogue between those committed to one or other end of the polarized options in Box 1.2.

One possible undesirable consequence is that an emphasis on the value of multiple, integrated methods may lead to a dilution of one or the other – a lowest common denominator position. It may also lead to a tendency to treat qualitative methodology (or quantitative) in an unduly homogenous way. As a corrective to this, we believe there is a need to develop the case for a dialectical mix of methods *within* qualitative research. This will need to proceed through the development of a set of critical features of knowledge for different qualitative methodologies. A helpful starting point for this is the paper by McKeganey and colleagues, in which they discuss the benefits and limitations of interviewing and observation methods as part of a study of professional decision-making when people may be offered a place in a home for the elderly (McKeganey et al., 1988; cf. Shaw, 1999a: 145–6). This initial analysis needs to be extended to a full range of qualitative strategies, and tied to the critical features of the associated knowledge claims (Greene and Caracelli, 1997: 12–13).

We have endeavoured in this opening chapter to turn on its head the conventional approach to the relationship between research and practice, which is pictured as the application of expert research to professional and agency practice. Hence, social work practice creates and sustains a broad agenda for qualitative research. Our starting point for this reorientation has been to focus attention on the significance of social work contexts and purposes for qualitative inquiry. The second strand in this opening chapter has been to explore where qualitative research fits within social research. We have argued that the methodology of social research has a real but far from linear relationship with paradigm positions. We have also entered a plea for constructive and circumspect dialogue between advocates of qualitative and quantitative inquiry strategies. We return through the book to both strands of this first chapter. In Chapter 2 we map the 'moments' and themes that characterize qualitative social work research.

Notes

1. Padgett, D.K. (1998a) 'Does the glove really fit? Qualitative research and clinical social work practice', *Social Work*, 43: 373–81.
2. This point was made to us by Will Housley in an email conversation.

Recommended reading

Almost all the issues introduced in this chapter are discussed in further detail later in the book, and the first port of call for further reading is the index to this book. Our recommendations here are deliberately for brief, illustrative discussions rather than book length statements.

Padgett (1998a) and Lang (1994) provide two contrasting brief discussions of the relationship between qualitative research and practice. The importance of taking contextual considerations into account is a central point throughout the edited collection by Miller and Dingwall (1997) and is persuasively illustrated in the chapter by Miller (1997).

Ian Butler (2000) has helpfully summarized literature of research ethics on social work, and his paper is especially helpful for this chapter, because he draws heavily on discussions of ethics in social work practice as well as research.

Growing misgivings have been expressed towards strong paradigm positions, partly in reaction to simplistic applications of Kuhnian ideas to social research. This reaction has almost arrived at the point of overstatement. Guba's edited set of papers (1990) is the best collection. The papers are lucid, varied and together provide a benchmark statement. Greene and Caracelli's 1997 collection of essays on the paradigm relationship between qualitative and quantitative methods succeeds in holding a more balanced, yet still provocative viewpoint.

2

A Review of Qualitative Research in Social Work

CONTENTS

**Mapping qualitative social work research – 'moments'
   and themes**   33
Emergent themes in qualitative social work research   40
Qualitative research and practice – a special relationship?   42
Annotated reading   45

> A study of social work research literature for information about qualitative methods would turn out to be a brief venture. (Goldstein, 1991: 101)

Goldstein's comment about the paucity of methodological discussion in social work research literature is both true and untrue. It indicates some of the apparent paradoxes which characterize discourse about qualitative research in social work. A cursory survey of recent (particularly North American) student texts on social work research finds qualitative research consigned to one chapter, the remainder of the books usually being dedicated to population-based and variable-centred research designs. The clear implication is that qualitative research is an exotic minority pastime, but inherently unproblematic in its execution. There are a few books given over to the topic of qualitative research in social work: for example, Sherman and Reids' (1994b) *Qualitative Research in Social Work* remains a valuable source; Riessman's (1994c) *Qualitative Studies in Social Work Research* brings together empirical studies focusing on grounded theory and narrative methods; more recently Padgett (1998b) has produced a manual for conducting qualitative research in social work contexts, *Qualitative Methods in Social Work Research*. The tenor of these books is often that qualitative researchers in social work are a beleaguered group struggling to open up the field to reflect a more tolerant methodological diversity.

However, a recent literature search conducted as part of work in progress for this volume confirmed that there exists a very large qualitative literature in the social work journals; a search of on-line bibliographic databases by the authors found nearly four hundred qualitative social work research studies. Empirical analysis of the content of US social work PhD dissertations also shows a strong upward trend in the numbers using qualitative methods (Brun, 1997). This may not represent a unified or self-conscious research movement but is indicative that qualitative methods are widely used by social work researchers. Indeed, one of the complaints of protagonists of 'evidence-based practice' is that the supposed weakness of social work's knowledge base lies in the dominance of qualitative methods in published social work research.

This chapter attempts to sift and systematize some of these claims and counter-claims, in order to produce some points for debate about the actual and potential contributions that qualitative research makes to social work (including direct practice). The chapter will firstly attempt to review the literature on two dimensions. First, whereas in Chapter 1 we considered the emergence of qualitative social work research in relation to paradigms, in this chapter we ask to what extent can the development of qualitative social work research be compared with the broader phases in the emergence of qualitative social research? Second, and more briefly, if instead of working from such a framework qualitative social work research is inductively sorted by subject, what are the major themes or topics that emerge? Third, having explored some of the cosmology of qualitative social work research, there will be a résumé of some of the current methodological debates around the contribution that such research makes to social work practice. What is the status of qualitatively derived evidence in the development of social work practice? This inevitably touches on questions of validity and reliability, the epistemology of practice and whether it has a special relationship to qualitative research, and the moral character of research, particularly the configuration of the relationship between researcher and researched.

Mapping qualitative social work research – 'moments' and themes

The periodization of qualitative research has come to be dominated by Denzin and Lincoln's (1994b) historical overview which they describe as five broad 'moments'. The *traditional period* runs from the beginning of the twentieth century until World War II, largely but not exclusively characterized by the dominance of the 'lone ethnographer', but also incorporating the Chicago School in sociology. The object of interest was the 'other', be it the anthropological field study of foreign cultures or the sociological observation of marginal or outsider individuals and communities within the researcher's own society. This gives way to the *modernist phase* existing until the 1970s, and typified by various projects to systematize and formalize the procedures of qualitative research. Thus, this would include Glaser and Strauss's development of grounded theory. Although Denzin and

Lincoln would see the high point of qualitative modernity as having passed by the 1970s, this moment continues in the work of writers like Miles and Huberman (1994) who advocate highly-proceduralized and systematic approaches to data collection, analysis and display. The third moment, *blurred genres,* describes developments until the mid-1980s and is evidenced by the co-existence of a plurality of approaches and a laisser-faire regard to their combination (from amongst, e.g. symbolic interactionism, ethno-methodology, phenomenology, semiotics, etc.). From the mid-1980s this phase gave way to the *crisis of representation* within which various critiques within the sociology of science and ethnography began to challenge the presumption that the researcher's account of events had a privileged relationship to an external reality, or that the author could escape the sub-jectivity of their own biography and cultural assumptions. Finally, Lincoln and Denzin's *fifth moment* indicates the influence of postmodernist decon-struction of grand theory, and the recasting of research as a series of narratives producing local, provisional accounts.

Lincoln and Denzin's periodization is not without its problems. Not least, it is a US-centric view of the research literature and in particular under-represents developments in non-English language literature: e.g. Flick (1998) has given examples of objective hermeneutics and Schutze's work in developing narrative interview research as quite distinct developments in the German literature. Lincoln and Denzin's framework also suffers the usual problems of such taxonomies by being over-schematic, not to mention short-sighted – the further back the perspective (for instance pre-War) the more homogenized and over-generalizing it becomes. Such historical frameworks tend also to focus on the doctrinal differences between certain researchers, and as we shall see, play down the persistence of pragmatic research approaches which deploy qualitative approaches as part of a mixed repertoire in addressing practice or policy-based research questions. Atkinson has been a particularly severe critic of the reduction-ist tendencies in schematizing qualitative research, emphasizing that often there are confusions made between theoretical traditions (symbolic interactionism, ethnomethodology, phenomenology), research methods (grounded theory) and meta-theories or concepts of broad generality which have no necessary connection to methodological issues (deconstructionism, feminism, critical theory) (Atkinson, 1995b: 121).

This overview is sympathetic to his view that research practice is not advanced by 'slavish' adherence to artificial historical boundaries, but nevertheless attempts to synthesize an overview of trends in qualitative research in social work. In particular we will show that 'moments' are not like geological seams which are mined to extinction, but overlap and are often worked simultaneously. Nevertheless, it offers a sensitizing frame-work for thinking about the evolution of qualitative research in social work.

The first moment is broadly indicated by the predominance in the social work literature of the clinical case study. Sherman and Reid briefly chart the place of the case study in social work journals from Richmond to Hollis:

Indeed we could justifiably say that the case study method developed by Mary Richmond in *Social Diagnosis* is a legitimate form of qualitative research. The case study has been defined as an in-depth form of research that may focus on a person, a cultural incident or a community. Certainly, the in-depth study involved in 'social diagnosis' could be construed as applied qualitative research in which research findings guide intervention. (Sherman and Reid, 1994a: 2)

For Sherman and Reid, from the 1950s until around 1970, social work experienced a qualitative 'dark ages' during which the dominant paradigm became variable-based evaluative studies with a psychological orientation. Ironically, within sociology this was a golden age of qualitative research, particularly with the consolidation of social constructionism. Until the 1970s the influence on social work (with a few notable exceptions) of qualitative research was from social scientists, primarily sociologists, who studied topics or issues which were of interest to social workers, such as institutions or the cultural life of marginalized groups of outsiders. Thus, the Chicago School of sociology produced Whyte's *Street Corner Society* (1981, first published 1943), Becker's *Outsiders* (1963), Liebow's *Talley's Corner* (1967), all of which revealed the assumptions and understandings of the worlds with which social workers sought to engage. Similarly, studies of institutional life such as Polsky's *Cottage Six* (1962) or Goffman's *Asylums* (1961) were important sources of sensitization to the socializing processes of working and living in institutional settings. The landmark study for social work of this period or moment was Mayer and Timms's *The Client Speaks* (1970) drawing on qualitative interviews with clients of social workers to gain their views on being the recipients of casework. This became the first in a series of qualitative studies, or 'client studies' giving voice to service users (Fisher, 1983).

However, university departments of social work, particularly in the UK, did not become significant producers of research until the early to mid-1970s. The modernist phase within the broader social sciences was about to give way to 'blurred genres', a pluralistic pick and mix of methods. In social work by the late 1970s a cluster of studies emerged within which ethnography was being used for studying the dynamics of social work organizations, either as a totality, or some sub-unit or functional aspect of their activity such as intake or assessment. A number of these studies took as their point of departure organizational pre-occupations of the time with intake processes and the functional organization of teams. For example, both Maluccio (1979) and Rees (1979) used ethnographic methods to explore the processes of intake: how the agency receives, prioritizes and allocates work relating to new referrals, and how the definition of problems is negotiated. In the UK, Carole Satyamurti (1981) showed how social workers cope with working within irreconcilable ideological frames of reference. Theoretically located within a Marxist tradition of sociological studies of work but methodologically grounded in ethnography, Satyamurti attempted to elicit the internal and external worlds of social workers during the post-Seebohm period of reorganization in social services. A case study of one department was constructed built on two years' part-time participant observation. This included talking informally to people, going on home visits with social workers, reading case files and other documentation, and general immersion in the life of the group, supplemented by structured interviews with a sample of 40 people. Other studies have continued to utilize ethnographic methods to describe and understand the contradictions and tensions, both personal and organizational, in social work: for instance, Pithouse's study of a UK social services department (Pithouse, 1998).

The 'modernist moment' supposedly had its apotheosis by the mid- to late-1970s, characterized by attempts to formalize qualitative research. However, it is argued (Flick, 1998: 9) that its legacy survives in the procedures of grounded theory (Glaser and Strauss, 1967) and the influence of Miles and Huberman in systematizing approaches to the structured analysis and presentation of qualitative data (Miles and Huberman, 1994). Certainly, within social work research, grounded theory has continued to be an influential and active tradition. Grounded theory has been described by Sherman and Reid as 'particularly promising for the development of indigenous social work theory and knowledge . . .' (1994a: 6) and, as we shall see below, has been drawn on as a source for arguing for the recognition of synergies between qualitative research and practice. Its claim is to be an approach and set of methods for developing theories, concepts and hypotheses direct from the data rather than a priori assumptions, other research or existing theoretical frameworks.

Grounded theory has continued to be an ongoing stimulus within the social work research field. With its emphasis on the inductive construction of categories through processes of constant comparison and analytic induction it has sought to analyse populations in terms of constructs which are more multifactorial and subtle than those produced by static, quantitative cross-sectional data analysis. The examples from the social work literature are many. Mizrahi and Abramson (1985) used grounded theory to study interaction between social workers and physicians, developing a typology of professionals which could be placed on a continuum of collaboration – traditional, transitional and transformational. Belcher (1994) reports on a grounded theory study of how people become homeless. Usually, homelessness research, based on cross-sectional data, tends to explain process in terms of one variable, e.g. mental illness. Using open-ended interviews Belcher and colleagues sought to develop a more complex model of multiple factors involved in the drift into homelessness. Similarly, grounded theory approaches to data collection and analysis have been used in studying the contribution made to change by community activists. Lazzari et al. (1996) studied the contribution of 21 Hispanic women who were active in their communities in facilitating change, be it improving conditions for local people, or developing collective approaches to community development. Ward et al. (1996) used continuous comparative techniques from grounded theory to compare how qualified and student social workers attributed motivation to sexual abusers of children. Lazar (1998) also used grounded theory to analyse the interviews with social workers to explore how they construed the relationship between gender and environmental influences.

The fourth moment represents a crisis of representation as, under the influence of feminism and postmodernism, foci emerge which problematize the processes of doing fieldwork and analysis, and foreground the subjectivity of the researcher in these processes. The exemplars of this fourth moment include the overlapping fields of feminist and narrative research. Both are fundamentally concerned with giving voice to those who may not be heard: 'At the core of feminist research, therefore, is the commitment to give voice to previously marginalized and silenced people' (Davis and Srinivisan, 1994: 348). This is also a diverse tradition but within which there is a broadly shared emancipatory agenda, summarized by Harding as: (1) knowledge is grounded in the experiences of women; (2) research should benefit women; (3) the researcher immerses herself or shows empathy for the world being researched (cited Hyde, 1994: 173). At the same time, as Padgett (1998b) points out, within this broad manifesto there is also to be found a plurality of epistemologies and methodological repertoires, one of which is narrative research.

Narrative research in social work draws on models of therapeutic intervention, e.g. narrative family therapy, as both research method and therapeutic intervention (Besa, 1994; Fish and Condon, 1994), and also the methods of oral historians. Thus, the construction of narratives about an individual life is not only a communication of the subjective experience of events, but also a process of re-integration for people whose lives may have been fragmented by violence or oppression (Riessman, 1994a: 114). 'Narrative analyses start from a specific form of sequentiality' (Flick, 1998: 204). The character of narrative research is both methodological and epistemological. Life is regarded as a biographical narrative which can be reconstructed through a procedure of elicitation although, for the critics of narrative research, this leads to methodological controversies. First, there is an over-confidence in the inference from narrative to external reality; there is rarely triangulation with other data sources. Second, the labour intensity of the method, and its idiographic rationale, mean that often studies are presented as individual case studies, or very small samples which can, at least to positivist critics, produce problems of generalizability. Despite these objections, for some social work researchers, narrative inquiry rescues the voice of the service user or those excluded from the margins, and contests the implicit hierarchies within positivistic research. For example, Krumer-Nevo (1998) has used narrative analyses of young women's perceptions of their struggles as mothers in families with multiple problems. Riessman in particular (see Chapter 5) has argued for narrative research as a counter to some of the perceived reductionist tendencies of positivism; she draws on narrative accounts by people experiencing divorce to contrast this with more quantitative studies of the divorce process which produce, for instance, gender bias within standardized symptom scores and the neglect of personal meaning in survey research (Riessman, 1991). Borden also used narrative methods with individuals who had experienced adverse life events to show how narrative identified the strengths and personal resources that they were able to mobilize, in contrast to the 'deficit models' which problem-centred approaches tend to produce (Borden, 1992). There are similar implications from Riessman's narrative case study of a man with advanced multiple sclerosis who uses narrative devices of restorying his life to guide the image others have of him (Riessman, 1990b). Again, Stevens (1997) uses narrative accounts by black female adolescents to show the complexity of their coping strategies to meet challenges in living.

The movements into narrative and postmodernism segue into Lincoln and Denzin's fifth moment of reflection, co-operative inquiry, empowerment and the positioned investigator. Here the concept of narrative moves from the more literal meaning of telling life stories towards the argument that research theories or methods are forms of rhetoric, persuasion or story-telling. This is where, as Flick has argued, 'narratives have replaced theories, or theories are read as narratives' (Flick, 1998: 10). The interest in subjectivities allies some strands of feminist research with postmodernism. Sands (1995) has suggested that postmodern theories of multiple selves and multiple identities as elaborated through the concept of 'voice' enable challenges to be made to patriarchal assumptions of conventional social work; drawing on narrative methods she uses the exemplar of an excerpt from an interview to explore the reconstruction of identity. Similarly, Trethewey (1997) has used qualitative interview data with clients and social workers to analyse strategies of resistance and empowerment amongst clients, arguing that their identities are not the passive recipients that is often presumed.

These developments are indicative of three emergent, interlocking themes in wider qualitative research, which are also found in social work:

- 'the crisis of representation' – a recognition that even within the ethnographic tradition there has been a tendency to write up fieldwork in terms which emulate the objectivity of positivism, so that the author is concealed as an agent who interprets, prioritizes and owns the research. This was not new to the 1990s; Geertz's seminal book, *The Interpretation of Cultures,* first published in the 1970s, gave rise to a 'confessional' style of ethnography acknowledging the hand of the author in the construction of research accounts (Seale, 1999). However, postmodern deconstruction more radically and fundamentally places the author at the centre of methodological argumentation;
- the reinstatement of the author within research accounts implies a declaration of the political position of the researcher and legitimates research as an intentional political project, which is intended to contri-

bute to the emancipation of the subjects of the research. This echoes Marxist conceptions of praxis, the dialectical interaction of theory and practice, and in particular the field of action research. But there are also implications for less overtly political traditions such as ethnography where the moral and political implications are identified:

> Ethnography is both a way to study justice as well as to 'do justice'. Furthermore we suggest that ethnographers are 'justice workers' in so far as they clarify the nature, process and consequences of human expectation which are manifested in everyday life as social definitions. (Altheide and Johnson, 1997: 173–4)

- the instatement of those who might traditionally have been viewed as the subjects or respondents of research as equal collaborators in research, the service user or practitioner as co-researcher. This reinforces the recognition of research as a reflexive practice, and the dissolution of traditional dualities between the researcher and the researched.

Shaw (1999a) has noted that participatory research is not a unified field and incorporates the influences of several approaches including co-operative inquiry, action science, action inquiry and participatory action research. From within these perspectives conventional, modernist qualitative research is a morally compromised endeavour in which respondents consent to participate without having opportunity to influence or control the research process. Some social workers have looked to the contribution to research methodology and epistemology of writers such as John Heron (1996) and Peter Reason (1994a, 1994b) to provide an alternative approach in which the formally designated researcher facilitates a process which is democratically steered by people who traditionally might be 'respondents'. There are already numerous examples within the social work literature. Bemak (1996) raises the possibility of working with children as co-ethnographers. Other examples would be Bess Whitmore's (1994b) work on user participation in programme evaluation or Baldwin's account of working with people with learning disabilities as co-inquirers into day centre services (Baldwin, 1997).

   What we often see here is a continuation of modernist research methodologies but located within a research sensibility which has become cautious of claims to universality or generalizability beyond the local. The postmodern concern with decentring the authorial presence to create space for a plurality of voices is not without problems, and it remains to be seen how this is developed within social work. At the more modernist end of the postmodern spectrum – as we have seen – there is already a long tradition of confessional ethnography which makes explicit the actions of the researcher. This is really still a form of realism; the researcher retains responsibility for selection and interpretation of the data, but by accounting for the process there is an attempt to deal with conventional research preoccupations of bias, reliability or replicability. As such, reflexivity can be a disguised form of realism, by convincing the audience that the researcher has 'really been there' there is a hidden attempt to persuade us that this is a credible and authentic research account. Moving along the continuum there is a commitment to making the researcher's theoretical position more explicit yet. As Seale (1999) argues, it is not always clear what is meant by 'theory'; sometimes this can refer to a cluster of attitudes, values or prejudices without really engaging with more technical conceptions of what might be construed as 'theory'. Such research can still be seen as a modernist aspiration to produce a narrative in a single voice, albeit one within which rhetorical devices are deployed to persuade the reader that the author is open and trustworthy. Most 'reflexive' qualitative research in social work is located within a research tradition which is essentially modernist – paradoxically it makes claims for the decentring of authorship but, through its use of the first person and declarations of subjective response to the field, the author is often more centre-stage than ever. In social work there is as yet little sign of radical postmodern reflexivity which engages with innovative or experimental textual formats, polyvocal texts where there is a genuine plurality of voices, although some researchers are writing and publishing with activists and service users (e.g. Evans and Fisher, 1999).

Emergent themes in qualitative social work research

Another way to 'cut the cake' of qualitative social work research, in contrast to the more deductive method of comparing social work research against a predetermined historical framework which emphasizes epistemology and methodology, is to sort it inductively to identify substantive themes or pre-occupations of qualitative social work researchers. Such a project has been undertaken by Popay and Williams (1998) in the field of qualitative health research. Some of the categories which emerge are in fact prefigured by our historical overview of qualitative social work research; there are identifiable clusters of studies which over time have addressed such topics as understanding organizational culture, investigating 'invisible' processes in social work, eliciting service user perceptions of practice and evaluating complex policy initiatives. Some of these studies are what Popay and Williams call a difference model, i.e. stand-alone qualitative studies; others are combined with quantitative methods as part of an 'enhancement' model, that is they compensate for some of the deficits of pure quantitative studies:

- *Analysing 'taken for granted' practices in social work.* For researchers and practitioners alike, familiarity makes many of the everyday routines and procedures in social work either invisible, or at least taken for granted. Submitting mundane or routine processes to scrutiny and analysis in order to learn more about their function and how participants construct their roles within the agency has been a fairly constant pre-occupation of qualitative researchers in social work. For instance, Maluccio's (1979) study of intake teams when, in the 1970s, this became an established organizational strategy for managing the bombardment of referrals on front-line staff. Dingwall et al. (1983) used participant observation to uncover some of the submerged professional assumptions in child protection practice which reveal how social workers and doctors negotiate the tensions within the liberal state between the regulation of public welfare and the private domain of the family. More recently, Parton et al. (1997) have drawn on discourse analysis to uncover shifts in mainstream child protection practice towards managerialist preoccupations with 'risk'.

- *Understanding service user and social worker behaviour.* Another cluster within the qualitative literature has been to probe and explore the behaviour of social workers as an occupational group, that of service users and the interactions between them. Thus, as discussed above, Mizrahi and Abramson (1985) studied the interactions between social workers and doctors and from their data constructed a typology of forms of collaboration between the two professions. Gilgun and Connor (1989) analysed interviews with perpetrators of child sexual abuse to understand how they construed their offending behaviour. Stenson (1993) used the analytics of discourse theory to show how in social work interviews a complex interplay of friendship and tutelage shapes the client into compliant and socially acceptable forms of response. As has been mentioned, Belcher (1994) employed grounded theory to understand the dynamics of individuals' drift into homelessness and the implications for service delivery.
- *Representing service users' voices.* As has been seen in relation to the emergence of client studies, and later narrative research, a consistent interest in qualitative social work research since Mayer and Timms (1970) has been to use qualitative methods to articulate the voice of the service user. Earlier client studies tended to draw their material from conventional in-depth interviews, but more recently the influence of narrative methods has produced more radical and reflexive approaches to promoting the voice of the service user.
- *Organizational culture and change management.* Under the emergence of conditions of post-Fordism and globalization, social work has become pre-occupied with organizational and professional adaptation as a continuous feature of organizational life. Satyamurti's (1981) study of adaptation in response to the the Seebom reforms of British social work in the early 1970s suggests that change is episodic, whereas more recent studies show that change is endemic. The management of change continues to be a focus of qualitative inquiry based on a plurality of methodologies, for instance Baldwin's (2000) use of co-operative inquiry to understand how social workers have adapted to their role as

care managers, or White's discussion (this volume, Chapter 7) of auto-ethnography to examine child care practice.

- *Understanding and evaluating complex policy initiatives.* Within policy analysis there are longstanding debates about whether policy making and implementation are driven by technical rational processes, or whether they are shaped by artistry and incremental adjustment (Majone, 1989). Social work has always had a brokerage role in relation to other services and arguably, in response to the interdisciplinarity of community-based provision, it takes on an even more strategic and complex role in service delivery. Shaw (1996, 1999a) has shown that qualitative methods have an established place in research and evalua-tion, and in both health and social work there is almost a rediscovery of qualitative methodology in relation to the analysis of complex policy initiatives. Some examples have been given earlier in the chapter, but further examples from recent years would be Lewis and Glenner-ster's (1996) analysis of the implementation of community care reforms in British social services departments, and Gould's (1999b) use of critical incident analysis to audit multidisciplinary practice in child protection.

Qualitative research and practice – a special relationship?

So far we have reviewed the qualitative social work literature in terms of empirical content and the development of qualitative social work research as a category within the wider sphere of social science research. As identi-fied in Chapter 1, in recent years there have been vigorous methodological and epistemological debates within the literature about whether qualitative research has a pre-eminent position in relation to the development of prac-tice. A superficially persuasive argument is that qualitative research should be the preferred approach in social work research because it has a natural synergy with the processes of practice. This view first strongly emerged in the writing of Jane Gilgun (1994) who has proposed and elaborated the metaphor that practice fits qualitative research 'like a hand fits a glove', but it is also an assumption of writers like Heineman Pieper, an advocate of 'naturalistic clinical research' (1994). Gilgun's argument is specifically located in grounded theory, though there has been a tendency by commen-tators to extrapolate from this to the general field of qualitative research. Essentially, Gilgun's case is that practice and qualitative research share a number of common features: the focus on how informants construe their world is congruent with the social work injunction to start where the client is; the contextualization of data fits with the social work emphasis on understanding the person within their environment; 'thick' description of individual case studies is parallel to the social work individualization of social work processes of assessment and intervention; grounded theory uses both deductive and inductive reasoning in the same way that social work synthesizes research-based knowledge and practice wisdom; both social workers and qualitative researchers use processes of constant comparison and analytic induction to construct, test and modify hypotheses; both take place in naturalistic settings, use similar methods of data collection such as observation and interviewing and involve maintaining a balance between empathy and analytic detachment.

Metaphors can be alluring forms of argument, and Gilgun's case seemed non-controversial until Padgett, herself a protagonist of qualitative research in social work, suggested that under closer scrutiny the glove really did not fit (1998a, 1999). Padgett reasserts the value of the contribution of qualitative research to the knowledge base of social work, but draws out a number of criteria by which she asserts that practice and research are very different undertakings, and that there are both scientific and ethical reasons for ensuring that the two are not conflated. Primarily she argues that both are located in different paradigms: practice is irredeemably theory and model driven, located within normative views of social or individual functioning, whereas qualitative research is concerned with theory generation and is non-normative. Padgett then argues that the goals of the two activities are divergent. Practice has a series of mandates established between legal duties, the agency and service user which may be contested or in conflict but are presumed to be contributing to a notion of 'helping'; the goals of research are the development of knowledge and scholarship. Furthermore, Padgett asserts that the practice and research relationships are different: the former is often time-limited and terminated by the judgement of at least one party that further improvement cannot be made; the latter is characterized by prolonged and unscheduled immersion in the field, brought to a close when the researcher judges that no further understanding will be elicited. Unlike in practice, with qualitative research the 'real work' begins when the engagement with the respondent is completed, with transcribing, data analysis and writing up. Padgett's sting that provoked the strongest reaction was her argument that the conflation of research and practice was inherently unethical with compromises around standards of confidentiality, informed consent and withdrawal from research/treatment (Padgett, 1998a: 376).

There have been a flurry of responses and counter-responses within the pages of the US journal *Social Work*. Essentially these have been that Padgett's argument caricatures social work, primarily that it construes practice within an outdated representation as a privatized, clinical activity located in anachronistic, psychological paradigms (Bein and Allen, 1999). Heineman Pieper and Tyson (1999) have focused their response on the allegation of unethical practice by arguing that in combining practice and qualitative research the ethical standards of the social work profession do not have to be somehow suspended while the research agenda is pursued. However, as Padgett subsequently points out (Padgett,1999) Heineman Pieper and Tyson seem to have a particularly narrow concern to 'rescue' their own brand of 'naturalistic clinical research' rather than to engage with the wider arguments about qualitative research which the debate raises.

Padgett does not perhaps really pursue the full implications of her argument. If doing qualitative research is different from doing practice, but makes an important contribution to the knowledge-base of social work, then how is that contribution made? Qualitative research in social work continues to develop within a range of theoretical and methodological traditions. Social work researchers draw eclectically from methods representing the diversity of qualitative 'moments', including ethnography, grounded theory, case studies, narrative, discourse analysis, conversation analysis, and co-operative inquiry, with little apparent concern about being conscripted to the paradigm wars. They bring these methods to bear on the kinds of questions which preoccupy qualitative researchers in other domains of social research. These include: exploratory research to describe and map out new fields of inquiry; researching issues of sensitivity where surveys are too blunt an approach; research to capture the frames of reference and meaning constructed by professionals and service users; evaluations of programmes and interventions where there is a desire to capture process as opposed to quantified outcomes; case studies where holism is more important than measurement of specified variables; and politically committed research which rejects the claimed neutrality of positivism. Although it would be difficult to show that social work has made an identifiably distinct contribution to qualitative methodology, qualitative social work research has made and continues to make a substantial contribution to social work's knowledge base.

Despite some of the rhetoric of (in the UK) protagonists of evidence-based practice and (in the USA) the protagonists of empirical practice, explaining how research-based knowledge contributes to social work practice and policy-making is not uniquely problematic for qualitative research; both quantitative and qualitatively derived knowledge have to be interpreted and mediated by practitioners to meet their needs (though both can be judged by explicit standards that are pragmatically relevant to practitioners). To restate the classic Wittgensteinian conundrum, rules cannot contain the rules for their own application; prescriptions do not follow deductively from knowledge – judgement, discretion and improvisation are some of the filters which intervene. As Reid (1994) has suggested, we need to reframe the epistemological debate in social work so that, rather than argue for the supremacy of a particular paradigm, we conceptualize or model the contribution that qualitative research makes to practice, in conjunction with quantitative research and practice-based knowledge. This acknowledges that social work as a form of practice is a complex, sophisticated activity involving the reflective synthesis of both inductive and deductive reasoning within which qualitative research contributes strongly to 'best attainable knowledge', in Reid's words, 'a network of propositions with origins in practice experience and research' (Reid, 1994: 464).

The scene is now set for the following six contributed chapters to this volume. Each has been written by a noted scholar who is a research practitioner of at least one qualitative methodological standpoint. We have seen that within the social work literature there is a significant and diverse body of empirical work which can be located both within the chronological development of social research, and also in relation to certain thematic preoccupations. Each contributed chapter can be read and interpreted in the light of a series of questions which are grounded in the overview in this chapter:

- How do the authors locate themselves within the moments of qualitative research?
- What is the theoretical or methodological contribution to the published body of social work research?
- How has the context of the research shaped the methodological choices?
- Do the voices of the researched stand in their own right or are they subjected to expert translation?
- What claims are made for the transferability of findings to other populations or settings?
- What relationship is argued between the research and prescriptions for practice or policy implementation?

These and other questions are returned to in the chapters following the invited contributions.

Recommended reading

In any assessment of the development of social research it is very difficult to avoid Denzin and Lincoln's chapter from their handbook as the point of departure (Denzin and Lincoln, 1994a). As has been stressed in this chapter, there are objections which can be made both to the particulars of their analysis, or to the overall project of periodizing the history of qualitative research, but Denzin and Lincoln's contribution has undoubted authority as a reference point within the ensuing debate. Readers who feel that the evidence for their argument is too partial in its dependence on English language and, particularly US, literature should consult Flick's *An Introduction to Qualitative Research* (1998), which provides a comparative framework making particular reference to European developments. Indeed, Flick's book is somewhat misleadingly titled an introduction as it is a serious text, and although the author is a nurse academic it contains much to interest social work researchers. Those who wish to challenge the whole Denzin and Lincoln approach to systematizing research moments and paradigms will find useful ammunition in Atkinson's critique (Atkinson, 1995b).

The debates around the contribution made by qualitative research and evaluation to social work practice have become more clamorous in recent years. A brief, general overview of the case for the contribution of qualitative research to social work's evidence base is set out in Gould (1999a). An overlooked but, in our view, important contribution to overcoming unhelpful oppositions between qualitative and empirical social work is made in Reid's paper, 'Reframing the epistemological debate' (Reid, 1994). Readers for whom life is too short to track through the extended debate in the journal *Social Work* about the contention that qualitative research and practice go hand in glove can cut to the chase by reading Gilgun (for) and Padgett (against) (Gilgun, 1994; Padgett 1998a).

Part 2

EXEMPLIFYING QUALITATIVE SOCIAL WORK
RESEARCH

3

Caught Not Taught: Ethnographic Research at a Young People's Accommodation Project

Tom Hall

CONTENTS

Introduction to a research project	50
Ethnographic research	51
Access	52
In the field	53
Caught not taught	55
Conclusion	57

This chapter is about ethnographic research. The aim is to provide the reader with a sense of the value of the ethnographic approach and a sense also of what it can be like to 'do' ethnographic fieldwork. The chapter draws, throughout, on research conducted at an emergency accommodation project for the young homeless. As is appropriate for a chapter on ethnography, the discussion builds, inductively, from this empirical example. It is characteristic of the ethnographic approach that the knowledge it makes available – theoretical or applied – has its starting point in the real and particular. Ethnography begins at ground level, with the lived experience of those in a particular social setting. Nor does it ever move too far ahead of this empirical reality. There is much to be said for this reluctance to move analysis too far, or to generalize too quickly, from the complex terrain of lived experience, and this commitment to a grounded understanding is something from which all of the distinctive features of ethnographic research flow.

Introduction to a research project

In the mid-1990s I undertook an extended investigation into youth home-lessness – a highly visible social problem throughout much of that decade and a continuing cause for concern today. The research focused, in the first instance, on a group of young people (most of them in their late teens) all of whom were homeless when I first met them and many of whom remained intermittently so throughout the 12 months that I was in contact with them. This was a study, then, of social exclusion. However, one of the first things one becomes aware of if one spends any time with the young homeless is that, however excluded they may be, they do not lead lives of isolation. Like many others on the social margins, the young home-less are often (almost invariably) in frequent contact with a range of agen-cies, organizations and professionals who are concerned to police, provide for, and intervene in their circumstances. In the town in which I carried out my research, a common point of contact for almost all the young homeless was the local emergency accommodation project, a short-stay hostel in the town-centre staffed by a small team of paid workers and volunteers. The hostel offered temporary accommodation for a mixed residency of up to ten young people at any one time. Staff on duty provided support and supervision for residents throughout their stay with the aim of assisting them in moving on into more permanent and settled accommodation. Life and work at the hostel were to become an important part of my overall research 'field', and the account of homelessness that I eventually produced (see Hall, 1997, 2001) encompassed not only the experience of a group of young homeless teenagers but also the working practices and deliberations of the hostel staff team.

Early on in the course of my research, visiting the hostel to speak to some of the young people staying there, I picked up a copy of the hostel's annual report which had this to say about the services made available to residents:

> [The hostel] aims to provide a breathing space where young people's needs are acknowledged so they can consider their options, decide how they want to spend their immediate future and make realistic choices . . . an opportunity for young people to take time to evaluate what has happened in their lives and provide them with resources to turn it around . . . a stable base from which to establish their goals and break the cycle of instability and homelessness.

At the time, I glanced at the report only to file it away along with other leaf-lets and documentation I had collected from the local offices of various other organizations. But as I came to see the hostel staff as key players in my research field, I grew curious as to how they interpreted and achieved such ambitions in their daily practice. In order to explore such issues further, I widened the ambit of my fieldwork activity – I was by this time already spending much of each day in the company of, and in conversation with, young homeless people in the local area – to incorporate the work of the staff team: spending time in the staff office, sitting in on team meetings, and accompanying staff members in the round of their duties.

In describing the experience of ethnographic research in this setting I will also discuss, briefly, some of the answers I think I found to the question of how the hostel staff 'deliver' services beyond that of the basic provision of accommodation.

Ethnographic research

Before detailing aspects of my research at the hostel it may help the reader if I state briefly and in the most general terms what it is I mean by ethnography, ethnographic research or fieldwork, and (although I have not yet used the term) 'participant observation'. I will use these terms interchangeably in this chapter to refer to a distinctive qualitative research strategy which enquires into social life and behaviour through first-hand intensive observation in naturally occurring settings; such research is also participant insofar as the researcher him or herself constitutes the primary research tool, participating in social activity in order to gain a close and unforced understanding of people's lived experience.

The ethnographer is thus both observer and participant, and while these two roles may each be given different weight at different times and in different places, ethnographic enquiry is not usefully reduced to either observation or participation alone. Instead, it is the combination of, and movement between, these two positions which enables the ethnographer to develop a richly informed but critical understanding. Thus in the course of my own ethnographic research at the hostel I was neither a known insider (a member of the staff team) nor an unknown outsider (a researcher calling in to conduct an occasional interview) but rather an (increasingly) familiar stranger. As fieldwork progressed – I was a daily visitor to the hostel for the best part of a year – I gained a detailed understanding of the work of the staff team, but whilst this afforded me something akin to an insider's knowledge I was not seeking simply to know and experience the work of the staff team as they themselves knew and experienced it, I was also, always, seeking to consider, record and question as an impartial observer.

This balancing act between participation and observation (familiarity and distance) is at the heart of all good ethnography. It can be difficult to achieve, and is of course not something that is ever achieved once and for all. Instead it is developed and re-worked throughout the course of any fieldwork endeavour. At the outset of an ethnographic enquiry one is usually much more of an outsider seeking to work towards familiarity (although see White's description of her research in Chapter 7 of this volume), whilst later one may have to consciously work to maintain a critical distance.[1]

Access

All fieldwork begins with the negotiation of access, not least in the corporal sense of arranging for oneself, the researcher, to be physically present in the research setting. Where the research setting is actual premises, such as a hostel, an office or organization, physical access is an obvious and immediate hurdle. And where such a setting is the site for the delivery of welfare services there is the double difficulty that welfare professionals will have both their own and their clients' interests to consider in granting research access; at the hostel, to know the staff's work was inevitably to know their private deliberations about individual young people.

However, there is also a sense in which public (and voluntary) sector welfare agencies can be open to research enquiries (more so than commercial organizations, for example). The anthropologist Ralph Grillo, reflecting on his research with social workers and immigrant communities in France (Grillo, 1985), remarks that he found agencies concerned with immigrants' families to be

> open to people like myself. Their staff were willing, indeed expected, to talk at great length about immigrants. My role as investigator fitted exactly their role as informants. (Grillo, 1985: 21)

Grillo's experiences resonate with my own. I was pleased to discover that the staff members at the hostel were, from the outset, very willing to answer any questions I might have about their work. They were in fact accustomed to doing just this for a variety of other visitors; the hostel manager and her deputy were specifically required, as part of their job description, to present and explain the work of the hostel to a range of local organizations and interested parties. But one should not confuse this kind of 'openness' with transparency. As Hutson and Liddiard (1994) have argued, when organizations like the hostel present a picture of the young homeless and of their work with this client group they are unlikely to do so impartially, for a number of reasons (for example, they may anticipate and seek to counter other 'negative' representations of the young homeless).

One of the strengths of ethnographic research is that, over time, it usually works its way behind such representations. The gap between what people say (about what they do) and what they actually do can be revealing in any setting, and participant observation, of all the qualitative methods, is best placed to reveal and explore such discrepancies. In my own research I was to become aware of such a gap between what staff members had to say about their work with the young homeless and how such work took shape in practice. However, such insights only came in the long run, and would not have been reached at all had I not been extremely fortunate in the initial access granted me by the staff team who, without being too sure where my research was leading (I was unsure myself), and without placing too many restrictions upon me, allowed me unencumbered access to their working lives.

Not every researcher is so lucky. That I was, on this occasion, may have had something to do with the informality that can be characteristic of voluntary-sector welfare organizations (particularly local and 'grassroots' initiatives). Researchers seeking access to statutory agencies and public service professionals are perhaps (more) likely to encounter more stipulations and conditions of access.

In the field

To say that one is a participant observer really gives little away as to what it is that one does all day. There are a number of strategies and techniques which sociologists and anthropologists employ as participant observers. Some of these are supplemental to the core of the method (questionnaires and surveys for example), quantitative pegs on which to hang a more qualitative account; interviews with key respondents/informants are often undertaken. At root, however, it comes down to spending intensive time not only alongside but also among those whose lives and practice one hopes to understand. Just how long one should spend in the field is a moot point. Certainly the longer the better, in almost any setting; a year is still widely considered the requisite minimum as a *rite de passage* for anthropologists. Fieldwork is about 'being there' as social activity unfolds, but the ethnographer cannot be everywhere at once, hence the value of prolonged fieldwork. Every extra day spent in the field enables one to see more, and also, just as importantly, enables one to guess at what one may be missing (see Bloor, 1997b: 305–6). During this time, as I have suggested, it is the ethnographer who constitutes the primary research tool, to whom any and all information is 'grist to the anthropological mill' (Fortes, cited in Drucker-Brown, 1985: 49).

In my case, whilst I did occasionally interview members of staff, and frequently questioned them, in conversation, about aspects of their work, the majority of my time at the hostel was spent in unobtrusive observation. Weekly staff meetings and scheduled key-working sessions with individual residents (see below) were among the more obvious venues in which the staff could be seen 'doing' their job. However, I did not confine myself to these. I also spent several hours of most days engaged in the much more domestic and routine round of activities at the hostel: preparing food with staff and residents in the kitchen, washing bed-linen, watching TV and chatting in the hostel lounge, sitting in the office listening to the staff members on duty recount recent comic incidents and share frustrations over coffee. That daily work at the hostel was pedestrian and prosaic at times could be frustrating, from a research perspective, but there was much here that was engaging. I sometimes spent several hours in casual discussion with staff members during quiet shifts at the hostel only to realize that I had been so effortlessly involved in the conversation that I had not been paying it 'serious' attention; at times like these it was only with a conscious wrench, and some regret, that I would put my ethnographer's hat back on.

At the same time as I was developing close and familiar relationships with the staff at the hostel, I was also fostering new relationships with a host of young people in the local area who were presently homeless or unsettled in their accommodation. Straddling these two sets of relationships was not without its tensions. I have written elsewhere about my field relations with the young homeless (Hall, 2000), drawing attention to some of the differences (and difficulties) I encountered here as a participant observer. With the staff team at the hostel I was on much more familiar ground from the very beginning. Although the members of the staff team were not known to me prior to my research, I had some familiarity with voluntary-sector provision for the homeless and was able to demonstrate that I was at least *au fait* with the work that they did and sympathetic to the difficulties it presented. The staff were broadly familiar with my work too; that is, the questions I was interested in asking made sense to them in essentially the same ways that they did to me. Such familiarity can be reassuring, but it also cuts two ways. At times, it required a conscious effort on my part to step back from overly identifying with the staff team, so as to develop a more independent perspective on their work in the hostel. Also the staff team's competency to engage with my research speculations took away from me the complacency that might have been afforded by my accounts of life at the hostel being the only ones of their kind. To begin with I found such familiarity a little too close to home.

On the whole I did not consider it appropriate to record conversations and activities at the hostel as these occurred. Conspicuously taking notes would have been both disruptive and impractical. Instead, often in the late evenings, I would sit down on my own (hopefully undisturbed) to make detailed notes of events and conversations to which I had been party. This proved to be a laborious process requiring a considerable effort of memory and a careful policing of my own observations for unwarranted elaborations. A small notebook, kept constantly on my person, in which I made shorthand notes whenever the opportunity presented, acted as a valuable *aide mémoire*. By the end of my fieldwork I had hundreds of pages of fieldnotes full of observations, incidents and remembered conversations. These fieldnotes were my primary resource, but I did collect other data: a few months into my research at the hostel I persuaded the staff to allow me to record their weekly staff meetings, transcripts of which proved to be an immensely useful supplement to my fieldnotes. I also conducted a small number of interviews with staff members, most of these at the outset of my research when both the staff team and myself were a little uncertain as to what shape my role as participant observer would take and were all grateful to seize on a tangible and recognizable research activity.

Caught not taught

My feelings about qualitative interviewing as a research technique are mixed. Interviews can be extremely useful and revealing, but the tape-recorder has a tendency to elicit particular sorts of narrative from respondents – those which respondents feel are appropriate to the interview context – I agree with Bourdieu here about the potential for distortion generated by the 'relationship of enquiry' (1977a: 166). It was certainly the case that in my early interviews with staff at the hostel I tended to get 'official accounts' of the work that they did. And as my fieldwork progressed I was to find these accounts to be incomplete in their explanation of daily practice at the hostel. The following discussion reports on just one instance of this.

The extract from the hostel's annual report that I included towards the beginning of this chapter makes it clear that there is more than just housing on the staff team's agenda. Young people coming to the hostel are to be encouraged to 'consider their options' and make 'realistic choices' in order to 'break the cycle of . . . homelessness'. Staff members were to confirm this agenda to me in interview:

> Our goal for them is to help them to leave into accommodation . . . and move on to having a more stable lifestyle. In order to give them the skills for having a more stable lifestyle, while they're [here] . . . the agreed goals, for example, are that they learn to budget, learn to have a realistic idea of their employment, sign on for benefits . . . with John [for example] we need to be thinking about his drug and alcohol problem while he's here.

They also identified a strategy for addressing any and all of these issues: 'key-working'. Each resident coming to stay at the hostel was assigned a key-worker, a member of the staff team with whom they would meet regularly, in private, to discuss those issues which may have contributed to their homelessness and to plan how best to address these. Plans made in key-working sessions – to re-establish contact with estranged parents, or to make an appointment at the drugs counselling service, or to put aside some money each fortnight in order to save for furniture – did not always materialize afterwards, and this could be frustrating. But nonetheless, key-working was represented by the staff as the principal, explicit and most evident mechanism through which they sought to make a constructive intervention into the young people's lives.

Had I taken the staff at their word and focused narrowly on key-working as the declared means by which they delivered on the hostel agenda I would doubtless have found much to write about – indeed those key-work sessions that I did sit in on were fascinating. But there was also a sense in which these sessions were removed (abstracted) from the usual round of activity at the hostel. Looking at my fieldnotes during the course of my research I was increasingly struck by how little of the time that staff and residents spent in each other's company was accounted for by the somewhat formal vehicle of key-work, and how much more contact was of a casual, informal and domestic character – reading the papers together, cooking meals, arguing over who should do the washing up, discussing last night's TV.

Also, listening to staff members talking amongst themselves, I noticed time and again that when the discussion turned to shared frustrations about work it was not so much key-work plans gone awry that featured prominently here as minor upsets and petty conflicts with residents over the daily rules and routines at the hostel:

> *Poppy:* I can't stand going into a room more than once to tell them to get up, it really pains me.
>
> *Ann:* Well, it's about discipline isn't it; being self-disciplined.
>
> *Kevin:* . . . I found a plate in the bathroom, under Roy's clothes, by the toilet bowl. I mean that's blatantly just saying 'I'm not cleaning up' . . . There's so many little things that we would do that they just don't want to do.
>
> *Ann:* . . . I mean the aim isn't for us to make life as difficult for them as possible, it's to keep the hostel clean and to make them responsible for cleaning. When we're at home we have to do something every day . . . so I don't think this is being unreasonable or autocratic or anything is it? It's just getting responsibility.

Over time, and in the light of exchanges such as this and my own daily observations at the hostel, I came to re-assess the relative importance and focus of the staff team's work.

It was evident (indeed obvious) that the staff spent a great deal more time in everyday and informal contact with the residents at the hostel than they spent working in more formal and structured ways. On its own this did not constitute a strong case for directing attention away from the latter to the former. What did, was a growing recognition on my part that the content of informal domestic interaction around the hostel was not as thin or inconsequential as it might have appeared to be at first glance.

In the course of my fieldwork I came to see that the everyday, informal interaction at the hostel was not merely background noise – a backdrop against which the real and tangible business of assistance and guidance (as manifest in key-working sessions) took place. Instead, much of what passed between staff and residents at the hostel did so at just this informal level. Central components of the staff team's agenda at work – the intention to elicit from and instil in the residents the kind of attitude, responsibility and outlook which will help them to stabilize their accommodation – were always at stake in the ongoing and everyday domestic traffic between staff and residents, where seemingly mundane exchanges or communications could carry a considerable freight of meaning and cumulative significance. The daily schedule at the hostel; the rules of occupancy; the shopping, cooking and cleaning rotas for residents: all of these and many other relatively minor arrangements – 'little things' as Kevin calls them – carried an ideological charge that had to do with establishing and encouraging certain attributes, standards and competencies. In the staff team's view these attributes (reliability, responsibility, self-discipline, organization) were exactly those that the young people would have to take on board if they were to make an adequate response to their own housing situation.

Similarly, as everyday and conversational exchanges between staff and residents filled my fieldnotes I began to see these as having a greater combined significance than the more formal discussions taking place in the context of key-work meetings: reassurance and advice over breakfast about an impending court appearance; a sympathetic but firm reminder, on giro day, to put some money aside for next week; or a verbal nudge about getting down to the Job-Centre. It was in this sense that while key-work may have represented the most tangible aspect of the staff team's work at the hostel (an aspect that they could easily communicate in a research interview), the domestic and informal character of life at the hostel ensured that much of what passed between staff and residents did so less explicitly; was caught rather than taught.

Once I had recognized this, my earlier puzzlement about staff members' propensity to fret about minor breaches of the hostel's domestic regulations started to make more sense. The multiple freight carried by these regulations meant that a breach could always be read as having significance beyond that of any immediate inconvenience caused. When residents like Roy left dirty plates in the bathroom, staff did not encounter this so much as an unwelcome distraction from the real business of work at the hostel (key-working) but as a direct challenge to their whole agenda, a challenge that was repeated daily.

Conclusion

This recognition of the tacit importance of the seemingly mundane and inconsequential is just one example of the way in which my understanding of the work of the staff team advanced during the course of fieldwork. The example is hardly an elaborate one, but I have included it here as a practical illustration of my earlier comment about the gap between what people say about what they do and what they actually do. Initial interviews with staff did not direct my attention in this direction; instead what was foregrounded in these interviews was the 'official' vehicle for intervention and assistance at the hostel – key-work sessions.

I do not suggest that what staff members said when they talked about key-working was somehow 'false'. What I do say is that what they gave was an account of their practice, prompted by questioning from an outsider and produced in a particular context (an interview). And key-work *was*, of course, an important component of the staff team's working practice: important as a means of assisting and advising residents and important too as a concrete focus for staff members working at a job that was in practice much more diffuse.

At the start of this chapter I referred to the grounded understanding that ethnography works towards. The participant observer works from the bottom up, as it were, attempting to engage with social life on its own terms and as he or she finds it; fieldwork is a sustained *holistic* engagement with what people observably do. It follows, inevitably, that ethnographic research lacks (or rather avoids) some of the structure of other research strategies. While ethnography can provide sophisticated answers to research questions, it does not anticipate the answers it might find, or indeed the questions that will prove to be important; the limits of the field of enquiry and the research focus are not fixed once and for all at the outset. Instead, ethnographic fieldwork is often messy and uncertain (like work, like life). This is to recognize an important feature of such an approach, its openness to the new and unexpected, offering the researcher what Willis has referred to as a 'profoundly important methodological possibility – the possibility of *being surprised*; of reaching knowledge not prefigured in one's starting paradigm' (1976: 138, emphasis in original). This holds true even when the 'surprise' arrives in mundane packaging.

I described earlier in this chapter the knowledge that ethnographic research makes available to us as being both theoretical and applied. In closing it is worth returning briefly to this question of research and its use and/or relevance. Given that ethnography works from the bottom up, one would expect it to be well suited to the production of concrete knowledge capable of informing developments in policy and service provision; this case has been well argued by anthropologists and others in recent years (see Edgar and Russell, 1998). Warren (1998) proposes that qualitative methods have the advantage over quantitative strategies for research in 'welfare' settings, not least for the opportunities that the former offer for the empowerment and participation of service *users*. Yet the grounded character of ethnographic research cuts both ways here. Its findings (complex and holistic) are not always easily translatable into specific recommendations, and it is poorly suited to addressing the macro-level processes (political, economic, ideological) which shape and inform social work and welfare (beyond explicating the ways in which such processes manifest at a local level). Speaking for myself, I do not like to think of research as being *either* 'academic' *or* applied. One can see what is meant by this distinction of course, but all social research, inasmuch as it is about and results from an engagement with the social world, is 'applied'. My own research may not have been geared to production of recommendations for the development of provision at the hostel (although I did share my findings with the staff team), but its relevance and impact depend upon much more than this – on what readers of this chapter take away with them, for example. This last comment should alert us to a deeply reflexive point about the nature of social research in modern society – the continual, diffuse, reciprocity between social activity on the one hand and what the social sciences enable us to think and know about this on the other (see Giddens, 1987).

Perhaps, in conclusion, we could say that there is a sense in which ethnographic insights are also caught rather than taught. This is not to suggest that such understanding is somehow tacitly arrived at through an immersion of the ethnographer's self in a particular setting (although this romantic notion persists with some). But there is an important sense in which ethnography generates understandings that are not prompted by questioning but are instead picked up or 'caught' in the course of intensive and sustained fieldwork.

Note

1. Recent years have of course seen an epistemological anxiety spread across the social sciences, calling into question the validity of 'objective' accounts and explanations of social activity. Whilst one could argue that the practice of participant observation always contained the potential to destabilize any simplistic subject–object separation (see Hastrup, 1995), ethnography has also gained from a new, reflexive awareness of what it is that is being undertaken both in fieldwork practice and in the writing of ethnography. Certainly '[n]o one comes to fieldwork as a *tabula rasa*' (Monaghan and Just, 2000: 14), nor does ethnographic study produce accounts of social reality that are objective and impartial in any naïve sense. That this is so does not excuse ethnographers from a duty to observe accurately, but it implies a duty to *watch oneself*, as an ethnographer, at the same time as watching others.

4

Interviewing Interviewers and Knowing about Knowledge

Jonathan Scourfield

CONTENTS

Researching gendered occupational culture   61
Interviewing social workers   64
Knowing about knowledge   66
Women as oppressed   67
Women making choices   69
Conclusion   72

Interviewing is an everyday activity. We live, Silverman (1993: 19) observes, in an 'interview society' where the mass media, human services and researchers generate a great deal of information through interviewing. For social workers, particularly those with a casework role, the interview is the dominant practice method. So too is it for social researchers from most mainstream traditions. Research mirrors social work practice in many respects, indeed social work assessment in particular can be regarded as a form of social research. Sheppard (1995) and White (1997a), amongst others, have argued the connection between the skills of qualitative research and social work assessment. This chapter will reflect on two aspects of the symmetry between social work practice and social research: the interview process and the analysis of interview data. The chapter will draw on a qualitative research study of the occupational culture of a child care social work team to illustrate the potential of using qualitative interviews in social work research.

The chapter will be organized as follows. Since I draw on examples from a specific qualitative study, the context of this study is described at the outset. The research questions are explained and the research process is described. I then move on to make some more general arguments about the use of interviews. I explain how the process of interviewing social workers mirrors their practice, and then discuss the opportunities and limitations of qualitative interviews in terms of what the researcher can find out from interviewing. The argument is then made that the process of gaining knowledge about social work from interviewing social workers mirrors the process of social workers forming judgements about clients, in that a key question in both arenas is the extent to which people are 'stuck' or free to act. I go on to argue, with reference to my data, that a post-structuralist emphasis on multiple discourses best captures the nature of occupational culture in social work.

Researching gendered occupational culture[1]

The focus of the research is the construction of gendered clients in the occupational culture of child protection social work. Many observers have noted the gendered nature of much child protection activity, with women typically being the focus of intervention and coming under scrutiny even when it is men who have caused harm to children (see O'Hagan and Dillenburger (1995) for a summary of this commentary). In the light of this existing work, I set out to explore the construction of men and women clients in the social work office.

The research was conducted during 1997 in a local authority children and families team in the UK, 'The Uplands'. The population covered by the Uplands team, their 'patch', was founded in the last century around a specific industry that barely now exists, except in its cultural significance. It is an area of social deprivation according to all the standard indices. I spent three months based in the social work team's office. The social work team comprised six women and three men social workers, and a woman team manager, all of whom were white. The population of the Uplands is 99 per cent white, and during the fieldwork all the child protection cases I studied were poor white working-class families. Because of sensitivity of access I did not observe worker–client interaction, but did observe collegial talk around the office, conduct an in-depth interview with each team member, and analyse in detail the files on all cases on the child protection register. Whilst the overall analysis depended on insights from all types of data, I shall restrict my examples from the study in this chapter to those from interviews with social workers. I certainly see interviews with clients/service users as an essential part of social work research, and some of my more general remarks will be relevant to interviewing users as well as interviewing staff at all levels. However, the empirical basis of the chapter is interviews with social workers and one team manager, so most of the chapter's argument relates more specifically to this kind of social work research interview.

In line with the reflexive tradition, my starting point for the research has been to accept that my biography, my own values and beliefs, and my personal conduct would be intrinsically bound up with the progress of the fieldwork and my gathering and analysis of the data. Some of my comments here are based on my presence in the social work team as an observer, though similar issues would have arisen if I had spent much less time with the team and only arrived in the office to conduct interviews. I approached the team as a university tutor doing a PhD. To avoid being taken as some kind of expert because of this status, I was careful to assure participants that child care work was not my field, in the sense that I do not have either a research or practice background in this area of work. My social work background (drugs work and probation) did, however, create a certain rapport due to participants' perceptions of common strands in work background and training.

As well as bringing my current and previous work to the research, I brought my sex/gender. Though much has been written about a gendered understanding of women researchers' effect on the field and the field's effect on them, there has been less reflection in the research methods literature on men as researchers (McKeganey and Bloor, 1991). In my case, others' perceptions of my masculinity varied considerably, often because of other mediating factors such as my age, assumed class background, educational status and university affiliation. People generally think I am younger than I am. I look to be perhaps in my mid-twenties rather than early thirties. My accent is middle class, I speak with received pronunciation. These factors inevitably affect the way the participants viewed me. Perceptions of me as a man varied greatly. One social work manager, interviewing me about research access, expressed the fear that I could be a 'paedophile', wanting to research work with men in order to make contact with other sex offenders. Some of the social workers made the very different assumption that the motivation to research such a topic implied I was a pro-feminist 'new' man.

Several authors have pointed to the difference in interview responses according to the sex of the interviewer (see, for example, Padfield and Proctor, 1996). Most often the conclusion is that women researchers are seen as more sympathetic and can therefore prompt greater depth of response from informants. Although I was not aware of any respondent obviously holding back, it is possible that my gender adversely affected their willingness to be frank about their views on their work. It was evident that the body language of interviews was gendered. One man in particular was confident and expansive, sitting with a very open posture, whilst I recall one of the women looking down, momentarily embarrassed, on my asking about working with cases of sexual abuse. It is not possible to eliminate such gendered effects. It is, however, important to acknowledge them, at the time of fieldwork and subsequently when analysing and writing. As Morgan (1981: 95) writes, 'the male researcher needs, as it were, a small voice at his shoulder reminding him at each point that he is a man'.

As well as presenting as a young, educated, middle-class white man, I presented as married and therefore apparently heterosexual, and as a father. Within a few days of starting fieldwork, in the course of small talk with social workers, these aspects of my life had come to light. My father-hood certainly improved rapport with some, since the social workers' own children were often discussed. As far as I was aware, all but two of them had children of their own, so this was a point of contact with the majority, though only the majority. This shared life experience perhaps added to the assumed common concern for children seen to be 'endangered'. Research with any proximity to the abuse of children is likely to have an emotional impact on the researcher (see, for example, Moran-Ellis, 1996; Scott, 1998). My fatherhood affected my emotional reactions to the data, in two very different ways. I found some of the descriptions of alleged abuse of children more difficult to hear than I think I would have done before parenthood (see also Moran-Ellis, 1996). I also found, though, that my experience of the stresses and strains of looking after a child made me question some of the expectations being made of clients, particu-larly in relation to standards of cleanliness and hygiene.

As Collins (1998) has observed, the research interview is often divided into two types: the 'structured' and the 'unstructured'. According to this division, mine would be termed unstructured interviews. I find this division unsatisfactory, however, since I agree with Collins that

> even the apparently most 'unstructured' interview is structured in a number of sometimes subtle ways. The interviewer, in the very act of initiating the interview necessarily determines the nature of the event: we are to engage in what is called 'an interview' – it is an event which most people will understand to consist of particular roles and rules: shaped, that is, by a particular structure. As the inter-view progresses an internal dynamic develops, a storyline emerges which becomes increasingly complex especially in those cases where further interviews are undertaken. (Collins, 1998: 1.3)

The term 'semi-structured' may in some ways be a more helpful description for those I conducted, although I did not use any closed response questions, and I allowed social workers to 'digress' from the planned topics since I considered everything to be potentially relevant to an exploration of gender construction. I am happier with the label of 'in-depth' interviews. Certainly the goal was the pursuit of depth. I aimed to achieve a rich con-textualized account of social work culture. It has become fairly common-place for the term 'ethnography' to be used in a very loose sense, to be synonymous with 'qualitative'. I do not agree that a research strategy based solely on conducting in-depth interviews constitutes ethnography. What makes ethnography distinctive is participant observation. It is also true, however, as Fontana and Frey (1998) assert, that many of the data gathered by observers do in fact come from interviews, albeit informal ones conducted in more or less natural settings. I am taking qualitative interviewing here to mean an exchange that is rather more formal because a time slot is arranged in advance, and typically the discussion is tape recorded and fully transcribed.

I decided to ask very general questions in the main, though I did ask those with cases on the child protection register to talk about these specific families, since these related to case files I had chosen to study in detail. The questions I used as prompts were in fact more of a reminder to me of topics to cover than actual wording used, since the flow of conversation required extemporizing. In many cases I followed Spradley's (1979) advice of asking fairly long questions with plenty of clarifying clauses, to allow respondents time to prepare their answers. I conducted two pilot interviews in another authority, 'Docktown', to test out my prepared questions. I drew on data from these as well as the Uplands interviews in my analysis.

My approach to the analysis of the Uplands team data was based on the idea of grounded theory. As Strauss (1987) reminds us, this is not a specific technique, but rather a methodological orientation that seeks to base theorizing in the data rather than imposing a pre-determined hypothesis. As already mentioned, a reflexive stance requires acknowledgement of the knowledge the researcher inevitably brings to the data. A reflexive grounded theory approach is possible, however. Such an approach involves examining the data with existing influences made explicit, but with an openness to the theoretical implications of the raw data. Coding was facilitated by the computer software NUD*IST 4. Strauss (1987) has identified 'open' coding, 'axial' coding and 'selective' coding as distinct elements of the process. I cannot claim to have carried out totally open coding, since the first few codes I tried out had their origins in analytic memos noted as the fieldwork progressed. Having constructed an initial NUD*IST coding 'tree', which is a structure that represents relationships between codes, I read and coded all data, adding to the basic tree structure where necessary. I then proceeded to axial coding – an intense analysis around one category at a time – combined with a selective coding – limiting data coded to those which relate to the core codes in a sufficiently significant way.

Interviewing social workers

As asserted at the beginning of this chapter, interviewing social workers for a research project mirrors social workers' interviewing of their clients. Social workers tend to rely very heavily on verbal exchange in an interview situation. Holland's (2000) research into child protection assessments found that the primary evidence on which decisions were based was gleaned from verbal interactions rather than observation of parenting. In these verbal interactions, clients construct accounts for social workers as social workers do for researchers. All the characteristics listed in Kadushin's book (1972: 8–11) on the social work interview that distinguish an interview from a conversation are also characteristics of research interviews. The same author makes the obvious point that social work interviews are distinguished from other kinds of interviews in that they are 'concerned with social work content, are scheduled to achieve social work purposes, and take place in social work settings' (Kadushin, 1972: 11). He makes the familiar observation that an emphasis on the relationship between people and their *social* environment is what marks out social work from other helping professions. Of course the same claim can be made for what distinguishes sociological research from other social research connected with other academic disciplines. The similarities between social work interviews and research interviews caused Rubin (1981) to observe that clinical social work training is a very relevant preparation for research interviewing.

In some respects, their familiarity with the interview process makes social workers one of the easiest professional groups to interview for research purposes. Theirs is a talking job; they believe talking helps people. They demonstrate their competence to colleagues through 'telling the case' (Pithouse and Atkinson, 1988), so they tell a good story. The common base of interviewing can also lead to some confusion, however. University colleagues of mine have found that training social workers in qualitative research interviews is difficult because they assume they know all about interviewing. There are, in fact, some distinct differences between the two types of interview. One key distinction of the interviewer's orientation towards their data is whether or not they have set out to evaluate, to make decisions about value and worth, to appraise. It may be that social workers, who necessarily have to make an evaluative judgement about a client's circumstances in order to complete an assessment, may assume a researcher is also in the business of overt evaluation. Some researchers will be. Others may be seeking to understand rather than make judgements about the rights and wrongs of practice.

We should not, of course, expect social workers' accounts of their practice to straightforwardly equate to what they *actually* do with clients (see Hall's chapter in this volume), just as clients' accounts of, for example, their parenting, do not straightforwardly reflect their actual everyday interaction with their children. As Parton (1999, WWW page) observes, 'what people do and what they say they do, and how people think in action and how people reflect on the way they think in action, are not necessarily the same things'. There is plenty of evidence for this gap between accounts and practice and for the ways in which different research strategies reveal different versions of reality. Lever's work (1981, cited in Hammersley and Atkinson, 1995) on sex differences in children's play, for example, found that children's versions of what they 'usually do' in response to questionnaires showed greater difference between boys and girls than the evidence of the diaries the children kept about day-to-day play activities. In a sense, qualitative researchers in the 2000s do not need to dig out evidence such as Lever's findings to prove to us that people construct different kinds of accounts for different kinds of audience. This realization has been a dominant methodological orientation for some time. I agree, however, with

Miller and Glassner (1997), who reject both positivist and constructionist extremes in relation to the knowledge we can gain from interviews. I do not think it is possible to sterilize interviews so they give a pure reflection of reality. Neither am I convinced that no external reality can be known from an interview because it reflects nothing more than the narrative version of the social world that each participant has constructed.

The perspective I find most helpful is what Best (1989) has called 'contextual social constructionism'. This perspective focuses on the making of claims about social problems, but accepts that knowledge about social context and objective information can help explain how claims arise. So it is necessary to make reference to material reality. *Actual* social work practice and clients' *actual* behaviour do affect social workers' constructions of clients. Clients' constructions of social workers reveal both received ideas about what social workers are like *and also* some direct reflection of their own experience. It is similarly important to hold on to a conception of material reality when considering gender relations. Whilst postmodernist theorizing of gender relations can liberate us from some overly rigid concepts, as Oakley argues, it also tends to be distanced from

> the situation of women out there in a world that definitely does exist, and that remains obdurately structured by a dualistic, power-driven gender system. (Oakley, 1998: 143)

To repeat the assertion made earlier, even though we may hold on to a conception of material reality, and regard this as an essential context to the social construction of knowledge, we should still not expect to establish what this material reality is from talking to people. We can, however, expect to gain some insight into occupational discourses. We may need to abandon any attempt at finding out any direct unmediated information about actual social work practice from interviews with social workers, but we can learn a great deal from what Hall (in Chapter 3 of this volume) calls 'official accounts' of work. For my project this means the ideas about men and women clients that have discursive power in the social work office. Harlow and Hearn's summary of theories of organizational culture (1995) outlines the breadth of different theoretical perspectives that have been applied to the topic. This chapter uses the perspective that Harlow and Hearn label 'culture as discourse'.

Knowing about knowledge

As well as the symmetry of interviewing interviewers, there is another respect in which my research process mirrors the social workers' practice. In this research project I am in the business of constructing knowledge about knowledge about people. In other words, the question of how I should understand the individual social worker in relation to occupational culture and professional knowledge mirrors the question of how social workers should understand individual clients in relation to their social circumstances. For both the researcher and the social worker there is tension between the individual and the social, between agency and structure. To explain this point further I shall draw on some interview data. I shall discuss some dominant occupational constructions of women clients. I identified three defining discourses of (client) femininity in the social work office: women as oppressed, women as responsible for protection, and women as making choices. I shall focus on the discourses of women as oppressed and women making choices, as these highlight the tensions in social work knowledge that I also faced in my interpretation of the qualitative data.

Women as oppressed

In contrast with some research, for example Swift's (1995) encounter with social work practice in Canada, the Uplands social workers are, to an extent, influenced by some of the messages of second-wave feminism. Traditional family structures are seen to be oppressive for women and to often have profoundly negative effects on them. So, for example, women's 'not coping' is often connected with the absence of help from the men in their lives. This failure to cope can be in relation to the practical demands of child care and housework, or failure to manage children's behaviour. Pete, in the excerpt below, sees responsibility for mothers' difficulties as being located with partners and those who live nearby.

> A lot of women feel as if they are on their own, as if they can't cope anymore because there is no help, they are not getting enough help. Well that is not a matter of social work help. It is a matter of community help, partner, etc. Some have their husbands as the disciplinarians and they are kept to one side and then wheeled in as and when necessary to administer punishment to the children. But over so much of the problems that the women are presenting is the fact of just not being able to cope anymore with the behaviour of the children. (interview with social worker 'Pete')

The experience of having been abused is seen as leaving women with very low expectations of quality of life. 'Debbie' (social worker) told me in an interview 'our women clients don't expect anything'. Mike, in the following interview extract makes the general point that he is struck by how much his women clients put up with. He describes a particular case in illustration where the woman finally asserted herself with her partner over something Mike considered to be a fairly minor offence in comparison with the physical abuse she has suffered. There is a cultural gulf here. Mike is sympathetic to the woman's oppressive situation, but cannot understand why she puts up with so much.

Certainly there is a fair number of women on my case load who aren't even really able to meet their own needs in terms of relationships, putting themselves first occasionally. A fairly common experience is women who for instance won't go to the doctor when they are feeling ill, or won't go to the doctor when they are obviously under an awful lot of stress and perhaps do need to go and see the doctor about that. I suppose another example of that kind of behaviour is women whose expectations from their partners seem kind of surprisingly low in terms of putting up with an awful lot, right up to physical abuse from their partners on a fairly frequent kind of basis. The most surprising thing that I ever encountered was someone who put up with years of really quite bad beatings from her partner and I went around there one day and she said I have chucked him out. And the reason why she had finally chucked him out was because he had bought this car and there were an awful lot of difficulties with it because it wasn't taxed or MOT'd. It was sitting outside and the police came around and happened to pick that one up and they ended up going to court and having a load of fines and things like that. She chucked him out then. She got cross about that and chucked him out, but she hadn't at all got cross about having to hide black eyes and bruises around the neck and things for years and years. That surprised me, but I think there certainly are quite a large number of women who will put up with an awful lot in terms of what happens to them. (interview with social worker 'Mike')

Social workers talk of patterns that women get into. Swift's research (1995) found frequent reference to the idea of cycles of abuse: the abused becoming the abuser. In the Uplands team, the notion of a cycle was much more often invoked in relation to men's sexual abuse of children. The pattern the social workers described in relation to some women involves abuse begetting abuse, but in a different sense. The idea is that being a victim of one form of abuse will make it more likely that you will be a victim again in a different situation, not that it will necessarily turn you into an abuser. In particular the pattern concept is invoked in relation to living with bad men.

The mother has low self esteem, a poor self image. She's grown up with a father who's violent, got herself into that kind of relationship. (interview with social worker 'Claire')

The reality of the lives of many of the women clients is understood to involve living with bad men. The priority of the social workers, as is constantly repeated, is 'the welfare of the child'. So although there is an appreciation of how an experience of oppression has negative outcomes for women, there is more practical concern about the effects of this on the children than on women themselves. The following excerpt illustrates how a social worker sees the effects on the children of living with a man who is violent towards their mother.

That can sometimes have two different effects on sort of child care. One is that partners who are abusive towards them are more likely to be abusive towards the children as well, and their own abilities to cope with the kids obviously get knocked back if they are being abused themselves or if they are not looking after themselves. To look after your kids you have got to look after yourself. (interview with social worker 'Mike')

Women making choices

Howe (1996) has claimed that contemporary social work practice, purged of psychodynamic influences, views clients as making free rational choices to act in the ways they do. I deliberately use the word 'choices' because a traditional social work emphasis on the social and economic context of clients' problems seems to be balanced by an ethic of ultimate individual responsibility. This balance is to be expected in a policy climate that has prioritized the targeting of dangerous families rather than broader social interventions (Parton, 1991). The following excerpt illustrates this. It is Mary's view that social policy can help many but not all.

> I think there is a hell of a lot that can be done in wider social policy, you know like housing, education, community services like play schemes, after school clubs, there are loads and loads of things. Benefits as well is the other thing. If a lot of those things were changed, a lot of the work that we do wouldn't be necessary. But that is not to say, I mean there was one point where I thought that would be the whole answer but I don't think that now. I think there are people who have got deeper problems and would always need some sort of social services. (interview with social worker 'Mary')

The most overt way in which women choose not to put their children first is in choosing a bad man. It is a very interesting and important aspect of the construction of gender because it illustrates the process (highlighted by Farmer and Owen, 1998) of attention moving from abusive men onto the women who 'allow them' to stay around and abuse them or their children. Women's responsibility for protection against abusive men is expressed as a clear choice: him or the kids.

> If domestic violence has a high profile within the family I am sure that as a department we would be saying to the woman that you must make a choice about whether you want to stay with this man or leave him. (interview with team manager 'Margaret')

> Where women are faced with the choice 'it's your children or your partner' quite often they don't make the choice. They choose the partner. (interview with social worker 'Claire')

> The child is actually with an adoptive family and to see her now, and how she has glossed and developed confidence, stature, that is rewarding. She is not a sad little girl now; she is brave and bubbly. It is sad for her mother, but her mother had choices and chose her partner. That's the kind of process that you go through. It is not always as clear cut as that. (interview with Docktown social worker, 'Lynne')

Lynne, in the last of these extracts, acknowledges there is not always a clear cut 'choice'. Claire's view that women often 'don't make the choice' also accepts that women do not necessarily make a calm, rational choice to give up their children. Despite these notes of caution, there is a strong culture of laying down ultimatums to women living with abusive men: if it is bad for the children, you have to get him out. Farmer and Owen's research (1998) has shown that many women living with violent men are afraid to go to social services departments for help, for fear their children will be taken into care. Coming forward for help is viewed positively, but failure then to throw the man out can indeed result in these fears being realized. Ultimatums do not consider the complex reasons why women may want men to stay, or be persuaded or coerced into letting them stay. This approach to the presence of violent or abusive men fits with Howe's observation (1996: 88) that in contemporary social work, change in clients is expected in response to the laying down of rules, rather than any therapeutic intervention.

I would reject Philp's (1979) structuralist assumption that it should be possible to identify a unitary discourse for the social work profession. I do agree with Philp, however, that the production of knowledge about subjects, subjects who can act and not get stuck (Stenson, 1993), does have a great deal of discursive power in the culture of social work. Gordon's (1988) study of gender and violence in historical case records also found that

> despite the environmental analysis, child protectors continued to feature moralistic appeals to will power, as if individual determination could hold off the centrifugal forces of modern urban life. (Gordon, 1988: 74)

In fact the application of Philp's theories to the Uplands team shows that women are expected to have will power, and men, when seen as abusers, are beyond subjectivity and therefore beyond clienthood. The emphasis on the subject who can act, despite a lifetime of identity formation and overwhelming circumstantial pressure, is problematic for feminist social work. Inevitably, it means a down-grading of social information that might explain a 'case', and makes interventions on a governmental or a community level seem irrelevant. As Swift observes,

> the contextual information that might help to explain problems in child care is stripped away from the mother, and she is looked at as an 'individual' a process that warrants the efforts of the state to focus its change efforts on her – in fact, which makes any other effort appear off the point. Poverty, class and race relations, gender issues, and fathers all vanish. Mothers are produced and reproduced as the 'causal variable' (Swift, 1995: 125).

Arguably, the emphasis on the 'will-power' of the subject does not take account of how gender works. It does not consider the effects of long-term oppression on the formation of social identities, the difficulty of thinking you ought to do one thing, but finding yourself doing another – the very thing you believe you should not be doing. It does not take account of limitations on opportunities for action such as, for example, the immense difficulty for a woman in acting to force a man to leave her house when he has threatened her life and she fears homelessness and the stigma of single parenthood. The subjectification of clients does not allow for a social understanding of gender relations, but brings everything back to individual responsibility.

The tensions between the individual and the social experienced by social workers in trying to explain their clients' circumstances mirror my own struggles to conceptualize the social workers' constructions of gender. The question they have to face as to whether clients are trapped in an oppressive social context neatly matches one of the most important theoretical dilemmas of my research, namely are the social workers trapped in occupational discourse or can there be alternative, oppositional constructions of men and women clients? There is symmetry here, and not surprisingly, since this is the oldest problem of social inquiry, the activity that both the social workers and I as researcher are engaged in. This is the dualism of sociology–psychology, structure–agency, work with individuals or work with collectivities.

A post-structuralist emphasis on multiple gendered discourses best captures for me the relation of individual social workers to their knowledge base, rooted as this is in occupational culture. It may also have potential for improving social workers' understanding of their clients. Weedon's (1987) feminist post-structuralism explains that the power of discourse constrains what can be known and what can be said in specific social and historical contexts, and her theoretical framework also allows for fluidity, and tensions between discourses. So, for example, it can explain how conservative discourses on the family operate, and it can also allow for feminist challenges. Post-structuralism challenges the liberal humanist notion of the knowing, unified, rational subject. Rather, subjectivity is seen as socially produced in language and as a site of struggle and potential change. So social workers are not simply free to construct their clients in any way they choose. As Weedon explains,

> Discourses represent political interests and in consequence are constantly vying for status and power. The site of this battle for power is the subjectivity of the individual and it is a battle in which the individual is an active but not a sovereign protagonist. (Weedon, 1987: 41)

Of course child protection social work is not just about knowledge and language, it is also about action. My use of 'discourse' is not restricted to what social workers say and write. It is not the intention to make a clear separation between 'knowledge' and 'practice'. Foucault's work (e.g. 1977) demonstrates that discourse is not abstract, impacting on minds only, but has a material relation to the bodies that are the objects of discourse (the clients in this case). As Connell (1998: 6) expresses it, 'domination is not a matter of disembodied discourses'. Discourse should be regarded as 'a material practice' (Haraway, 1992: 111).

Conclusion

I have tried to convey in this chapter some notions of symmetry in social work research, using the example of my study of the construction of gender in child protection work. The first symmetrical relationship is that qualitative researchers are engaged in interviewing people who are themselves experts in interviewing. The second is that in interpreting aspects of occupational culture and occupational discourse in the social work office, the researcher is faced with the same tension between structure and agency as the social worker who has to struggle with the social understanding that her professional identity demands and also the practical imperative of making a judgement about an individual's capacity to change. An awareness of this symmetry does not make the researcher's task easier, but could potentially make it more interesting.

Note

1. A full account of the research that this chapter draws on can be found in Scourfield, J.B. (1999) *The Construction of Gender in Child Protection Social Work*, PhD thesis, Cardiff University.

5

Personal Troubles as Social Issues: A Narrative of Infertility in Context

Catherine Kohler Riessman

CONTENTS

Constructing social identities in personal narrative   75
Discussion   81

Social work practice, in all its diversity, is united by a commitment to social and economic justice – decreasing inequalities and increasing life chances of all citizens. Social work research can support these values by documenting inequalities in lives and analysing precisely how social structures and social policies enhance and restrict opportunities for individuals and groups. In this chapter I focus on the substantive issue of infertility – a 'personal trouble'. I examine its relationship to gender inequality, and one woman's efforts in the face of the stigma of infertility, made possible by a context of progressive social policies in her south Indian state. My methodological approach is narrative analysis.

There is currently a large body of research based on a variety of narrative methods, including applications in social work. The burgeoning literature has touched almost every discipline and profession, particularly in the USA. No longer the province only of literary study, the 'narrative turn' in the human sciences has entered history (Carr, 1986; Cronon, 1992; White, 1987), anthropology and folklore (Behar, 1993; Mattingly and Garro, 2000; Rosaldo, 1989; Young, 1987), psychology (Bruner 1986, 1990; Mishler 1986, 1999; Polkinghorne, 1988; Rosenwald and Ochberg, 1992; Sarbin, 1986), sociolinguistics (Capps and Ochs, 1995; Gee, 1986, 1991; Labov, 1982; Linde, 1993), and sociology (Bell, 1988, 1999; Boje, 1991; Chase, 1995; DeVault, 1991; Frank, 1995; Holstein and Gubrium, 2000; Williams, 1984). The professions, too, have embraced the narrative metaphor, along with investigators who study particular professions: law ('Legal Storytelling',

1989), medicine (Charon, 1986; Greenhalgh and Hurwitz, 1998; Hunter, 1991; Hyden, 1997; Kleinman, 1988), nursing (Sandelowski, 1991), occupational therapy (Mattingly, 1998), and social work (Dean, 1995; Laird, 1988). Storytelling, to put the argument simply, is what we do with research and clinical materials, and what informants do with us.

Narrative analysis takes as its object of investigation the story itself. I limit discussion here to first-person accounts in interviews of informants' experience,[1] putting aside other kinds of narratives (e.g. about the self of the investigator, what happened in the field, written narratives, media descriptions of events, or the 'master narratives' of theory). My research has focused on disruptive life events, accounts of 'personal troubles' that fundamentally alter expected biographies (divorce, chronic illness, and infertility), and I draw on the example of infertility later. Narrative analysis, however, is not only relevant for the study of disruptive life events: the methods are equally appropriate for studies of social movements, political change, and macro-level phenomena. Plummer (1995: 174) argues that 'stories gather people around them', dialectically connecting people and social movements. His investigations of identity stories of members of historically 'defiled' groups (rape victims, gays and lesbians) reveal shifts in language over time, which shaped (and were shaped by) the mobilization of these actors in collective movements, such as 'Take Back the Night' and gay rights groups. 'For narratives to flourish there must be a community to hear; . . . for communities to hear, there must be stories which weave together their history, their identity, their politics' (Plummer, 1995: 87).

Storytelling is a collaborative practice, and assumes tellers and listeners/ questioners interact in particular cultural milieux – contexts essential to interpretation. Analysis in narrative studies opens up forms of telling about experience, not simply the content to which language refers. We ask, why was the story told *that* way? (Riessman, 1993).

Study of personal narrative is a form of case-centered research (Mishler, 1999a). Building on the tradition of sociology articulated most vividly by C.W. Mills (1959), the approach illuminates the intersection of biography, history, and society. The 'personal troubles' that participants represent in their narratives of divorce, for example, tell us a great deal about social and historical processes – contemporary beliefs about gender relations and pressures on marriage at a juncture in American history (Riessman, 1990a). Coming out stories, similarly, where narrators proclaim their gayness to themselves and others, reveal a shift in genre over time: the linear, 'causal' modernist tales of the 1960s and 1970s give way in contemporary stories to identities that blur and change (Plummer, 1995). Historical shifts in understanding and growing politicization occur in the stories of women with cancer whose mothers were exposed to the drug DES during pregnancy, reflecting changes in understanding made possible by the women's health movement (Bell, 1999). As Mills said long ago, what we call 'personal troubles' are located in particular times and places, and individuals' narratives about their troubles are works of history, as much as they are about individuals, the social spaces they inhabit, and the societies they live in.

Attention to the social in a 'personal' narrative can embolden social work research, and unite research and practice around the values of social justice and equality. What research participants' stories take for granted – the 'real', the way things are – can be analysed for social meanings and effects. A participant's understandings of her 'troubles' contain the seeds of her social analysis that, in turn, can be interpreted for the ways it supports and/or undermines larger systems of domination. The approach attends to contexts (local, cultural, and historical) in the interpretation of personal narratives. Here, for example, I attend to the locality of Kerala, arguably the most progressive state in India, which provides opportunities for women not easily available in other parts of the subcontinent, along with constraints. The approach leads to insights about lives in context and the workings of oppressive social structures – not portraits of an 'authentic' subject or 'true' self, as critics have claimed (Atkinson, 1997; Atkinson and Silverman, 1997).

Constructing social identities in personal narrative

I illustrate a social perspective to narrative analysis with a segment from a research interview. Detailed transcription is included so that readers can examine the narrative in dialogic exchange. My theoretical interest is in women's identity construction when they face the 'personal trouble' of infertility. I analyse how a woman performs her social identities in a story: her 'private self' is shaped by contradictory realities – gender inequality, on the one hand, and public policies that foster social justice, on the other. The interview is from a larger corpus of interviews with married childless women completed during fieldwork in Kerala, south India, in 1993–4. Interviews, conducted at a single point in time, were taped and subsequently transcribed and translated where necessary. My research assistant (Liza) and I conducted them (seven were in English and the rest in Malayalam[2]). We encouraged women to give extended accounts of their situations, including the reactions of others: husband, other family, the neighbours. We did not interview husbands, so their perceptions of infertility are not included except as wives represent them. (For a full description of method, see Riessman, 2000a, 2000b.)

The woman whose life story I examine – I'll call her Asha – was chosen because she is among the oldest in my sample, and probably past child-bearing age. Constructing a meaningful gender identity without biological children is a major issue for her. Asha lives in India, a strongly pronatalist society – women are expected to marry and bear children – but she lives in the state of Kerala, which has a long tradition of fostering women's autonomy and economic sufficiency.[3] Like other childless women in

Kerala, however, she faces severe stigma because she is not a mother (Riessman, 2000b). For example, neighbours treat her 'like a *machi*' – a word in Malayalam that has no English equivalent: It refers to a farm animal that cannot breed.

In Asha's narrative, I pay particular attention to social positioning in relation to identity claims. 'The act of positioning . . . refers to the assignment of fluid "parts" or "roles" to speakers in the discursive construction of personal stories . . .' (Harré and Van Langenhove, 1999: 7). When we tell stories about our lives we perform our identities (Langellier, 2001; Mishler, 1999). Several levels of social positioning are my analytic points of entry into the 'personal story'. First, it developed in an immediate discursive context, an evolving interview with a listener/questioner. At this level, Asha positions herself in a dialogic process. She performs her preferred identity for a particular audience – my research assistant, and me in this case. We are also located in social spaces and bring views about infertility to the conversations, positioning Asha. Second, Asha's narrative is positioned in a broader cultural discourse about women's proper place in modern India, a 'developing' nation that is developing new spaces (besides home and field) for women to labour. The narrative is also located in the gender politics of Kerala, where women have been advantaged by progressive social policies, but also constrained by gender ideologies. I show how attention to the shifting cultural context, and the proximate interview context, is essential to interpretation. Third, Asha positions herself in the particulars of her story in relation to physicians (and medical technology), and vis-à-vis powerful family members. Taken together, the angle of vision of social positioning in narrative provides a lens to explore how a middle-aged woman works to construct a positive identity when she cannot conceive.

Asha, who has never been pregnant, is a 42–year-old Hindu woman. She completed secondary school and is employed as a government clerk. Typical of women in Kerala, she has benefited from the state's educational policies: girls attend school as often as boys and, because of similar levels of education, secure government jobs are occupied by both women and men, in contrast to other states in India. She and her husband, from a 'backward' (Dalit) caste, also receive some food and housing assistance from the government.

On the day we met Asha, she was making her second visit to the infertility clinic of a government hospital. She had previously gone for biomedical treatment for infertility in another hospital, as her narrative describes. Biomedicine is widely available in Kerala's towns and villages; the hospital where she came this time is the tertiary care centre for a large district. Asha had come reluctantly we learn in the excerpt (below), but she was not reluctant to be interviewed; we spent nearly an hour talking together in a private room while she was waiting to be seen by the doctor. Liza, my 26-year-old research assistant, told Asha we wanted to understand 'the experience of being childless from women's points of view'. The open-ended interview was in Malayalam, translated periodically for me, and Asha said she felt 'comforted' by it. Although our questions focused mostly on issues of infertility and societal response, Asha directed the interview to other topics of importance to her. During the first few minutes, for example, when asked about the composition of her household and other demographic 'facts', Asha's extended responses hint at complexities in gender relations: her husband is 12 years her junior, and will become unemployed shortly – 'we will be managing on my income alone'. The meaning of these issues only became clear later in the interview. At this point, Liza asks, 'What do you think is the reason why you do not have children?' We enter the interview at this point.

Lisa: What do you think is the reason why you do not have children?
Asha: I think that it must be because I am so old
          That is my opinion
          Other than that, no other problem.

          There is this [name] hospital in Alleppey
          There – I had gone there for treatment
          Then the doctor said that – after after doing a scan
          the way through which the sperm goes
          There is some block
          And so they did a D&C.
          When the results came – when we gave money to the lab
          They said they did not see any problem.
          After that they said I must take 5 pills.
          I took them.
          Then that also did not work.
          Then they said that I must have an injection.
          I had one.
          They said I must come again after that.
          After I had the first injection
          I was disappointed when it did not work
          I had hoped that it would be all right after the first injection.
          When that did not happen
          Then I was very much disheartened.
          Then when they said to come again –
          Then I didn't go after that.

          – [describes how a neighbour persuaded her to go to Infertility Clinic]
          –
          If God is going to give, let him.

Asha's response takes a classic narrative form: she emplots a sequence of events related to medical treatment, which she locates in time and place, and she provides evaluation or commentary on their meanings. Typical of 'fully formed', bounded narratives identified by sociolinguists (Labov, 1982), hers is tightly structured and uninterrupted by the listener. Asha was 40 years old at the time of the events, had been married 2 years, and could not get pregnant. We do not know, at this point in the conversation, why she married so late – the average age for women in Kerala is 22 (Gulati et al., 1996).

Looking at how Asha positions herself, she answers our question directly and offers her present understanding of 'the reason' for infertility ('it must be because I am so old'), which contrasts with the technical diagnosis offered by a physician she consulted in the past ('there is some block'). It is her location in the life course, she says, not some internal flaw, that is responsible for the infertility. The narrator is agent, the real expert, wise and realistic about the meaning of age for fertility; she positions the physicians as 'they' – the other – who depend on medical technology (a scan, D&C, pills and injections). Her positioning aligns the listener with the narrator in a moral stance: the 'I' knows better than the 'other'. As the knowing subject, Asha deflects blame – age is not something she is responsible for. The narrative suggests self-assurance rather than self-blame – a marked contrast to the speech of women visiting an infertility clinic in north India, who typically said 'there is something wrong with me' (Jindal and Gupta, 1989). Asha carefully and knowledgeably names every medical procedure. She reports how she followed the prescribed regime, perhaps because of the setting of the interview and expectations about us. She positions herself for the medical context – she would be viewed as a 'good historian' and 'compliant patient'. But biomedicine failed her. It also failed to make room for her emotions: no one relates to her disappointment in the narrative performance. Asha became 'disheartened' when treatment didn't work, and did not return to the hospital.

In a lengthy episode (not included in the transcript) Asha performs a conversation with a neighbour in her village, who got pregnant after treatment at the infertility clinic where our interview took place. 'She told me if I came here [to clinic] it will be alright.' Asha said to the neighbour, 'I will still have this problem of my age.' The neighbour responded by saying she had seen 'people who are 45 years' in the waiting room of the clinic. Asha then agreed, very reluctantly, to try the clinic, as 'a last resort'. As she reasoned, 'there will be no need to be disappointed' because she will have tried everything.

Asha concludes the narrative with a coda that looks to religion rather than science ('If God is going to give [children], let him'). Like the first line of the narrative or abstract ('I think it must be because I am so old'), the coda acknowledges that health involves more than narrow, technical problems in the body that doctors can fix. A theodicy frames the account of infertility – beginning and ending it – suggesting resistance to the bio-medical model and secular beliefs about health (Greil, 1991).

There are several ambiguities in Asha's sparse narrative. Because the interview was translated from Malayalam, close examination of word choice is not appropriate but other narrative strategies can be examined: for example, the characters she introduces in the performance, and the way she positions herself in relation to them. Absences are striking: there is no mention of husband or other family members; only once does she use a plural pronoun ('we gave money to the lab'). She does not say that her husband accompanied her for treatment or if he was examined by doctors – customary in Indian infertility clinics. In contrast to the richly peopled stories about infertility told by other south Indian women, there are few characters in Asha's: anonymous doctors ('they'), a neighbour, and Asha herself. We get the impression of an isolated, singular 'self', negotiating infertility treatment on her own – a picture that is at odds with the typical family-centred fertility search I observed in other interviews, and with Indian views of familial identity (Riessman, 2000b).

Information from later in the interview forced me to consider additional meanings, suggesting other provisional interpretations of Asha's identity performance in the excerpt. As our conversation progressed, she introduced a series of topics that went beyond the interview's focus on infertility, enabling the construction of a life story in which the bounded narrative about infertility can be situated.[4] Her life story is in some ways typical of the life course of women from the rural areas of Kerala, although in key respects it is unique.

Asha related that her natal family was large, very poor, and when marriage proposals came for her, the parents could not raise the dowry. Asha also says she was not interested in marriage ('married life, I did not want it from childhood on, I was one of those who did not like it'). An independent self is performed in this utterance, not unlike Asha's identity performance in the infertility narrative. Resistance to marriage by young women is somewhat unusual in India, although marriage can be postponed for girls to complete educational careers. For Asha, however, other events interrupted the inevitable path toward marriage. Both of Asha's parents died when she was a young woman. She received a small inheritance when the property was divided among the siblings. With it, she bought a little gold, secured a small loan, got a job, won some money in the lottery, and eventually accumulated enough to buy a small piece of land with a thatched hut ('all of it I bought by myself'). Such autonomous actions on the part of a woman contrast with stereotypes about women in India, but Asha's actions are not entirely atypical in Kerala. Government policies are fostering women's power and economic independence as part of rural development efforts, including micro credit schemes and enterprises, in addition to affirmative action policies for women and historically disadvantaged castes (Gulati et al., 1996; Jeffrey, 1993).

Asha did eventually marry. I asked about her 'change of heart' and she educated me: 'if you want to get ahead in the future you must have a husband, a child – only then [do you have] a family; when we become old there must be somebody to look after us'. Like women in India generally, she needed 'a family' to move forward and receive social recognition – to 'get ahead'. As she must know, unmarried women are severely stigmatized in Indian villages, and some migrate to large cities to achieve anonymity if they remain unmarried. Asha needed a husband to legitimately have 'a family', that is, a child – necessary in a country without universal social welfare programmes for the aged. (Instrumental views about having children to insure care in old age were common in my interviews.) In a word, Asha's life chances are profoundly shaped by gender constraints, even in the context of Kerala's emphasis on women's status and independence (Jeffery et al., 1989; Uberoi, 1993).

Asha went to a marriage broker to fix a marriage at age 38 – an unusual move, necessitated by the fact that her brothers had left the region. The arranged inter-caste marriage (Asha married 'down') concealed a significant age discrepancy – Asha was 12 years older than her husband – which she discovered later. It may be that she was exploited by the increasingly commercialized world of marriage arrangements – data are sparse here. With the recent influx of foreign goods into India and increasing consumerism, coupled with high unemployment, dowry (or the selection of a wife with good earnings) has become a way for poor families to imagine having more. Asha has a higher level of education than her husband does and a secure government job; her husband faces unemployment (he has a sales job and the small enterprise is closing).

He, however, expects children. She performed a conversation with him in our interview that voices his disappointment: 'What kind of life is this, without children? Two people sitting and looking at each other.' Her in-laws blame her for the fertility problems ('it is my fault that we do not have children, their son has no problem – that is her [mother-in-law's] opinion'). His family is pressuring her to get treatment – a typical manifestation of gender inequality in perceived responsibility for infertility. Stigma, I learned in other interviews, falls overwhelmingly on the woman when pregnancy does not occur, and they face abandonment by husbands who can remarry (Riessman, 2000a, 2000b, 2001b). Asha intimates this will be her fate ('if we do not have children, the marital relationship will break up').

In this context, the narrative episode (excerpt above) makes sense – 'as a last resort' Asha decides to try infertility treatment again, at age 42, even as she wisely knows she is 'too old'. The absence of family and husband in the excerpt masks their large role in the decision. The husband's absence raises other questions, however. Given the precarious status of her marriage, is Asha readying herself for life again as a single woman? A reader might be tempted to read her story as one of victimization – a south Indian woman who faces divorce because of infertility – but her narrative performance as a competent 'solo self' suggests a more complex reality.

Discussion

My social analysis of a personal narrative highlights several issues in work with interview narratives. First, they do not speak for themselves. Narrative excerpts require interpretation, expansion, and analysis – 'unpacking' to uncover and interpret the inevitable ambiguities contained in any form of language. Second, narratives are situated utterances. They unfold in particular interactions with particular listeners, and these contexts shape what is said, and what cannot be spoken. (Remember how Asha educated me on how she needed a family to 'get ahead' in India and achieve status as an adult woman, despite her financial independence.) Narrators do not tell *their* story, that is, reveal an essential self – but *a* story that shines light on certain aspects of identity, and leaves others in shadow. A different listener/questioner would undoubtedly see other identities. For example, Asha performs her competent self for a Western woman professional (me) and my assistant, Liza – a south Indian social worker. For a different audience, Asha's narrative performance might have included greater sadness, worry, or fear. We might also ask how her texts might be read by native speakers and others sharing indigenous gender ideologies. Elsewhere (Riessman, 2000a) I open up this issue by examining a south Indian woman's narrative that was read differently by different participants (and the same participant over time). The 'translating' nature of interpretation cannot be ignored in ethnographic research (Clifford, 1997).

Finally, narratives of personal troubles, such as infertility, are situated in cultural and historical time. Social work research can bring these contexts to bear in the interpretation of personal stories. Asha's life story, for example, is contingent on social policies and contemporary rural development efforts, even as it is constrained by gender ideologies and age hierarchies, including the motherhood mandate and the power of in-laws over a wife. As Amartya Sen (1999: xii) argues, 'There is a deep complementarity between individual agency and social arrangements.'

The absence of a social movement in India to support Asha's position as a childless, and possibly divorced woman, is also significant. Although there are long-standing feminist interests and organizations in India, the difficulties of women who attempt to live outside of families without children (or outside of marriage) remain private issues. As Patricia Hill Collins (1997) cautions, individual women may benefit from local resistance practices, but there is no substitute for sustained improvement of women as a group, which is possible in collective movements that target structural power.

Acknowledgements

I thank Liza George, Leela Gulati, and Drs Kaveri Gopalakrishnan and P.K. Shamala. The Indo-US Subcommission on Education and Culture,

Council for the International Exchange of Scholars, provided financial support for fieldwork.

Notes

1. There are, of course, other narrative sites besides interviews. For examples of so-called 'natural' storytelling, see Ochs et al. (1989) and Polanyi (1985).
2. Malayalam is a member of the Drividian family of languages spoken in south India. My representation of the translated interviews has benefited from conversations with Liza while in India, and with India specialists since my return to the USA. Translation can open up ambiguities of meaning that get hidden in 'same-language' texts. When we have a common language with our informants, we tend to easily assume that we know what they are saying, and alternative readings tend to get obscured, or even ignored. For more on issues of translation and meaning see Riessman (2000a).
3. Kerala, located along the southwestern coast of India, is an exceptional state on a variety of indicators: a 75 per cent literacy rate (vs 39 for India) for women, a life expectancy at birth of 73 (vs 57) for women, and a sex ratio of 1,036 females (vs 929) per 1,000 males. The effective female literacy rate in Kerala approaches 86 per cent (Gulati et al., 1996). There is debate about the precise causes of the state's advantaged position (Letters, 1991). On the political economy, special ecology, and unique history of Kerala, see Jeffrey (1993), Nag (1988), Sen (1999).
4. Analysis of brief, topically specific narratives organized around characters, setting, and plot – the approach pioneered by Labov (1982) – contrasts with analysis of extended accounts of lives that develop over the course of entire interviews – the narrative approach of Mishler (1999). For more on different definitions of narrative and associated analytic strategies, see Mishler (1995) and Riessman (2001a).

6

'People Listened to What We Had to Say': Reflections on an Emancipatory Qualitative Evaluation

Elizabeth Whitmore

CONTENTS

Introduction: A Drop In Centre in search of an evaluation   83
The Drop In Centre: a thumbnail sketch   83
Some key elements of emancipatory research   84
The practice of emancipatory qualitative research   86
Building a research team   86
Figuring out how to get the information   87
Introduction of interactive (PLA) methods   87
Reporting   89
Action: So what difference did this make?   90
Issues: Bumps and detours along the yellow brick road   91
Locating the self   91
Exploring political and power dimensions of empowerment   93
Being explicit about the tensions   96
Linking research to wider questions of social inequality and justice   97
Conclusion: Not an afterthought   98

Introduction: A Drop In Centre in search of an evaluation[1]

> The agency has a long history of delivering services to high risk youth . . . We currently do not know what works or who benefits from our Drop In services for street involved youth. (Evaluation Funding Proposal, 1996)

The Drop In Centre: a thumbnail sketch

A Drop In Centre for street-involved youth, one of a number of services offered by a large, youth-serving agency in a Canadian city, had been operating for four years. It provides support services to 'high risk', street-involved youth ten hours daily, every day of the year. Services are free and include a hot lunch, showers, laundry facilities, referral to other agencies and crisis counselling. An average of 80 youth visit the Centre daily. The majority are marginalized by poverty, have histories of abuse, and lack education and employment skills. Often they attempt to overcome these barriers and avoid their problems through criminal activity and drug and alcohol misuse. Because the Centre is staffed by only three front line workers, the large numbers of youth facing serious issues can create a chaotic environment that can sometimes raise concerns about safety.

After four years, it was time to do an evaluation, to take a look at what was happening, whether the services offered were meeting the needs of the target population and to assess their effectiveness. The Centre's mission and clientele were controversial. While some felt that the youth needed a safe place to 'hang out', allowing staff to reach out informally, build trust and intervene in crises, others wanted more structured activities and stricter rules. Still others saw the Centre as attracting 'undesirable' youth to the downtown area and wanted it closed down entirely.

My involvement began in response to an agency staff member who had approached faculty at the school of social work in my university around the possibility of forming research partnerships with local agencies. An evaluation of the Drop In Centre was one option. I have long had a personal interest in participatory action research and evaluation, particularly the methodology – how does the process actually work (Whitmore, 1998)? It is certainly philosophically consistent with social work values, principles and practice (Dullea and Mullender, 1999). This seemed a perfect opportunity to combine my social work background with my interest in participatory/emancipatory approaches to research.

I approached the idea with several assumptions: one, that street-involved youth know their reality far better than anyone else, and are thus in the best position to evaluate their own services; two, that the youth would be reluctant to trust any adult in authority, let alone a stranger and an academic; and three, that qualitative methods are generally more compatible with such a setting and with social work practice in general. So, the challenge was not whether to involve youth in the evaluation process, but how.

The purpose of this chapter is to present a case example of emancipatory qualitative research. I will begin by outlining some key aspects of emancipatory research, and then describe how this approach was applied in the Drop In Centre evaluation. Finally, I will explore some of the issues emerging from this experience and how they relate to social work theory and practice.

Some key elements of emancipatory research

Four key aspects of the emancipatory research model guided our work in this project. First, the influence of social, political, cultural, economic, ethnic, gender and disability values was recognized as an integral factor in this research (Mertens, 1998: 20). It was clear that our differing personal, social and institutional 'locations' had a great deal to do with how each one of the participants understood and interpreted the world and how each was perceived. This directly challenged the notion of neutrality or value free inquiry. We understood that multiple perspectives needed to be captured and the hidden values made explicit (Patton, 1999; Stanfield, 1999). Emancipatory research examines what is assumed to be 'real', taking a critical look at social structures and policies that may be reified and oppressive to groups outside the mainstream. It is argued by hooks (1984) that the view from the margins is in fact more complete in that it encompasses the realities of those at the margins *and* those in the centre. In contrast, people at the centre of power are often unable, or unwilling, to understand the experience of those with less power.

Second, issues related to power were considered to be central. Who creates knowledge? Who controls the research? Who conducts research on whom and for what purposes? Who benefits? The transformative potential of the social research process is manifested in how knowledge is produced, who produces it and what happens to it (Truman, 2000). Mertens (1999) refers to the importance of including otherwise-silenced voices in a diverse world. The majority of research on street-involved youth (using the word 'on' advisedly) fails to include their voices in any significant way. At best, they are 'subjects' in survey designs or they may have opportunities to respond to some open-ended questions.

This research was designed to 'hand over the stick' to the youth (Chambers, 1997). That is, as much as possible, they were to be in charge of the process, and my role (and that of the staff members) was to facilitate and support that. The explicit intent was to enhance the power of the service users to have the research process and results reflect their knowledge and experience (cf. Evans and Fisher, 1999). We wanted them to benefit both directly as individuals and as a collective, and indirectly in improving the Drop In services. 'In addition to a willingness to engage in inclusive, demystifying practice, social workers also need the ability to analyse the power and control implications of their research role' (Evans and Fisher, 1999: 114).

A third aspect involved receptivity to 'other' ways of knowing as legitimate and indeed necessary. This implied interactive and culturally appropriate ways to *fully* engage participants in the process. It means 'connecting' with what people know, learning to listen in unfamiliar ways and thinking outside of our customary understandings (Riessman, 1987). It means using methods and techniques of information gathering and analysis that are adaptable and perhaps less well known. It does not, however, mean less rigour; indeed, there is evidence that in these circumstances, they provide more-valid results than conventional methods (Chambers, 1997).

Finally, linking the research directly to action focuses on inclusion of otherwise unheard voices. That is, there was a clear and explicit goal not only to change the Drop In Centre but also to demonstrate a model to the agency as a whole of how young people could be significantly involved in decision-making processes. This goes well beyond promoting 'utilization' of evaluation findings by 'decision-makers' to changing who is included, to what extent and for what purposes. Together, these four aspects formed the foundation of our approach to the evaluation design and to its implementation.

The practice of emancipatory qualitative research: Participation is an attitude, not only a set of methods

> It kept me out of a lot of shit. People listened to what we had to say and I even got paid for it. . . . (young woman, reflecting on her participation in the evaluation)

There were a number of phases in actually doing this evaluation, beginning with recruiting the participants through to the reporting of the final results and follow up. We began with a commitment to working together as a starting point and being open to where the journey would take us (Evans and Fisher, 1999: 115).

Building a research team

Given the population, I was well aware that the youth were likely to need consistent, ongoing support from trusted adults. This I certainly could not do myself, so I began by recruiting two Drop In staff members, Colette and Rick, as part of the research team. (Staff team members were selected on the basis of interviews with those expressing interest. The grant funds were used primarily for replacement staff time, salaries for the youth researchers, teaching release time for me and research-related expenses.) We then focused on youth, advertised for the job – using posters and word of mouth – and interviewed applicants on the short list. Six young people were hired.

At the beginning, I took a leadership role and gradually, as the youth gained confidence and understanding of the process, they assumed leadership. We began team building using standard group work theory and practice, balancing task with group maintenance and individual needs (Burke, 1998; MIT Theory, 1975).

Everything was done on flipcharts, which helped focus attention and enhance collective input and ownership (Arnold et al., 1991; Avery et al., 1981). As a group, we started by establishing a set of rules to guide our work together, and develop some routines – check ins and check outs, regular breaks, and snacks (Oreo cookies were deemed to be one of the four basic food groups!). For the first month or so, we did team-building exercises to build trust and confidence. We also built in relaxation and fun, through monthly outings.

Figuring out how to get the information

I introduced the evaluation process, being careful not to use academic 'big' words or jargon. Instead of design, data collection and sample, we asked ourselves questions such as, what do we want to know, how are we going to find out, and whom should we ask (Barnsley and Ellis, 1992)? My role was one of teaching and support. We went round and round with these three questions, and gradually a design emerged. We began, interestingly enough, with rather conventional strategies, by deciding to do a series of surveys – of the youth who used the Drop In, of those who did not, of staff, local businesses, police and other social service agencies. Figuring out what questions to ask and how to ask them in a youth friendly way in the first survey (of Drop In users) took a long time. After they got the hang of it, the other surveys were developed more rapidly. Each survey contained a combination of closed and open-ended questions. We worked back and forth in subgroups (each with one of the adult members and two young people) and as a whole, working on questions, and getting feedback from the others. At appropriate times, I did introduce jargon so that they would become familiar with the terminology of research and be able to use it with understanding and confidence (Kirby and McKenna, 1989).

Introduction of interactive (PLA) methods

At first, the youth were unreceptive to more interactive techniques, such as Participatory Learning and Action (PLA) (Chambers, 1997). These involve highly visual and unconventional methods originally used with villages in the field of rural and international development. Three basic principles underlie this approach: the behaviour and attitudes of outsiders (who facilitate rather than dominate), the methods (from closed to open, individual to group, verbal to visual and from measuring to comparing) and a commitment to partnership and sharing (of information, experience, food and training) (Chambers, 1997: 105–6). Methods include mapping, transects (systematic walks and observation), diagramming, visual representations and matrices.

Perhaps the youth hesitated because they were insecure as a group and therefore were reluctant to engage the wider population of street youth. They needed to build confidence and trust first. In addition, they had never been exposed to 'other' ways of knowing as legitimate, so felt more comfortable staying with what was familiar.

There were several key ingredients in introducing interactive methods. One staff member, Colette, had attended a workshop on PLA methods and came back all fired up. (She recognized the relationship between these and social work practice methods right away.) The youth, however, did not share her enthusiasm and were quite resistant to methods they saw as 'game playing'. A second opportunity arose when we were trying to figure out how to sample local businesses. The Business Improvement Association (BIA) had given us their fax tree and as we looked at it, the youth noticed that many of the places they knew (the corner stores, fast food restaurants, tattoo parlours, etc.) were not there. These places do not have fax machines!

It was around this time that one of the young people exploded in frustration – 'this is so boring. All we're doing is stupid surveys! I applied for this job because I wanted to help change the Drop In and nothing's happening.' Here was an opportunity to switch gears and move to more interactive data-gathering techniques – to 'other' ways of knowing. Colette suggested that they draw a map of the downtown area and highlight the places where youth congregate. Then they filled in the businesses in the vicinity, and targeted those places for surveys. The youth certainly knew where the key businesses were! Without knowing it, the team had gotten into PLA techniques, and once we 'named' it, they recognized its value and relevance. We developed a very short and easy survey which the youth themselves took around and had people fill out on the spot.

From here, Colette introduced ways of engaging the wider Drop In youth population. The youth planned and carried out a series of focus groups. One group did a huge matrix (on flipcharts, covering a whole wall), rating each Drop In service (bad, needs improvement, good, excellent) with colourful sticky notes. The effect was quite immediate and dramatic, in that those services the youth regarded as positive were easily identifiable, as were those they found negative. The participants wrote specific comments on each note, so the particulars could be discussed. There was a similar exercise around suggestions for change (what should the Drop In continue to do? do differently?). From the ensuing discussion, the larger population of youth developed a keen interest in ensuring that their ideas were incorporated, that change did occur and that they got to participate in the process. The youth themselves would hold the agency accountable for follow through!

Another exercise involved mapping the downtown – colour coding safe and unsafe areas, squeegee corners, areas of prostitution, sleeping, hangout and eating spots, and localities where drugs are sold. Then the participants 'interviewed the map' – what is it that makes an area safe or unsafe, why do we eat, hang out or sleep where we do, etc.? This map could be used as a catalyst in engaging the youth in broader discussions about safety and street life, and collectively developing strategies for addressing them.

Making sense of the information   How were we to analyse and interpret all this information from so many different sources? More importantly, how could I fully engage the youth team members and even the broader youth population in such a complex and time-consuming process?

I began by explaining the basic data analysis process: figuring out how to summarize and make sense out of mountains of information. This involved summarizing (frequencies) and comparing (cross tabs) for the quantitative data, and summarizing, picking out key words or phrases and developing themes and patterns for the qualitative data. Then we would look at how the parts 'fit' together to make a whole, using the analogy of a puzzle.

After photocopying each data set twice, and putting the original away for safe keeping, we divided into teams (two young persons and one of the adults), each taking a data set. Each team read through the data and discussed their sense of the whole and some preliminary impressions of what respondents were saying. They then cut up each survey questionnaire, putting all answers to Question 1 in one envelope, Question 2 in another envelope, and so on. The next step was to take all the answers to each question and sort them into piles of similar answers. Then, they named each pile. After a fairly intensive process, this produced a set of categories. Team members recorded these on flipcharts to share and discuss with the whole team.

Lots of discussion ensued about what was meant by certain phrases, or how to interpret this or that comment, both in the small sub groups and whole team. These we were often able to clarify by referring back to the original interview or survey. As we compared the responses from each source, a set of overall themes gradually emerged. At the same time, we were developing a list of recommendations for change. It was a slow process, but as the results came into focus, so did our excitement about the possibilities for change at the Drop In.

Reporting

We first listed all the different ways that we could report what we had learned. These ranged from the usual written report to interactive presentations with the Drop In service users, and seminars and demonstrations to other audiences.

It was totally unrealistic to expect the youth, most of whom had not finished high school, to write a detailed formal report (needed for the agency Board and also for the funders) (although cf. Bowen, 1993). So how was I to engage the youth in drafting the written report, if I was to do the actual writing? I had faced this dilemma before (Whitmore, 1994b) and this time, I wanted to devise a process that would result in real ownership of the product by everyone on the team.

Team members began by brainstorming the various parts of the report and then, bit by bit, the content – all recorded on flipcharts, of course. I then drafted these into a narrative, which the group then went over (and over and over . . .). One young woman, after proclaiming that she did not read and this was boring anyway, pointed out a number of misspelled words and factual errors in one of the drafts – 'This is not spelled right. That is wrong!'. We did eight drafts of the report, and in the end, the youth fully understood and identified with the results. The youth themselves produced as many pieces of the report as possible – cover, index, graphics, charts and tables, appendices. They were deservedly very proud of the final product.

We also did a number of presentations, in which the youth took the lead. We spent quite a bit of time preparing for the first one – a public presentation about our process to the local social work professional association – which got an enthusiastic response. Thereafter, their stage jitters gradually diminished with each one. They presented to the agency board, to the AGM, did a workshop with the wider population of Drop In service users, and were guest speakers at a university seminar.

Perhaps the most interesting reporting mechanism was 'The Kit' – a guide for other youth evaluators interested in how to do their own evaluations. 'The Kit' was designed and produced entirely by the youth team members, who collectively brainstormed the contents – 'what we did', 'how we did it' and 'tips' (lessons learned) – and then divided up the work. It is the youths' representation of what they learned; its style, content and graphics speak to young people. The result is a boisterous, colourful guide, full of life, energy and humour.[2]

Action: So what difference did this make?

Though perhaps the main reason the youth participated in this project was that they got paid ('cash' was always their first response to this question), they also wanted to see changes in what was happening at the Drop In. Two rationales for choosing an emancipatory approach to this project were related to empowerment and social change – empowerment of the youth (individually and collectively), and changing how the Drop In was run and what it did. Beyond that, we also hoped to initiate a process of dialogue with key community players (e.g. local businesses, police, other agencies) related to street-involved youth.

This project did change the Drop In, which has since implemented virtually every recommendation made in the report. The fact that many youth had been involved in the process and had a personal investment in seeing the changes happen, contributed to the accountability of agency management to follow through on the recommendations. A Youth Advisory Council has been established and is very active in programming and decision-making at the Centre. Management, staff and youth all report a much improved atmosphere.

Were the youth empowered through this process? Individually, there is some evidence that this occurred. Some of the youth reported increased confidence, knowledge and skills. There is indirect evidence as well, as seen in the behaviour and choices some of the youth have since made (to leave abusive situations, for example, or return to school). Collectively, the Drop-In youth population as a whole has a greater stake in their Centre. Many have taken up the opportunity to participate in activities or decision-making bodies.

Issues: Bumps and detours along the yellow brick road

Truman et al. (2000) identify four key elements in what they call 'anti-exclusionary' research:

1. locating the 'self' in the research process
2. exploring the power dimensions
3. tensions
4. linking research to wider questions of social inequality and justice.

These are closely related to the key aspects, noted earlier, which provided the guiding principles for the project. I will use this framework to explore issues of emancipatory research as seen through the Drop In Centre evaluation.

Locating the self

Locating the 'self' in the research process in terms of personal, social and institutional influences on research and analysis includes asking, how did I identify myself within the research project? This relates directly to the nature of knowledge and how it is produced – who produces it and the importance of social location of those who produce it (Stanley and Wise, 1993: 228). 'The values, assumptions and cultural beliefs of those who shape the research agenda . . . should be treated, like data, as evidence' (Everitt, 1998: 112).

My personal reality and theirs – can the twain meet? I am a middle class, white, heterosexual, able-bodied woman. The privileges related to these locations are well known. I have never experienced real poverty, homelessness or physical, sexual or severe emotional abuse.

This is obviously a very different reality from that experienced by most street-involved youth. So rather than pretend that I 'understood' or could empathize with their position, we all recognized the limitations of my experience and that experience 'on the street' was expertise that the youth brought to the process. One team-building exercise, for example, involved their teaching me about the different groupings among street-involved youth. They drew pictures of a skater, a Goth, a rapper, an Anarchist, etc. and got a big kick out of my struggles to figure out the differences. This helped to 'level the playing field' in recognizing that each person brought something to the research and that I was not automatically the only 'expert'. What I could do was put my knowledge and skills as an experienced social worker and researcher at the disposal of the research participants (Truman, 2000).

My social experience: Same city, different worlds   My location as a professional and an academic puts me squarely in the mainstream of society. It is a respected and highly valued position. Its power, prestige and relative security allow me to experiment, take risks, and try out new and innovative approaches to research. This contrasts markedly with the powerlessness, insecurity and marginalization of street-involved youth. This enormous difference in class can be, and usually is (no matter how well intended we may be), a huge barrier to understanding, trust and the ability to collaborate. In a previous evaluation (Whitmore, 1991) I conducted with single expectant mothers on social assistance, one participant expressed it this way:

> You're dealing with a lot of people on social assistance and welfare. You're dealing with real hard-to-reach, low self-esteem people. And when they see anybody coming in that they think is high class or has anything to do with welfare . . . they are scared to death that you're going to squeal on them . . . [The respondents] are just scared that you work with these [social workers], that you're high up there so that they can't trust you 'cuz you're right in with them.

What right do I have, given my location, to undertake this research? Does one need to have experienced street life, abuse or racism in order to achieve empathy with participants, or to conduct research with a community? These are lively debates in the field. Some communities (for example, many African American communities and First Nations' communities in Canada) have developed specific guidelines to control research done *on* them rather than by or with them as subjects. Such 'spectator knowledge' reinforces the researcher's position of privilege (Truman, 2000: 28) through the appropriation of others' knowledge for research purposes.

The privileges related to my social location come with responsibilities, including the obligation to share my knowledge, 'being there' for them as much as possible, in personal as well as professional ways (which involves time, commitment, follow through, influence and sometimes even in material ways), and bringing them with me when opportunities arose where they could benefit from or influence decisions affecting their lives. I, and particularly the team staff members, spent considerable time with the youth helping them to resolve personal and material problems. We took pains to follow through on commitments. We intervened with welfare workers, helped to secure housing, got them to medical services when needed; we were able to serve as references for jobs the youth found. They were included in discussions with managers about the future of the Centre.

There was a different set of social relations constructed through this research process because it was seen as a form of activism. One major goal was to change the Drop In and this we, as a team, accomplished. We saw ourselves as part of the team, all wanting to make a concrete difference in how youth were served at the Drop In. The common process and goal helped to reduce some of the distance between us.

Institutional influences Institutional influences played themselves out particularly through me. As an academic, I brought the credibility and authority of the university to this project. That gave it a status it might not otherwise have had, certainly in the minds of the funders as well as the agency (Truman, 2000). This also played a key role in the importance given to the final report, especially the set of recommendations for change, by agency management and Board members. Management knew that structural and programmatic changes were needed at the Drop In Centre, but they lacked solid data on what was happening and how things needed to change. The final report was key to this process. In addition, the broader population of youth, having been involved in the process, were watching and expecting change. This significantly enhanced our own accountability as a team and that of decision-makers to follow through.

In the follow up process, the whole project has influenced how the agency as a whole includes youth in decision-making.

> It used to be token. Now the degree of youth involvement has shifted significantly, in research and at the Board level. Before, the youth rarely spoke, now they speak first. Half the audience at Board meetings is now youth. . . . (Agency staff member, personal communication).

It is well known that indigenous groups are suspicious of professionals. The extent to which social workers truly believe in the capacity of local people to deal with problems and create change is played out in our attitudes and in what we actually do in our work. As social workers, we need to recognize our own locations in relation to poverty and injustice. We need to understand that we can be part of the problem and not simply assume that, somehow everything we do invariably benefits the poor (Novak, 1996: 91, cited in Martin, 2000). 'Respect, humility, adaptability, empathy and patience *born out of critical consciousness* are among the most important attributes of those working in this field of research. These qualities may not be much valued or fostered in professional training and conventional research contexts' (Martin, 2000: 197).

Exploring political and power dimensions of empowerment: Redressing the imbalance

Issues related to the nature and role of power in the research process have been raised by feminists (Fonow and Cook, 1991; Harding, 1987; Reinharz, 1992) and participatory action researchers (Gaventa, 1993; Hall, 1981, 1992; Maguire, 1987; Tandon, 1981; Whitmore, 1998).

> The key issue is not how to empower people, but once people have decided to empower themselves, precisely what research can do to facilitate this process . . . the social relations of the research production have to be fundamentally changed; researchers have to learn how to put their knowledge and skills at the disposal of research subjects. . . . (Oliver, 1990: 13–14)

Social research can redress the power imbalance in a variety of ways. One way to do this was through the use of everyday language, by demystifying the jargon used in mainstream research (Dockery, 2000; Lishman, 1999). Another way was to really *engage* the broader Drop-In population in the process by expanding the ways of knowing. The mapping and matrix exercises were designed and facilitated entirely by the youth. The process involved elements of 'theatre', allowing emotions and dialogue – to say nothing of fun – to enter the process. Interviewing the matrix was a messy, noisy affair, full of laughter, shouting, agreement and disagreement. Eventually, they arrived at a consensus around what existed at the Centre, what was more (or less) important, and what needed to change. One 'outcome' was that they recognized their power to articulate, in a systematic and coherent manner, what needed to be changed and to demand accountability – of each other, staff and management.

Though the youth were not involved in initiating the evaluation itself, they had considerable control over the rest of the process (Hick, 1997). It was they who planned and conducted the research, they who decided what the key questions would be and whom to ask. The youth controlled how the data got interpreted and how the findings were reported. They *owned* the results. The youth may not have actually written the specific words in the final report, but they were intimately involved in formulating, reviewing and presenting them. The recommendations came out of *their* process. The fact that the youth had engaged the wider Drop-In population meant that the final decision-makers – essentially management and the Board – had to act on them (and they did).

A major factor in empowering the youth was our control of time (Whitmore and McKee, 2000). The team was able to take the time needed (within some bounds, of course) to fully comprehend the process and formulate the recommendations for change. Originally, it was to have taken one year. We ended up taking 18 months to complete the project. Had we not had that control and the 'space' it gave us to work carefully and at *their* pace, the balance of power could not have been maintained. Having enough time was a key factor in producing both a credible report and 'The Kit'. The parallels with social work practice with individuals or groups or communities seem obvious – at whose pace do we work and who controls the pace?

We also had control over the budget. We established a Financial Subcommittee, made up of two young people (who rotated membership) and one staff member. They kept track of the funds, what we spent, how we spent it and reported regularly to the team as a whole. The fact that, in addition to time, we had the flexibility to move funds around and stretch them over the time needed, was another key factor in making this project work.

Did the evaluation process described amount to real empowerment? Or was it a subtle form of co-optation – that is, the youth could speak but had no real power to make change? To what extent did I, and the two staff members, 'shape' what the youth wanted, manipulate them into doing what we thought was best – what Lukes (1974) calls the third dimension of power (Dullea and Mullender, 1999; Feuerstein, 1988)? There's no question that this relationship, as any in social work practice, is a delicate balance, one that demands rigorous self reflection around these issues. Who is *really* in charge? Can, or should we, as Oliver suggests, put our knowledge and skills at the disposal of research subjects *for them to use in whatever way they choose*? (Oliver, 1990: 13–14). Do we, or should we, really 'relinquish control of the research to marginalized groups' (Mertens, 1998: 15)? Emancipatory researchers need to be careful with such statements, for they could imply that we should be mere tools for others' uses (as long as the 'others' are seen as oppressed), without regard to what those uses might be. It also tends to romanticize those at the margins, when they are as vulnerable as any group to being co-opted or asserting goals that could be harmful to others. I certainly am not prepared to put my knowledge and skills at the disposal of those whose goals or values I regard as repugnant or unethical, and I have to take responsibility for drawing that line myself.

Perhaps the best answer, in this example, is that though we did share decision-making power and it was a collaborative process, there is no question that some members were more influential than others. The words and ideas of some carried more weight. This will be true in any group, as it was in this one. I must also recognize my own power, for all the effort to be responsive to and inclusive of the youth. Had some team members wanted to support a course of action that a staff member or I felt was unethical, for example, we cannot deny our considerable power to persuade them of our view. Given my key role, a threat to withdraw from the project would have carried definitive weight.

A defining moment in the process was when one youth – one that others tended to look up to and follow – threatened to quit because the process was boring and no change was happening at the Drop In. When Colette re-introduced the PLA methods and supported them in figuring out what to do, the change was dramatic! Though we all continued with the surveys (several team members continued to feel much more comfortable doing them than leading the interactive activities), several youth picked up this ball and ran with it. Eventually, all of the youth became engaged, as they saw the results and recognized their value. The gains in knowledge, confidence and engagement became a source of power for the youth, both in the team and in the wider Drop-In population.

'Such a shift in power and in patterns of working requires a change in both the attitudes and skills of professional social workers . . . and a willingness to work with service users as colleagues' (Evans and Fisher, 1999: 113–14). This involves a 'strategic alliance between service users and professionals to develop organizational openness to service user involvement' (p. 114).

Being explicit about the tensions

A number of tensions arose in this process (see Whitmore and McKee, 2000). Particularly relevant to this discussion are issues of equality, confidentiality and trust.

Some in the larger Drop-In population resented the privileges obtained by the youth team members. This created unintended tension among an already marginalized population. 'Our' youth got extra attention from the staff members on the team; they got paid; they decided what snacks to get for our meetings. This tension was reduced once the PLA activities got going, when at least some of the privileges got shared with the larger population.

One major problem arose around confidentiality. When internal staff conflicts and management politics at the Drop In got shared in staff focus groups with me, how much could or should I share with the youth? Such 'raw' information might well undermine their confidence in the agency and agitate a clientele already operating 'close to the edge'. To what extent could I trust the youths' commitment to confidentiality when it came to internal battles among people who were their counsellors in time of crisis? On the other hand, my withholding this information might imply that the youth could not be trusted or that I should decide what was good (or not good) for them to know. The dilemma was resolved by team members themselves, in negotiating for me, as the only real outsider, to conduct the focus groups. We agreed – and I could assure the staff – that I would craft the issues into a set of general themes and that no individual be implicated. These themes could be shared with the team and included in the final report. This process not only worked well but also appears to have been a positive factor in moving the staff and the agency toward constructive change.

Another tension arose as a result of the mapping exercise in which the youth specified areas in the downtown where certain illegal activities took place (e.g. drugs, prostitution). How much of this information should be shared with police and other authorities? If we as social workers and responsible staff members remained silent, this could be seen as condoning such activities. If we 'told', we would be seen as 'rats', violating the trust so painstakingly built up. Again, we discussed this as a team and agreed to summarize the data in the report, protecting the confidentiality of the information and of the youth, while respecting the value and importance of the picture they painted through that exercise.

Insider/outsider issues were complex and created tensions. There was the 'them' and 'me' tension – I was always the outsider, not ever fully trusted or respected. I was simply not physically at the Drop In, or available, except for the times when we met as a group. As a result, on several occasions when neither staff member was present, I could not effectively mediate among the youth themselves when tensions threatened to get out of hand. This was where staff participation became critical, for Colette and Rick could, and did, intervene when tensions boiled over into violence (or potential violence). Insider/outsider splits were also present among the youth themselves. Some of the youth were 'insiders' and separated themselves, in subtle and sometimes not so subtle ways, from those considered 'outsiders'. These smaller cliques clashed and there were times when the staff members and I had to work very hard to get them to work productively together. Some of these tensions were never fully resolved (Truman et al., 2000: 16).

Linking research to wider questions of social inequality and justice

The final element in the framework focuses on the relationship between research and social inequality and justice. Research should do more than merely describe the world; it should change it (Cook and Fonow, 1986). It is based on the idea that knowledge can and should result in action for positive social change. This evaluation was designed with certain action-oriented goals in mind. It was intended to provide a basis for concrete programmatic changes at the Drop In, and also to provide a positive personal and collective experience for the youth.

Did the research generate social change? Did the emancipatory process result in an emancipatory outcome (Kent, 2000)? There is no question that there have been significant programme changes at the Drop In and that our report served as a clear guide for these. The Drop In is a very different place now than it was before we started.

Individually, there is some evidence of 'empowerment', though this is far more difficult to measure, of course. There are the broad questions of inequality and social exclusion; that is, the homeless and certainly street-involved youth are seen by many in the larger society as 'druggies', 'losers', drop outs with limited potential. This affects how they see themselves, so any positive change in their self perceptions is a plus. The fact that five out of the six young people that we originally hired completed the project says volumes. Some youth reported feeling more confident – 'I know I've grown throughout the project. I mean . . . I'm not lashing out at people, hitting people, stuff like that . . . ' said one youth. Greater confidence was also observable in their behaviour. For example, two of the more timid members stepped into the breach at one of the public presentations (the Annual General Meeting of the agency) when those who were supposed to present could not do so at the very last moment. The report may not have been as polished, but in getting up in front of an audience and delivering the report, they did something they could not have imagined themselves doing just a few months earlier!

New possibilities and autonomy opened up for one young woman who decided to leave the city and return to her home town. This involved breaking free from a destructive relationship with her mother, a huge step for her. Another member took the important decision to admit herself to a long term drug and alcohol rehabilitation programme. This took considerable courage and commitment. It is, of course, impossible to determine whether or not these actions had any direct connection with their participation in the project. Did it have an influence? I have no doubt that it did.

The youth were very proud indeed of the 'products' and outcomes of their work. They realized that they actually could do a credible job and stay with it for an extended length of time – not a common experience for these youth. They certainly gained new knowledge and skills – they knew their stuff and could field any and all questions about the research at public presentations. Participation in this project was also a positive addition to their résumés for future education and employment. Several indicated that they wanted to do more of this work in the future. Some talked of upgrading their education; one enrolled in a community college programme and is talking actively of going to university.

> It is imperative to remember that social and personal transformation is not an event but a process that takes time. We all operate on our own very personal time lines and it is important not to examine the validity of our efforts towards emancipatory acts as the end results but rather as a process of struggle that should be celebrated at all points of the process. (Cohen-Mitchell, 2000: 172)

Conclusion: Not an afterthought . . .

> Initially, we made a commitment to do the evaluation of the program, but hadn't really thought about . . . the implications . . . I'd like to say 'Boy, this was a gutsy move that we made', but I'm not sure we realized how much it was going to change the face of the Drop In. . . . (Follow up interview with team staff member)

Most social workers do not think of research as a place where we can support marginalized groups or influence social institutions. Yet it is one place where we can 'make a difference'.

We assumed that street-involved youth were in the best position to evaluate their own services and we were right. They could not have done this alone, however. As much as we want to believe in 'community control', this has to be seen in context, and the reality is that marginalized populations will need our professional support and commitment in working with them. Nor could I as an outsider, whatever my academic credentials and experience, have done this without staff members whom the youth trusted on the team. Other pieces were also in place. We had the luxury of time and some resources; we also had the agency's commitment to experiment and management's readiness to follow through on recommendations. The timing, in terms of the agency's readiness for change, was right as well, although this is not always something one can plan for.

The combination, then, of a commitment to inclusion, willingness to try a different approach to evaluation, resources and a careful plan of incentives and support for the youth made this emancipatory process work.

> I felt a sense of accomplishment. I mean, we actually finished something rather than running away . . . We created something really good. . . . (Youth team member, reflecting on her experience in the project)

Notes

1. I would like to thank everyone involved for their participation and support, including the youth (Karen, G, Tammy, Iffie, and Bobbi), the youth who participated in the focus groups, the two staff members of the evaluation team (Colette McKee and Rick Perley), the agency management (Dan Paré and Denise Vallely), and members of the Evaluation Sub-Committee (Mark Totten, Diann Consaul and Ken Hoffman). Thanks also to the Trillium Foundation for funding this project.

   I would also like to express my appreciation to the Editors and to Dr Donna Mertens for their helpful comments on an earlier draft of this chapter.
2. 'The Kit' is available on the following website: <http://www.ysb.on.ca>

7

Auto-Ethnography as Reflexive Inquiry: The Research Act as Self-Surveillance

Sue White

CONTENTS

Reflexivity: Beyond introspection?   101
**Researching at home: The problematics of being on the
  inside 'out'**   103
Marginals and natives: collapsing the distinction   103
Defamiliarization and 'practitioner research'   104
**Reflexive inquiry as defamiliarization: Towards a more
  realistic realism**   106
Being a fish   106
Discovering water   108
A fish out of water?   111
Conclusion: Towards a realistic practice ethics   112

> We've got a little girl of nine. It's quite difficult, this rejection. It's not the same rejection as other families. What they are rejecting is a child . . . who they feel very guilty about bringing into the world and they would actually say, when they really get distraught, things like, 'really if she died it would be better for everyone concerned', and the father saying, 'well let's put it this way, if there was a shipwreck, I would save my wife and sons'. (Team Leader, Children and Families Team)

Social workers are very accustomed to providing accounts of their actions. For example, they may have to justify their decisions to the courts, to other professionals, to 'consumers' of services, or may be questioned as part of the audit activity which is increasingly a feature of welfare organizations in the UK and elsewhere. In the extract above, a team leader, working in a statutory child care team in the UK, is describing her thoughts and actions in relation to a case involving a child with a disability. There are a number of ways in which we could approach this account. Conventionally, it may be used to make a judgement about the team leader's practice. For example, was she following the imperative of the Children Act (1989) and treating children with disabilities as 'children first'? Had she properly assessed the risk to the child? Had she provided appropriate services? In this chapter, I should like to introduce you to a different way of reading professional accounts of various kinds. I shall argue that, by using transcripts of social workers' talk and by undertaking detailed description and analysis of every-day business, we may open up for debate previously unquestioned aspects of practice. Professional conversation (talk) and case files or reports (text) can be used to explore and make explicit taken-for-granted ideas about practice and hence can open these up for debate.

The study on which I draw is a multi-method ethnography of child care social work which I completed in 1997 (White, 1997b). During two years of participant observation, I adopted a 'complete-membership' role (Adler and Adler, 1996). That is, I conducted the study at 'home', in the department in which I was employed as a team manager. Hence, I have referred in the title to '*auto*-ethnography as reflexive inquiry'. This is a rather fancy way of saying that doing ethnography at home, or indeed reading ethnographies about ourselves, can help us to examine, more self-consciously and analytically, what we are thinking about and doing in our professional practice. This does not mean that we will necessarily want to change it. We might want to debate, or to change some things some of the time, but we might even feel rather proud of other bits. However, I shall argue that we can only make these judgements once we have developed a particular kind of 'reflexivity' about our routines and practices. We may help nurture this reflexivity by undertaking the kinds of analysis I have referred to above and I shall illustrate in more detail in due course. However, first, we must consider what is meant by the rather peculiar term 'reflexivity', and how it differs from the more familiar concept of 'reflection'.

Reflexivity: Beyond introspection?

In recent years, researchers and welfare professionals alike have been told they must be 'reflexive' in their practices. However, reflexivity is a slippery term and there is considerable ambiguity and variety in the way it is inter-preted (Taylor and White, 2000). It is often treated as a form of what, for the purposes of differentiation, I shall call, 'reflection'. This is a form of 'benign introspection' (Woolgar, 1988: 22): a process of looking *inward*, and think-ing about how our own life experiences or significant events may have impacted upon our thinking, or on the research or assessment process. Typically, this form of reflection involves the researcher or practitioner keeping confessional diaries, which include narrative accounts of their actions 'in the field', and particularly in the context of social work may make reference to 'power differentials' or to (often failed) attempts to 'empower'. As one interpretation of the concept of reflexivity, self-disclosures of this type have become rather fashionable of late. Clifford Geertz, in pejorative tone, dubs this trend 'the diary disease' (1987: 90). There is, indeed, a danger that we learn little about what is claimed and a great deal about the struggles and torments of the researcher or practitioner. Moreover, paradoxically, by 'confessing' to some misdemeanour, or error in the *past* and displaying their capacity to learn from such mistakes, the researcher or practitioner constructs their *current* interpretations and practices as new, improved, and hence more robust and less fallible. Although it is by no means true in all cases, the researcher or practitioner can cast themselves as a kind of born-again truth broker. This very effectively closes down opposition and fruitful debate – the very thing that reflective diaries are supposed to create.

Academics interested in the sociology of scientific knowledge have generated a more radical version of 'reflexivity' (for a collection of papers on reflexivity, see Woolgar, 1988). They argue that scientific knowledge is constructed through social and linguistic processes. However, since these sociologists also make knowledge claims of their own, this inevitably begs the question of how social scientific accounts of the social construction of scientific knowledge are themselves constructed through language, and so on. This interpretation of the concept of reflexivity has led to the development of innovative textual devices such as attempts to convey 'multi-vocality' (multiple voices or versions) by simulating conversations and arguments between the researcher/writer and themselves (cast in another role), about the production of the account. These 'literary' forms can be very revealing and useful (see Hall, 1997 for a particularly illuminating and worthwhile example of this technique applied to social work). However, some suggest that, in its extreme forms, this movement has drifted towards solipsism, producing a good deal of 'self-deconstructive' work about reflexivity, at the expense of detailed claim-making accounts on the sociology of science itself (Latour, 1988; Law, 1994; Pinch and Pinch, 1988).

Whilst both these forms of reflexivity are a good deal better than failing to think at all about what one is saying, writing or doing, in exploring the concept of reflexivity in this chapter, I shall be advocating a rather different reading.[1] Using the research experience as an exemplar, I want to interpret and apply the concept of reflexivity to denote a form of destabilization, or problematization of taken-for-granted knowledge and day to day reasoning. Treated in this way, reflexivity becomes a process of looking *inward* and *outward*, to the social and cultural artefacts and forms of thought which saturate our practices. So, for the reflective diary to become reflexive, it would need, as it were, to reflect upon the narrative forms themselves and upon their socio-cultural origins and effects (cf. Ixer, 1999). Bourdieu has termed this process of problematization 'epistemic reflexivity'.

However, the process of problematization is not so simple. If something is taken for granted, if we are no longer aware of it, how may we open it up for study? This links to a larger, recurrent question from social science and philosophy – 'to what extent can we know ourselves?'. This question has generated a good deal of methodological debate, which we should consider before proceeding further.

Researching at home: The problematics of being on the inside 'out'

Marginals and natives: collapsing the distinction

Before examining the specific ways in which the debates relate to social work and social work research, it is worthwhile summarizing some of the social scientific opinion on auto-ethnography. There is a rich literature, originating particularly within social anthropology, on conducting research within one's own culture. Some anthropologists, with their traditional predilection for the exotic and remote, appear to have been rather troubled by questions of reliability and validity within what has become known as 'auto-anthropology'. One of the guiding metaphors, transported into ethnographic studies from anthropology, is that of the ethnographer as a naïve 'child', 'apprentice', 'stranger'. Of course, when conducting research within familiar surroundings, it may be extremely difficult to achieve this 'anthropological strangeness'. However, the 'marginal native' metaphor sits uncomfortably alongside the imperative that the ethnographer should develop 'deep familiarly' with the setting and its members.

> The fieldworker is always a marginal person who, if he [*sic*] is *successful*, is permitted relatively free access to the backstage area of the social scene. (Pelto and Pelto, 1978: 248)

In other words, roll up your sleeves and muck in, but under no circumstances 'go native'.

However, as anthropologists have debated the in/out, stranger/native, familiar/unfamiliar dichotomies, it has become clear that either/or distinctions of this kind are difficult to measure or sustain in ethnographic fieldwork. An understanding of the setting is allegedly built for the ethnographer, through the search for regularities, involving the collection and analysis of descriptive data, leading to the gradual discovery, over time, of insights into 'the interpretations of reality as seen by the group members' (Agar, 1980: 195). Clearly, in order to access these interpretations, the researcher must place considerable dependence upon informants (insiders), and this blurs the ostensible boundary between inside and outside. The ideal-typical ethnographer may be on the outside 'in', but the informants selected by researchers may themselves, in some way, be on the inside 'out'.

The requirement for reflexivity on the part of the researcher *and* the informants is explained further by Geertz (1979), who points to the necessity for translation back and forth of 'experience-near' and 'experience-distant' concepts:

> Confinement to experience-near concepts leaves an ethnographer awash in immediacies as well as entangled in the vernacular. Confinement to experience-distant ones leaves him stranded in abstractions and smothered in jargon. (Geertz, 1979: 227)

The collection and abstraction of experience-near concepts is not simply a matter of extracting accounts from those who know best. Experience-near concepts are characterized by their high level of integration into the natural attitude, or, in Bourdieu's (1977b) terms, the habitus, of subjects. Thus, experience-near concepts will not be treated as *concepts* at all, but simply as the only right and proper way to think. Hence, there is a need for reflexive activity on the part of researcher *and* informants for whom the ordinary and everyday must already have been problematized.

Moreover, there are few settings so homogenous that they contain no one on the inside 'out'. For example, Strathern, referring to Okely's (1987) ethnographic study of Travellers, casts doubt on the distinction between the familiar and unfamiliar, saying that such a criterion would involve 'impossible measurements of degrees of familiarity' (Strathern, 1987: 16). What defines being 'at home' for Strathern is whether the researcher and researched share the conceptual frameworks which inform ethnography, thus:

> whether anthropologists are at home qua anthropologists, is not to be decided by whether they call themselves Malay, belong to the Travellers or have been born in Essex; it is decided by the relationship between their techniques of organizing knowledge and how people organize knowledge about themselves. (Strathern, 1987: 18)

So, it seems that validity and reliability do not depend on the ethnographer being an alien, or outsider in the setting. Indeed, as I shall go on to argue, the advantage of turning the ethnographic gaze upon the familiar is precisely that it holds the possibility of *defamiliarization* of certain routines and practices (Aull Davies, 1999). So, how does all this relate to social work?

Defamiliarization and 'practitioner research'

To answer this question, we need to examine some of the arguments for and against, so called, 'practitioner research'. You will see from Jan Fook's contribution to this volume, and the discussion in Chapter 10, that there is not one single variety of practitioner research, and there is no doubt that increasing numbers of social workers and managers are undertaking 'research' activity of various kinds. For example, in the UK, during the 1980s and early 1990s, as a consequence of neo-liberalism and the new managerialism, professionals were urged to monitor outcomes, demonstrate effectiveness and generate performance indicators with enthusiasm and vigour. The concepts of evaluation and outcome measurement have gathered momentum and have, in some services, become routine activities. Moreover, a particular rational-technical variety of practitioner 'research' has been fuelled by New Labour's 'modernization' agenda (e.g. Department of Health, 1998a, 1998b), reaching its pinnacle in the evidence-based practice movement.

Whilst some have argued that *only* practitioners in a particular field can produce research which is relevant to practice (see Hammersley, 1992 for a counter-argument to this view), the idea that practitioners can or should research themselves is not uncontroversial (e.g. Hammersley, 1992; Atkinson and Delamont, 1993). It is sometimes said that practitioner research is undertheorized, and that its problem-driven and solution-focused nature can preclude proper 'unfettered', critical engagement with the phenomena in question. In short, the argument runs that practitioner research sometimes moves far too quickly from exploring what *is*, to advocating what *ought* to be the case. There is some cogency to this argument, and elsewhere, with John Stancombe, I make a similar point in relation to psychotherapy process research. With the fundamental and unshakable belief that therapy is a good thing and an impassioned desire so to prove, we argue, clinician-researchers rarely find anything other than what they had commonsensically anticipated at the start of their enquiry (Stancombe and White, 1997).

This may be the case, but any *wholesale* dismissal of practitioner research must rest on the presupposition that it is impossible, in some sense, to research oneself. One cannot, it is implied, be on the 'inside' and achieve any 'distance' from the forms of thought one is researching. Under such circumstances, the argument runs, practitioner research becomes self-referential, simply reproducing dominant forms of thought. However, we have seen from the debates about anthropological fieldwork that the inside/outside distinction has proved extremely tenuous. I should like to suggest here that it is perfectly possible for practitioners to develop a critical, or analytic orientation to their practices. Reflecting on my own case, it seems that there were two principal ways in which this orientation developed.

First, it was in part a product of particular personal and professional experiences. For example, I remember that, on one or two occasions when my second child was very small, I took him into work with me for a short while. He would sometimes be clingy and sometimes very independent, preoccupied with play, or other people, and hence almost indifferent to my presence. In the company of a group of my social work colleagues, I became acutely conscious that his behaviour could easily be read on any of these occasions as one of the many varieties of 'attachment disorder'.

Had this been a clinical assessment, I thought how vulnerable I would have been to such a diagnosis, and how resistance to it could easily have been written off as defensiveness or denial. Having used the theory routinely in my work for many years, this experience made me much more aware of its incredible malleability and virtual incorrigibility. There are few permutations of infant behaviour which escape its prolific explanatory potential. I came to see attachment theory (indeed all theory) less as a convenient tool, or template, and more as a powerful coloured lens, with the capacity to clarify (by eliminating the 'glare' which we experience when we try to make sense of complex relationships), but which may also cast the world in an over-simplifying monochrome.

The second way in which a more meta-analytic orientation to day-to-day practices may develop, has been noted by Strathern above. It is related to 'techniques of organizing knowledge' (Strathern, 1987: 18). If practitioners are exposed to different analytic and meta-analytic frameworks from outside their primary discipline, this increases the likelihood of them understanding their practices in new ways. In my own case, this influence came from my academic studies in sociology and social theory.

Of course there must be many more routes to 'marginality', and echoing the anthropologists, I should like to argue that social work is 'heterogeneous enough to provide its own outsiders' (Shokeid (Minkovitz), 1970: 113). However, this does not mean that the defamiliarization upon which reflexive practice depends is straightforward or easy, or that all practitioners have the motivation to acquire it. It is important now to examine in more detail the processes involved and their effects.

Reflexive inquiry as defamiliarization: Towards a more realistic realism

Being a fish

Clearly, the main advantage of researching amongst one's own kind lies in the familiarity and ordinariness itself. This means that one can avoid the sorts of problem Law describes below:

> I had been told that I could sit in on meetings . . . But I could only attend meetings if I knew when and where they were taking place. And this was not so easy. 'You can't ask about something if you don't know it exists' . . . I'm not implying that anyone deliberately tried to stop me learning about meetings . . . It was more that they thought I wouldn't be interested. For it turns out . . . that people think that sociologists will not be very interested in 'technical details'. And what of the discussions and conversations that didn't take place in meetings? I had no way of plugging into these at all. (Law, 1994: 44)

In contrast to Law, I found that my relationships with practitioners and managers facilitated access to sensitive material, and my 'insider' knowledge helped me to identify effortlessly what were the important meetings. So, a 'complete membership role' (Adler and Adler, 1996) has some advantages. It allows for the checking and rechecking of observations and analytic inductions against constantly accessible 'business as usual' (cf. Pollard, 1985).

However, that is not to say that there are *no* difficulties and dilemmas associated with conducting an ethnography 'at home', indeed there are many. However much one desires it, defamiliarization does not come easily. The 'invisibility' of 'experience near' concepts referred to by Geertz above amplifies the need for reflexivity on the part of the researcher. This can take considerable effort and will always and necessarily be partial. It will be helpful at this point to examine my own ethnography of child care social work in more detail (White, 1997b).

As I explained earlier, between 1989 and 1995, I was employed as the manager of a hospital-based, local authority 'children and families' team. In 1993, I began two years of participant observation research in my own authority. By this time, 'doing being' a team manager was second nature to me. Like other professionals, I had my own 'cook book knowledge' (Atkinson, 1995a: 116) and I had learned the recipes by heart. Although my academic background in sociology had given me the kind of alternative interpretive repertoire referred to by Strathern above, defamiliarization was not unproblematic. For example, at the beginning of the research, I found myself able to spot *unusual* practices (often in a very critical 'I wouldn't have taken that decision' manner!), or to discuss attachment theory at a meta-theoretical level, or to comment sociologically on cases that were somehow distinctive, or on organizational cultures or bureaucratic practices. However, many of the *ordinary and everyday* explanatory frameworks and models of causation seemed to me to be quite simply the obvious and only way to think about cases. At this stage, I had barely approached the first stage of analysing the construction of social work practices – the task I had set myself in the research proposal. I was unable to see that some things could be other than the way they were. I had failed to see that 'X as it is at present, is not determined by the nature of things, it is not inevitable' (Hacking, 1999: 6).

For example, during fieldwork, I undertook an analysis of documentary sources of data. I had recognized the importance of case files, because it is in such records, and in the reports contained within them, that social workers produce their rationalizations for past interventions. Records are also time travellers and form the basis for sense-making in the future. They are thus of considerable significance both organizationally and analytically. Taking notes from an initial sample of a hundred of these files was a very time-consuming task, and at the beginning of the exercise, I had the alarming experience of not being able to see the wood for the trees. All I could see was 'ordinary' and highly predictable case recording. Similarly, I had identified the weekly 'allocation meetings' as a rich source of data. In these meetings, cases which have been referred during the previous week are talked through and allocated by the team manager to a particular social worker. I taped these meetings in two separate teams over several weeks, but during the initial transcription I was unable to imagine what I would possibly find to say about them. The forms of thought were so very familiar to me – like the proverbial fish, I had yet to discover water.

Discovering water

Gradually, by reading and rereading these data it became clear to me that there were certain preferred ways of ordering cases in professional narratives of various kinds. Incidentally, it is for precisely this reason that research instruments like tape-recorded talk can be useful, because they allow for a more distant and microscopic analysis of the taken-for-granted pragmatics of the ordinary and everyday (West, 1996), whether the analyst is outside 'in' or inside 'out', and whoever they are.

For example, by persevering with the transcription of the contents of the case files, I began to perceive patterns, routines, typifications and strategies which comprised 'competent' recording. For example, the records revealed what I called a hierarchy of accounts, with the versions of events offered by some categories of referrer or referred more likely to be reported as factual (e.g. child, other professionals and sometimes mother), and others more often coded as uncertain or contestable (e.g. fathers, particularly estranged fathers or step fathers, neighbours, some professionals with a reputation for over or under reacting, sometimes children denying abuse had taken place).

I also began to see subtle 'blamings' and to notice that certain causal accounts offered by families were usually reported with scepticism. For example, in the absence of corroborative medical or psychiatric diagnoses, parental reports that their children were temperamentally (intrinsically) difficult were routinely subverted and an alternative professional reading offered, which redefined the 'problem child' as a product of deficient parenting or family relationship problems. Amongst the hundred case files analysed, I could find no 'disconfirming' cases. That does not mean that none exist, but it does suggest that the assumption of 'parental culpability' (used here to mean 'responsibility' – Pomerantz, 1978) forms part of social workers' 'prototypical causal *gestalt*' (Bull and Shaw, 1992: 640).

In relation to the allocation meetings, by preparing and reading the transcripts it became increasingly clear to me that the notion of 'risk' is actively produced, or artfully accomplished in social workers' talk. This does not mean that social workers make it up. Rather, through active selection and assembly, fragmented and ambiguous information is ordered into a coherent story. This story, in the telling, attains the status of fact, attributes causation, accomplishes subtle blamings and anticipates certain effects. It also silences or quietens other potential readings of the case (cf. Hall et al., 1997). Again, scepticism about parental accounts, and a display of personal commitment to 'child-centred practice' is integral to competent professional performance. Here, again, social workers both invoke and reproduce a dominant cultural notion of childhood as an age of passivity and *potential* personhood (Burman, 1994; Marks, 1995; Rose, 1989, 1998; Stainton Rogers and Stainton Rogers, 1992; White, 1998b). Reaching personhood depends, not on the child's 'programming' (biology or nature), but on them receiving 'good enough parenting' (nurture).

This discourse of parental culpability is at its most apparent when it is challenged or breached. This occurs when a child's embodied character-istics are classified and defined by biomedicine as, in some way, deviant or pathological. In these circumstances social workers' accounts explicitly seek to reconcile biological explanatory frameworks with their dominant professional imperative to assess risk and judge parenting. This can be illustrated in the following, heavily edited extract in which a team leader is describing to me a very 'difficult case'.[2]

We've got a little girl of 9. It's quite difficult this rejection. It's not the same rejec-tion as other families. What they are rejecting is a child . . . who they feel very guilty about bringing into the world and they would actually say when they really get distraught things like, 'really if she died it would be better for everyone concerned', and the father saying, 'well let's put it this way, if there was a ship-wreck I would save my wife and sons'. You are getting a very clear message that really this child they wish she wasn't there. They wish they had never produced her. From the child's point of view she's autistic as well as deaf, totally deaf. We know that she recognizes her family and we know that she gets excited when she wants to go home with the family and we know that she has got into a certain routine that she knows her mother and father and her brothers, now she has got some kind of relationship and communication with them whatever their feelings are. . . .

I certainly spoke to child protection on a couple of occasions. I remember when we investigated it. Well the child was – we had a complaint that the child was outside on her bedroom window, sitting outside on the first floor window. When we investigated it the child was sent to her room quite a lot, and there were no safety bars on the window, so we talked about, well the mother said if I find myself getting uptight the only thing I can do, she actually has this screech, is put her in her bedroom, which is a coping technique . . . so what we did was to put bars on the window, which was in the child's interest, but it still bothered us that they were using that perhaps to excess and this is a time when I was offering the family resource worker because she was saying 'it's terrible I can't spend anytime with my two other sons at tea time', and yet when I offered a family resource worker she tells me she employs a nanny every-day at tea time, so she really wasn't making much sense and I couldn't respond to what she was saying. The other thing that we had was this child was made to wear a hat all the time, and she wouldn't go anywhere without this hat, but we were worried why she had to wear this hat and it was that she was pulling her hair out, so they insisted on her wearing a hat. Now you can say, this is the dilemma with disability, is it cruel to make her wear a hat or is it really the only thing you can do to make her stop damaging herself and people . . . The wearing of the hat has improved in that she has different kinds of hats now and she likes to wear a hat, but they are not actually these bonnet type things that tie under her chin, so she can wear a summer hat and she can change them and increasingly she is being encouraged to leave the hat aside for certain activities that she enjoys and we'll concentrate on that and actually her hair is growing. So, I think the parents resort to very serious preventative measures rather than coaxing and distracting that we would want them to do, so it's whether they've got that kind of investment. She started biting, biting her clothes and what they did was give her a horrible rubber ring. I don't know what it was off, it was almost like one of those dog rings, to bite on. The school refused to give her this rubber ring and with my backing we said we are not prepared to do it, if she wants to bite her clothes we'll attempt other methods of distraction, but we are not introducing a dog ring to this child.

As I said at the start of this chapter, there are several ways of reading this account. For example, it could be used to make a variety of normative judgements about this team leader's competence. However, it could also be examined for its fundamental organizing principles. What knowledges or rationalities does it invoke, and what are its effects? This latter form of analysis, which operates with a position of 'indifference' (Garfinkel and Sacks, 1970) as to the adequacy of the explanation, or the actions it purports to describe, can yield insights into taken-for-granted aspects of contemporary social work.

From this position of 'indifference', we can see that, throughout the story, the team leader seeks to reference the child's humanity – 'We know that she recognizes her family and we know that she gets excited when she wants to go home with the family.' At the same time, she assigns the child to 'deviant' categories – 'she is autistic, as well as deaf, totally deaf'; 'she's so damaged'. The team leader struggles to assign culpability to the parents for aspects of their parenting which would usually be defined as 'bad' (e.g. wishing the child had never been born; confining her to one room for long periods when she is distressed; insisting that she wears a hat at all times; giving her a rubber ring to chew on). The account continually juxtaposes 'blaming' talk about parental management techniques, with the more 'expert' strategies recommended by the social workers. For example, we are told 'the parents resort to very serious preventative measures rather than coaxing and distracting that we would want them to do', and also 'we'll attempt other methods of distraction, but we are not introducing a dog ring to this child'. The deviant nature of this action is amplified by the phrase 'we are not introducing a *dog* ring to this *child*'. This is a ring not fit for a child (it could have been called a teething ring for example), it is a *dog* ring.

The team leader's problems are multiplied by the pragmatic difficulty in 'measuring' any damage to a child whose development patently deviates from the usual markers of developmental psychology. The team leader finds it very difficult to mount a challenge to the parents' moral accounts of their situation, and is 'forced' to accept the story that they are providing the best care that they can. This is further reinforced by the team leader's practical knowledge that they are providing the best care *available*. That is, that she would struggle to find an alternative placement for the child. This sits uncomfortably alongside normative judgements about 'rejection', and their style of parenting which would 'normally' have resulted in the child being 'removed'.

Thus, although moral judgements *are* made about the parents of children with classified and named 'intrinsic' problems, the usual practical responses to these judgements (e.g. 'investigation', 'case conference') are rendered exceedingly problematic. However, the fact that stories are constructed by practitioners in the manner illustrated above, underscores the dominance of the 'parent as culpable' discourse, in that deviations are clearly recognized as 'accountable' phenomena, which require that social workers and managers tender justifications and disclaimers.

A fish out of water?

Thus, through the fieldwork experience, I became aware of the pervasive and unquestioned nature of the notion that children are 'made not born'. This does not mean that I am asserting that the discourse of child centredness is wrong. However, once one has become aware of it, one develops in response a critical control over one's thinking. Moreover, some components of 'sense-making' become more explicit and hence are opened up for debate. For example, it became increasingly clear to me that, although formal knowledge (e.g. developmental milestones, attachment theory, immunization status, medical, forensic and psychological opinion) is palpably displayed in social workers' forms of talk and written records, many narratives have a transparently qualitative, evaluative and profoundly moral design. Indeed, rational-technical or evidential materials are often invoked to authorize *moral* judgements. So, a mother may be 'blamed' for being 'emotionally unavailable' to her infant and hence for failing to 'promote a healthy attachment'. In short, it became clear to me that theory and even apparently 'forensic' evidence could sometimes be invoked to provide *ex post facto* a normative warrant for decisions taken on other grounds.

Once routinized forms of thought have been destabilized in this way, it becomes extraordinarily difficult to continue to think as usual. Towards the end of my fieldwork (and of my career as a team manager), I became increasingly conscious of a dialogue between myself as researcher and myself as social worker. As the research progressed, I became more and more self-conscious about this, which was a rather strange and destabilizing experience. However, rather than this being a bad thing, it opened up to question my taken-for-granted presuppositions. Practice is inevitably remoralized, and rendered more contestable and debatable as a result of the epistemological and ontological shift (cf. Giddens, 1984). I have often been asked whether this destabilization was the catalyst for my departure from practice into an academic post. It may well have been, since the published results opened up that possibility. However, it was and is perfectly possible, if not always comfortable, to continue to act, and also to 'see' oneself acting. Academics, too, have their cherished discourses about pedagogy, student assessment and research which can themselves be problematized. Exam boards are as fruitful a source of rhetoric and moral accounting as any allocation meeting! There is no escape. So, yes, defamiliarization can be hard work, but it is worth it. As I shall conclude below, it is worth it because it offers the possibility of more realistic realism about professional judgement and hence of more robust ethical debate.

Conclusion: Towards a realistic practice ethics

> One may realize that something, which seems inevitable in the present state of things, was not inevitable, and yet is not thereby a bad thing. But most people who use the social construction idea enthusiastically want to criticize, change or destroy some X that they dislike in the established order of things. (Hacking, 1999: 7)

As Hacking notes above, the kind of analysis I have undertaken in this chapter can easily be read as a criticism of social workers' understandings and practices. The idea of normative critique is so embedded in our modern, reforming consciousness that it is almost impossible to study and describe anything without being accused of wanting to change or destroy it. That has not been my intention. For example, it remains a *material* fact that children's bodies are damaged by their parents, and it is social workers and other child care professionals who are charged with the task of dealing with these situations. It is an occupation dealing with life *in extremis,* and this is reflected in the forms of thought, in particular the quest for certainty in assessment. Moreover, social workers have room only for invention within limits. Their activities and professional mandates are heavily circumscribed by statute.

However, 'grounding' professional activity in the very material, embodied *facts* of child abuse and neglect and in the prescriptions and pro-scriptions of policy does not have to lead back into an acceptance of a linear relationship between theory, policy and research and professional practice. I have tried to show here that social work practice depends on a variety of 'rationalities'. For example, in relation to causation or risk, 'objective' or 'forensic' criteria are vitally important, but social workers must also make judgements about the veracity and moral adequacy of particular accounts, and about the creditworthiness and blameworthiness of various parties, including the other professionals. Obviously, these judgements are not arbitrary, but neither are they neutral. Moreover, the grounds for the judge-ments are rarely fully self-conscious. They are influenced by taken-for-granted tacit presuppositions which are socially and historically constituted and often intrinsically moral. For example, social workers may find a mother's account of her reasons for 'not knowing' that her child was being sexually abused either morally adequate, or in some way inadequate based on common-sense criteria such as consistency of the story over time, and by making judgements (and that is what they are) about whether she is in other ways a 'good mother' (as currently understood).

I am not suggesting that these forms of sense-making are inferior, bad and must be dispensed with. Rather, they are essential and unavoidable in many, or dare I say all, health and welfare occupations (for examples from other professions see, Atkinson, 1995a; John, 1990; Latimer, 1997; Marks, 1995; Stancombe and White, 1997; Taylor and White, 2000). They become problematic if they are treated as though they are a detached and neutral 'mirror' of reality. Social work is a practical moral activity and, as such, its judgements and 'rationalities' need to be explored and debated. This kind of analytic rigour, paradoxically, is spawned by a recognition of undecidability and indeterminacy. Decisions should be warranted not by sustaining the myth of certainty, but by looking at the problem of judgement for what it is, and opening it up for debate.

On this note, I am struck by the relevance of a debate between Rorty and Derrida on the subject of judgement. I have sympathy for Derrida's position when he states:

> . . . whatever choice I might make, I cannot say with good conscience that I have assumed my responsibilities . . . If I conduct myself particularly well with regard to someone, I know that it is to the detriment of another . . . And this is why undecidability is not a moment to be traversed and overcome. . . . (Derrida, 1996: 86–7)

However, against this, Rorty argues that the only criterion needed for the justification of action is the prevention of cruelty, and that Derrida unnecessarily complicates the issue:

> Derrideans tend to think that the more questioning, problematizing and *mettant-en-abime* you can squeeze into the day's work, the better. Deweyans, on the other hand, think that you should only question when you find yourself in what Dewey called a 'problematic situation' – a situation in which you are no longer sure of what you are doing. You may not be sure what you want, or you may not be sure that your old tools are the best way of getting what you want, or your perplexity may involve both kinds of uncertainty at once. But unless you suffer from some such uncertainty, you should save problematizing for the weekends. (Rorty, 1996: 44)

Social workers and their managers need to be helped to steer a course between Derrida and Rorty. Practitioners do not have time for the kind of self-indulgent epistemologizing beloved by Derrida. They resolutely must continue to judge and to act upon their judgements. However, where

Derrida falters in undecidability, Rorty strides forth a little too sure-footedly. Rorty refuses to acknowledge the critical potential of the work of the likes of Foucault and Derrida, but it is not always clear whether something is broken until one has deconstructed it and made it problematic (Critchley, 1996). What is needed is an approach to practice, which is at one and the same time, problematized and 'doable'.

The acknowledgement of uncertainty does not lead inexorably into a descending vortex of relativism. We do not need to maintain the simplistic dichotomy between realist and relativist approaches. For example, Bruno Latour advocates a more 'realistic realism' (Latour, 1999: 15) (which he also calls 'sturdy relativism' – Latour, 1999: 4) which acknowledges that we can be relatively sure about quite a few things, but that we still need other sorts of judgement. The acknowledgement of the complexity of social workers' different ways on knowing makes reflexive and analytic practice more not less important. In the absence of algorithmic methods to help us resolve uncertain situations, we must think very carefully about what we do.

Foucault points to the need for agents to build an ethics based on an understanding of the socially and historically constituted nature of their knowledges:

> People have to build their own ethics, taking as a point of departure the historical analysis, sociological analysis, and so on that one can provide for them. I don't think that people who try to decipher the truth should have to provide ethical principles or practical advice at the same moment, in the same book and the same analysis. All this prescriptive network has to be elaborated and transformed by people themselves. (Foucault, 1994: 132)

They cannot do this, however, whilst their presuppositions and shortcuts remain taken-for-granted. By using detailed ethnographic data as part of a dialogical model of applied social science, social workers can be helped to see the problem of versions and hence to become more reflexive, analytic and systematic in their sense-making activities. By attending to *how work gets done*, rather than to how it *should* be done, ethnographic data can form the basis for fruitful dialogue between research and practice.

Acknowledgements

I should like to thank the practitioners and managers who allowed me access to their meetings and case records, Rob Flynn for helping me to discover water and Ian Shaw for helpful comments on an earlier draft. The research on which this chapter is based was supported by an ESRC studentship.

Notes

1. My reluctance to deconstruct or disavow the ethnographic claims I make in this chapter does not mean that I consider them to be infallible. Rather, because all such claims are constructed and inevitably interpreted we may as well get on with making them, so that people, if they so wish, may argue with us (cf. Latour, 1988; Law, 1994). However, this is not the place for a detailed analysis of my own ethnographic findings (see, for more detail, White, 1997b, 1998a, 1998b, 1999b), nor is there space here for a systematic consideration of the important issue of validity. For a wide ranging discussion on validity in ethnography see, *inter alia*, Hammersley, 1992 and in social work, *inter alia*, Shaw, 1999a.
2. The general claim I have made is supported by many different sources and types of data (e.g. documentary sources, interview transcripts and tape recordings of naturally occurring talk). This is not the place for me to provide analyses of these sources. I am using this exemplar to illustrate a general point about reflexivity. You may of course contest my reading of this extract, and that is precisely why recorded talk is so valuable.

8

Identifying Expert Social Work: Qualitative Practitioner Research

Jan Fook

CONTENTS

The politics of topic: The research question in question   117
**The voice of practitioners: What is qualitative practitioner
    research?**   119
The embedded culture of positivism   123
Evolving a methodology   123
Alternative criteria and processes   125
Reflexivity   127
Creating a framework for qualitative practitioner research   129

What are some of the major methodological issues involved in qualitative practitioner research? In 1998 I completed a major qualitative study of the development of professional expertise in social work with two colleagues, Martin Ryan and Linette Hawkins (Fook et al., 2000). The project spanned a decade of our experiences as social workers, researchers, theorists and educators. Although the project was a joint effort, we each came to the work with different perspectives, and took on different and changing roles, all the time developing a process which would allow three very different individuals to work together to produce material which we felt would adequately represent what our participants communicated to us. In this chapter I discuss what I regard as some of the major methodological issues regarding qualitative practitioner research and illustrate them with reference to our expertise study. However, the chapter represents my own concerns, rather than the shared view of my colleagues.

The basic issues I discuss revolve around the politics of qualitative practitioner research. By politics I mean the more hidden issues in the practice of such research, and the hidden interests which may mean that particular groups or positions are unwittingly privileged at the expense of others: what are the purposes and legitimate forms of qualitative practitioner research; what embedded values and cultural assumptions guide our decision-making in qualitative research practice; whose interests are involved and how are these best represented; and to what extent, and how, should practitioners be involved in research?

The politics of topic: The research question in question

What is expert social work and how is it developed? The question seems straightforward and well meaning. Yet the choice of topic in research is determined and influenced by a complex interplay of different factors which can loosely be termed political. Punch (1994: 84) describes politics as ranging from the micropolitics of personal relations, to broader con- textual issues such as institutional concerns and funding arrangements. In our case, it seems to me most of these were ever-present, and I would argue that in the case of qualitative practitioner research, where both the methodology and the focus of research are contested, political dimensions take on a significant role.

Although I was aware that perspectives on what was considered 'expert' practice would differ according to political standpoint, since the notion of 'expert' is value-laden, I felt confident enough in our academic and research ability to fashion the design in such a way that theoretical and value con- siderations would be appropriately taken into account. However, I had not thought through enough the *context of cultural orthodoxies* in which we were planning our research. A 'positivist-inclined' camp actually exer- cised power over funding, and our project suffered several grant rejections, because, among other things, we had not successfully defined 'expert social work' in our applications (despite the fact that almost no research existed on the topic and the stated purpose of our study was to develop such a defi- nition) (Ryan, 1996). However to pre-determine a definition of expert social work and then to investigate its existence, would have been to undermine the very reasons for undertaking the research, and would not have allowed us to see how practitioners themselves understood and practised 'expertly'. The research assessor's requirements were not picking up on a simple design fault, but were rather based on more positivist assumptions. If we had designed the study along the lines proposed we would not have been able to investigate the problem we were posing.

This issue of the pervading culture of positivism which guides research thinking and practice is well-noted as a major impediment to qualitative practitioner research. Everrit et al. (1992: 8) argue that practitioner dis- enchantment with research is actually a disenchantment with positivism. They also acknowledge the relative disadvantage of qualitative projects in receiving research funding (Wells, 1995; Colquhuon, 1996; Daly, 1998). Whilst I do not wish to argue exclusively for qualitative approaches over quantitative, there are many good reasons that social work researchers might wish to undertake research which is more open-ended, and which seeks to represent experiences about which little has been formally documented. In the case of researching 'expert' social work, we believed that a qualitative design, which simply took as its starting point descriptions of the practice of professionals *who were deemed by their peers to be 'expert'* (Fook et al., 1997), would maximize the depth and amount of learning about a phenomenon which had been so little investigated. The irony of course with much qualitative practitioner research is that it is messy, complicated (Gilgun, 1994) and time consuming, but that it stands to yield much new knowledge. It is often the research which needs the most doing, precisely because it focuses on the difficult areas, about which less may be known. Yet it is the research for which it is hardest to receive funding, and therefore it is less likely to be undertaken in this increasingly cost-driven environment.

Other politics were implicit in the ultimate *purposes and uses of the research*. Practitioner research can serve many different purposes, including the generation of new knowledge from practice (Everrit et al., 1992; Goldstein, 1994) particularly in reflective ways (Bernstein and Epstein, 1994); the improvement of practice and professionalism; and the evaluation of practice (for example, Shaw and Lishman, 1999). In my own case, I had yet other reasons which were explicitly political: I was particularly motivated by a desire to reaffirm the nature and value of social work in a competitive context, and I had become increasingly annoyed with trends which I believed had reduced social work, particularly direct practice, to a more psychologistic orientation (Fook, 1993). There was a sense in which I saw our research as crusading work, the results of which should allow us to carve out a legitimate space for social work, and I saw this as a laudable aim in itself. However, the question of the ultimate purposes and uses of the research became the seat of revolving tensions throughout the course of our project in particularly pragmatic ways. For instance, one ongoing question was what right had I to assume that practitioners would want to participate in research which might represent social work differently from the way they saw it? Another issue was also ethical: should participants be asked to participate in research, the findings and outcomes of which would be largely uncertain at the time of interview? What is informed consent under these circumstances (Kellehear, 1998)?

Another question which I had not thought through was what other changes might result from our work, and the extent to which our study should try to incorporate material which would allow us to address these directly. In particular there was the question of how and whether our research should specifically address how notions of expertise should also influence social work education. This question became a foremost tension, since one of our team members subscribed strongly to a more explicit participatory action research framework (Hawkins, 1996) in which the express purpose of any research project is direct change. I took the view that this was an important goal, but to address it properly would require another type of research study. It was, however, very difficult to compart-mentalize our thinking and actions in line with this distinction, particularly since all of us were engaged in social work education, and naturally we wanted to apply our ongoing research learning to our ongoing teaching experience. Whenever we met to discuss the analysis of our material, the discussion would inevitably turn to what it meant for our educational prac-tices. The present and ultimate uses of our research were therefore ques-tions which required constant revisiting, and were questions inextricably bound up with our espoused paradigms in relation to research, and the context of our current professional experiences. This meant that it was very difficult to put boundaries on the scope of our research, an issue which was particularly frustrating in a climate which demands quick and measurable outcomes from research.

The voice of practitioners: What is qualitative practitioner research?

The genesis of our study was quite pragmatic in that our decision to replicate Benner's (1984) research on nursing expertise meant that we attempted to modify it to fit social work contexts. This of course is one of the basic points which needs to be made about qualitative practitioner research: since it is contextual, and contexts may vary, it may not be possible to replicate existing studies. In the event we devised a complicated design which consisted of two parts: a longitudinal aspect which followed a group of approximately 30 social workers for five years, from the beginning of their social work studies to the end of their third year of practice (inter-viewed at nine different stages); and a 'one off' aspect in which a group of 30 experienced ('expert') workers were interviewed. We used a number of different tools to collect different types of data, allowing us to make com-parisons in a number of different ways. Unfortunately Benner's design did not fit neatly at all, since the practice situations of nurses vary markedly from those of social workers. Benner had used matched pairs of experi-enced and student nurses, acting in the same situation. This was impossible in social work, given the more individualistic work of social workers, and the variety and unpredictability of settings in which they practice. Ultimately we adopted one of her instruments, the critical incident tech-nique (Flanagan, 1954; Benner, 1984) in which practitioners choose and describe an incident which exemplifies something significant for them. We also extended the design through the use of hypothetical practice vignettes (Walden et al., 1990), to which practitioners were asked to respond. Our aim was to collect data which was as 'pure' a description of concrete specific practices as possible, rather than to interview practitioners about more abstract theorizations of practice. We wanted to hear about their subjective descriptions of practice, rather than their more objectified view of it (Baldwin, 2000: 10).

We termed our approach as loosely qualitative, again for the pragmatic reason that it involved for the most part relatively unstructured interviews (Kellehear, 1998). The thinking through of what this meant in theoretical terms was to come much later, as I struggled with keeping the study 'on target' in terms of our aims and ethical considerations. However, at this stage, we deemed a broad qualitative design as appropriate, since our main intention was to inductively identify notions of expertise and its development from the accounts of practitioners. In these initial stages of design, broader questions of alternative ways to create this material were not asked. However, after we conducted the first stage of interviews, ethical and methodological questions of what right we had to make particular judgements and interpretations of interviewees' transcripts began to enter. Was it ethical that they be asked to participate in research whose findings might ultimately judge their performance as lacking in some way? Hyde (1994) grapples with similar issues, particularly wondering how she could pass judgement when not having to confront the daily realities of her research participants (Hyde, 1994: 177–8). This underscores the privileged role of the researcher, even in qualitative research which claims to represent the world of the researched.

Other doubts were constantly present. Were the voices of practitioners being heard and represented accurately? Should qualitative practitioner research be conducted by practitioners themselves, or is it also legitimate for non-practitioner researchers to represent their voices? How could we theorize the material in ways meaningful to us, but at the same time not imply negative judgements of participants' practice, and be respectful of their different experiences and perspectives?

Some of these issues I will revisit at the end of the chapter, in discussing a view of qualitative practitioner research. However, in the case of this latter question, the politics of how we represented our findings were crucial. For instance, how could we find a language for our findings which would not imply criticism of 'non-expert' practice, but at the same time would value, and help improve, existing social work practices? In framing our theory of expertise, we were also aware of avoiding simple behavioural descriptions of 'competency' (Gould, 1996). Yet at the same time, we were aware that unless we were able to frame our descriptions of expertise in ways which were meaningful and attractive to *both* practitioners and managers, much of the political value of our work would be lost. Accordingly we decided it was important to 'name' the competencies of expert practice, but to name them in terms which we thought represented the complexities of practice most closely, as embodied in our participants' descriptions of their practice. Our descriptions of expert practice and its development therefore include value and attitudinal, as well as behavioural and critical dimensions (Eraut, 1994), since practitioners tend to speak about their work in these more holistic ways. In order not to appear negatively judgemental of practice which we might not consider 'expert' we focused positively on describing the elements of expertise, rather than the dimensions of 'non-expert' practice. The theory of expertise which we developed from our participants' interviews and existing theories thus comprises eleven different elements (substantive knowledge, procedural knowledge, skills, values, contextuality, reflexivity, breadth of vision, flexibility/creativity, use of theory, approach, perspective on profession), which develop variably over six stages. The seventh 'stage' of the expert, is not a necessary stage, in that it is not an automatic progression. However, it is characterized by: the ability to create theory and knowledge directly from practice experience, and to translate this into different contexts (transferability); an ability to work with uncertainty and change (flexibility and creativity); an ability to prioritize and to develop forms of continuity and meaning which transcend the particular job; to work in a connected and integrated way with context (contextual abilities); and to work with complexities (Fook et al., 2000). This very summarized list represents our attempt to create a language to both describe and value the uncertainties and complexities of social work practice.

Another major and ongoing tension was the degree of involvement practitioners should have as researchers themselves. Linette Hawkins writes about this issue in some detail (1996), the question of the division 'researchers' and 'researched' constituting a major problem for her. Linette subscribed closely to a participative action research model as developed by Wadsworth (1984), as mentioned previously, in which the researcher acts as facilitator, and the research process is expressly emancipatory (Reason, 1994b: 328–9; Hawkins, 1996: 99). Whilst valuing this type of approach, I particularly felt that to follow such a model would actually constitute a different type of research study, which would achieve different, although equally laudable aims. It would necessitate starting over, rather than a modification of the existing design. For pragmatic and other reasons, I was not keen to start again. For one thing, we had already received funding for the project as originally proposed, and had already spent most of this funding. We took a decision to continue with the established design, and to try to involve participants in ways which would have minimal influence on subsequent responses. Whilst I also felt some disquiet with this practice (as I was aware that we were influencing the participants simply by involving them in the research process) there were other pragmatic reasons why an expressly participatory and emancipatory design might not have been appropriate. Linette documents some of these (Hawkins, 1996), such as the fact that the group of participants did not see themselves as a coherent group with common interests. Linette also expressed some disappointment that the participants themselves did not often have a critical view of their educational experience, and were not seemingly interested in changing social work education, or the ways in which our research might do so.

One of the processes we did try to institute to encourage participant involvement was regular meetings with participants to feedback ideas, and to discuss and develop our own theorizing. A few very dedicated participants attended these meetings, but often we were not able to focus the discussion well enough so that it was meaningful in terms of our own current thinking. From my own memory, these sessions functioned more as an opportunity for people to catch up on each other's news, and to reflect a little about how they viewed their social work education in the light of their subsequent work experience. I suspect part of the difficulty was that these groups had never been set up as research groups, and had not had the opportunity to develop as such. Perhaps if the design had been directly participatory from the start, participants might have better developed as involved contributors in the theory development exercise. Wuest (1995) notes the potential for differences in interpretation between the participants and the researchers, and that this can be problematic if the goal is to produce a single truth. In the case of our study, I took a very definite decision to privilege our interpretations, since they were based on an overview of many different stories in which we had immersed ourselves constantly over several years. The experience with this material was necessarily more sporadic for the participants, which meant it was difficult for our different meaning systems to connect. Wuest contends (1995), and I would agree, that full participation and inclusion of participants is difficult, if not impossible, as the balance of power is ultimately in the researcher's favour. The opportunities might be maximized with participatory designs, such as in explicitly co-operative designs (Heron, 1996; Baldwin, 2000) but ultimately the roles of researcher and participant emerge from different motivations, political positions and interests. They might only converge where designs are explicitly reflexive, and/or where practitioners are themselves the researchers. I will return to some of these issues further on, as the implications for good quality practitioner research are significant.

This basic question, however, of what are the appropriate paradigms and designs for qualitative practitioner research does not I believe have a simple answer, and it is not even clear to me that this is an appropriate question to ask. There is room within qualitative research for a variety of perspectives. Denzin and Lincoln (1994b: 3–4) note the multidisciplinary nature of qualitative research, and the commitment to naturalistic and interpretive perspectives. They quote from Nelson et al. (1992: 4):

> At the same time the field is inherently political and shaped by multiple ethical and political positions.
>
> Qualitative research embraces two tensions at the same time. On the one hand it is drawn to a broad interpretive, postmodern, feminist and critical sensibility. On the other hand it is drawn to more narrowly defined positivist, postpositivist, humanistic and naturalistic conceptions of human experience and its analysis.

This way of understanding qualitative research means for me that qualitative practitioner research can therefore involve any type of research which seeks to understand or represent the experiences of the practitioner in ways which recognize the political and value contexts of those experiences. Whilst methods can differ on a continuum ranging from 'soft' non-complex statistical measures to experiential tools, the focus is more on generating rich data from an 'emic' insider's point of view. This view of qualitative research does not dictate who the researchers must be, or narrow parameters for the relationship between researchers and study participants. Practitioner research can therefore be undertaken by practitioners themselves, or by other researchers studying practitioners. It is qualitative if it is focused on the practitioner's view. Qualitative practitioner research in this sense is *inclusionary* of a range of methods and ways of knowing.

The embedded culture of positivism

This way of viewing qualitative research is enabling in hindsight, since it appears acceptable that some qualitative research might occur at the more positivist end of the continuum, so to speak. Throughout the life of the research project, though, it was a constant tension for me to try to keep the study, its processes and practices, 'true' to what I believed to be a non-positivist orientation. This became a major issue at three particular points: in evolving a methodology; in finding an appropriate language; and in devising alternative criteria for evaluating the research.

Evolving a methodology

The design of our study was complex in that we used a number of similar and different tools at different times to allow patterns and also comparisons to be developed. Because of the huge amount of data generated (an average of 5 typed pages of material for each of the total of 300 interviews, making a total of 1,500 pages of transcripts), and the complexity of the responses, there were obvious tensions between finding an efficient way to analyse the material and at the same time doing justice to the richness of detail and quality of the stories. We swung between a more positivistic type of content analysis (Kellehear, 1993) and a more grounded theory approach (Strauss and Corbin, 1990). In the early days of analysis, we constructed 'lists' of practice features derived from classic works like Biestek's (1961) principles of the casework relationship and from later works detailing assessment categories (for example, knowledge of biomedical/material, psychological, social and structural factors) (Fook, 1993), so that we could construct an analysis of practice against preformulated ideas of sound practice. This proved not only time consuming, but almost impossible and meaningless, since we could not reach a consensus about how each of the categories was to be interpreted in responses. However, when we tried more grounded approaches, and tried to guide research assistants in the details of inducing patterns from the transcripts, we could do little more than to advise they read and reread the material, taking note of patterns which emerge, and reworking them to fit emergent patterns. This is the type of activity which makes sense once you have done it, as Sue White notes in her chapter in this volume. But to people unused to the tradition of qualitative data analysis, it calls for a huge leap of faith to trust in one's intuitive ability to understand and appreciate the text. The positivist assumption that you cannot trust your own judgement since it is by definition subjective, and therefore not objective, and therefore not research, proved difficult to unseat. Hyde (1994) talks about similar difficulties in determining which themes are truly significant.

Ultimately we developed two ways of analysing the data to ensure that we had both ends covered, so to speak. We devised a more structured, what we termed a 'deductive' schema, in which the material was analysed against a pre-existing theory of expertise, the Dreyfus and Dreyfus model (1986). This comprised five stages of skill acquisition which involved: moving from the use of context-free rules to situational rules and the development of an involved intuitive (rather than a detached analytical) perspective. The content analysis deductive side was clear enough, in that we were able to stipulate, fairly simply, how we derived categories from the Dreyfus and Dreyfus material, and indicate what sorts of practice fitted these. For instance, context-free rules were relatively easy to identify, since they involved the use of generalized adages which applied regardless of context. We also conducted what we termed the 'inductive' aspect, which was the grounded theory approach, in which we tried to describe the patterns which emerged. This combination of inductive and deductive analysis is relatively common (Gilgun, 1994).

In doing this though, I was acutely aware that there were shortcomings. With the inductive aspect, there was the ongoing pragmatic issue that not all of us could conduct the interviews and also perform the inductive analysis of the transcripts. We in fact employed a research assistant to conduct most of the interviews and do the bulk of the detailed data analysis. The principal researchers conducted a small number of interviews at each stage in order to 'get a feel' for them, and we also ended up collaboratively doing a more 'macro' analysis of the transcripts as well. For instance, an initial analysis of interviews at one stage might indicate a reluctance to deal with men continuing on from early stages. However, a more 'macro' analysis might note that this reluctance is more associated with people who work in less structured settings. Therefore our broader analysis might be that workers in more structured statutory settings gain some confidence from the use of authority their employment position gives them. The methodological problem for me in this was that I did not feel it was possible to conduct what felt like an accurate in-depth analysis of rich data, without having conducted the interview. It felt like trying to make meaning from experience which has been divulged in one context, in a completely different context. Nor is it very easy, or perhaps even 'authentic' to theorize from material which one has not collected first hand on a personal basis. Yet there was no other way we could have conducted research of this scale, unless our own salaries were totally funded to undertake it (a prospect which is exceedingly unlikely for research topics of this kind). Research funding protocols seem founded on the positivist premise that data can be collected separately from its analysis and recording.

We also developed our research design as we went, in order to help us cope with the large amount of data. We devised a type of 'theoretical sampling' (Gilgun, 1994) whereby we picked up on issues in subsequent stages which had been identified in earlier stages, to allow us to track the features of professional development a little more explicitly. For instance, in one of the early stages the theme of a reluctance to deal with men, and with anger emerged quite clearly, so we ensured that the practice vignettes given in subsequent stages included situations with these elements. In some instances we worried about the lack of reference to collective ways of working, so we deliberately included vignettes of situations which allowed for collective strategies.

Alternative criteria and processes: questions of reliability, validity and objectivity

Probably the most embedded way in which the culture of positivism prevails is in determining the criteria against which soundness of research is judged (Mullen, 1995). The issues of reliability, validity and objectivity raise constant problems for qualitative researchers, as they are concepts which arise from a positivist frame of reference. In the expertise study, they assumed paramount importance, particularly because of the controversial nature of the topic.

In the earlier years of the research one of our research grant application reviewers questioned how we would ensure 'inter-rater reliability'. The process we eventually devised was one in which all three of us would independently conduct an initial analysis of the material, and then meet and discuss interpretations. When we reached a consensus, that was the interpretation recorded. What was also interesting about this process was that we were also engaging in a type of negative case analysis (Finch and Mason, 1990) in which different interpretations were tried on until one which fitted was identified. It was also a process of increasing cycles of macro analysis, in which basic descriptive details developed into successively more sophisticated theorizing, as different perspectives were taken into account and used to modify each other.

The question of validity was also problematic for us, and is a question which arises repeatedly for qualitative researchers. How generalizable are the findings from a small sample (Shaw, 1999a: 62), and is this even an appropriate question to ask? Years later, I concluded that what we were doing was not devising a theory in order to *generalize* it across all populations, but rather developing an understanding of expert social work which might be *transferable* to other situations, in that it might help provide meaning in other contexts. Using theories developed in one context to explicate experiences in another context (transferability), is different, in this sense, from imposing the meanings gained from one context on another (generalizability). This problem is not in fact unique to qualitative research.

Some qualitative researchers have coined terms like 'trustworthiness and authenticity' (Guba and Lincoln, 1994), 'adequacy and credibiltiy' (Olesen, 1994) or 'credibility and fittingness' (Beck, 1993) as more befitting questions of the extent to which qualitative findings can be said to represent the experiencers' views of the phenomenon being researched. The same questions are caught up in the debate between 'relevance and rigour' (Shaw, 1999a: 62). Later presentations of our findings and theorizing have 'validated' our work in that practitioners say it 'rings bells' for them, and helps articulate what they think they do. Its relevance appears to far out-weigh questions of the accuracy of our representation of our participants' views.

One way in which we tried to establish the 'trustworthiness' (internal validity) of our findings was to obtain some examples of students' own accounts of their learning. We were troubled by the notion that our own theorizing of students' learning experiences was just that, and that students themselves might describe their own learning experiences quite differently, if given a more open opportunity to reflect on these in 'hindsight'. Accordingly we interviewed three participants, some four years after the study ended, and asked them to talk about what had been significant learning experiences for them. We were right to be concerned. What we received in accounts from students was not on the whole couched in any of the terminology or discourse that we had used. Whereas we had talked about dimensions like identification with the profession, they tended to refer to the learning derived from significant others. Neither set of discourses is necessarily mutually exclusive – indeed, it may have been that if we laid out our whole theory and explained its terms to our participants they might readily have seen themselves in this picture. We have never attempted this. However, these observations of disparities in stories lend force to the idea that research may in fact simply be a type of 'translation' process (Steier, 1991) in that research involves translating one set of meanings into another set which can be understood by other parties. In our case, we as researchers turned the participants' stories into a meaning system which we hoped could be appreciated by social work educators, theorists, expertise researchers, and other social workers.

The question of objectivity was early recognized by us, and relatively easily addressed. We were aware, from the beginning, that definitions of expert social work practice would be inextricable from value and political positions (Fook et al., 1997), and we were clear from the beginning what our own subjective stance on 'good' social work was. We shared a critical perspective on social work, and were therefore aware that we were likely to be disappointed in practice which individualized social problems, and that we were also likely to notice these features more. To some extent our choice to conduct a deductive analysis of the material against an established theory of expertise enabled our analysis to incorporate other dimensions. In other cases we simply declared our position, and took it into account when analysing the material. We also actively searched for other types of value positions, whilst at the same time being aware that we could not avoid making implicit judgements about the standpoints taken by some practitioners. From my point of view I did not find this stance problematic, as I must self-reflexively recognize that all research is situated in personal context, and that my interpretations are necessarily made through the lens of my own embodied experience. This issue of reflexivity is integral for qualitative practitioner researchers.

Reflexivity

From a reflexive point of view, subjectivity is not a problem but an asset. In the course of our study, I moved towards this more reflexive position, from seeing subjectivity as a problem to be minimized, to a stance which potentially enhanced the research, and which might even be a creative part of the research process. In simple terms, I see reflexivity as the ability to recognize the influence of the researcher's whole self and context (social, cultural and structural) on every aspect of the research, and the ability to use this awareness in the research act itself (Fook, 2000b). Sue White, in this volume, notes a similar understanding, that of reflexivity as a process of 'looking inward and outward to the social and cultural artifacts and forms of thought which saturate our practices'. Initially, as I indicated earlier, I felt that whilst I knew my own value position on expert social work would unavoidably colour how I interpreted the material, I felt that simply declaring this would minimize whatever deleterious effects there might be. I also wanted to minimize the reactivity effects of informing participants of our interpretations of findings, thereby colouring their subsequent responses to us. A further concern was that my own commitment to a 'critical' social work perspective would limit the scope and relevance of the work to people who did not share my perspective. I did not simply want to 'find out' what I thought I already hoped to be the case.

Interestingly, after some years of rereading, analysing and discussing the transcripts, it has become clear to me that we have gone through several different processes and levels of analysis. This is to me a type of reflexivity, whereby we have successively interrogated our own interpretations of the material, so that with each successive interrogation, we have created new meanings from the material. Certainly, as each successive piece of 'micro' analysis was completed, the emerging 'macro' analysis influenced the way in which subsequent material was understood. It is instructive to compare early formulations (Fook et al., 1996) of expert practice with the most recent (Fook et al., 2000). The earlier versions tended to be relatively superficial descriptions of practice (for example, we used terms such as 'holistic' and 'generic'). Later descriptors tended to develop these holistic and generic orientations in terms of contextual work and a whole complex of skill areas (for example, we speak later of 'connectedness' and 'contextuality'), as we were able to see broader patterns from the overview of all the material.

I have no doubt that if I were to revisit the raw transcripts again tomorrow, I could make yet another set of meanings. Whilst this awareness might have alarmed me, even two years ago, I have now come to recognize that this is in fact the way that the meaning making process must work. Guba and Lincoln (1994: 107) talk about the theory-ladenness of facts, that 'facts' are only 'facts' within some theoretical framework. What has happened for me in the course of analysing the expertise material, is that different 'facts' have emerged, depending upon which theoretical framework I was operating in at the time. For example, ten years ago I was heavily into structural and feminist notions of social work, and an exponent of the liberatory pedagogy of Freire (1972). I then became interested in reflectivity (Argyris and Schon, 1974) and how it helped link practice, theory and research (Fook, 1996). Later I moved onto incorporating postmodern ideas, and returning to critical social science to examine the overlap (Pease and Fook, 1999), I also managed to link critical reflection with the postmodern turn. What is interesting is that it is possible to trace a similar pattern in my own theory building of the expertise material. Early on, my engagement with the material bordered on the positivist and modernist – I had fairly structured notions of how to read and understand the material. The earlier types of skills and knowledge we traced reflected themes of individualization and notions of social structure. As time has gone on, I have become more empowered to trust my own interpretations, my own theory-building prowess, to the point where I have attempted, with my colleagues, to build a theory of expertise which attempts to conceptualize professional expertise for and in postmodern times (Fook, 2000a). The skills and knowledge we focused on have been more to do with practices surrounding knowledge creation, and the practitioner's reflective ability. It is no coincidence that theory building has paralleled theory use.

One way of characterizing this process is that I have been building different theories of expertise (from different 'facts') depending upon which theories I have been using to build and understand these 'facts'. The 'facts' have changed as my theories have changed. In this sense the constructions I make might therefore primarily be reflections of the materials I am using. This phenomenon is both exciting and frustrating, given that for me the heart of qualitative research is its theory- or meaning-making potential. It is exciting for its creative capacities, but it is frustrating, because it is impossible to ever escape from the lens of one's own making. However, in studying the lens itself, it is possible to create new ways of seeing – by examining ourselves, we create new ways of seeing others.

This reflexive constructivist process leads me to examine the whole idea of theory building as research, and its use as a framework in qualitative practitioner research.

Creating a framework for qualitative practitioner research

In a strange way, I have arrived back at where I started ten years earlier. Back then I was heartily engaged in creating theory (a theoretical model for the practice of radical casework) solely through my own reading and reflection, without the undertaking of systematic empirical research. I became engaged in the expertise study primarily because of university workplace pressures, under the notion that empirical research was some-how more valued than theoretical research. I now question this assump-tion, and also the suggestion that there should be any imperative to privilege one type of research over another. I can see now that theory build-ing is an integral part of any type of research, but that we may simply go about collecting the raw material for that theory building in different types of ways. What makes the theory-building process terribly exciting for me is the creative possibilities that a reflexive interrogation of my own theoretical assumptions opens up in my awareness and ability to under-stand other people's experiences. As Steier says (1991:177):

> . . . as we reflexively understand our research to be about ourselves, we open up greater (rather than fewer) degrees of freedom for the voices of others. It allows us to begin to question where our own categories do not fit, and where we have created 'false' notes out of good music.

The research story for qualitative practitioner researchers, myself included, doesn't end here, however. It is one thing to recognize and value reflexivity, it is another thing to recognize it as a legitimate form and framework for research. Where a recognition of reflexivity can help in the quest to legiti-mate and undertake good qualitative practitioner research, is in the recog-nition that the tacit knowledge of the practitioner is not only a legitimate, but necessary, focus for practitioner research. If the qualitative researcher is self-reflexive, then she or he recognizes that the self is the lens through which they see the world. The lens itself therefore becomes an important part of the research, as instrument but also data. Unfortunately, many of the features of the lens itself may not be explicit, and it is these tacit aspects of the lens, what Lincoln and Guba term 'tacit knowledge' (1985: 195–8) which must often be experienced to be understood. These may be the aspects of practitioner experience which only the practitioner researcher can unearth her or himself, and may include the unexamined assumptions and experiences which result from the practitioner's social, cultural and structural position. From this perspective, qualitative practitioner research undertaken by practitioners on their own practice, is absolutely vital to the identification of all aspects of practice.

Where does this discussion leave us in terms of the major issues confronting qualitative practitioner research? There is some debate about whether practitioners themselves are best placed to undertake research, particularly on their own practice. Sue White (this volume) notes the criticism that practitioners may uncritically move to solution-focused research. Padgett (1998a, 1998b) argues that there are significant differences (in roles, paradigmatic assumptions and disciplinary background) between qualitative research methods and social work practice, so that practitioners are ill-equipped to be researchers. Gilgun (1994), however, in an oft-quoted chapter (Padgett, 1998a; Bein and Allen, 1999) argues convincingly for the fit between qualitative research and direct practice. However, there may still be some major practical and contextual impediments for practitioners who wish to undertake their own qualitative research. Some, such as the time-consuming nature of qualitative research, and the lack of funding support, and the dominant positivist culture we have already noted, although these conditions do not constitute, in my view, sufficient argument for practitioners not to undertake research, since there are often efficient and pragmatic ways of connecting the two (Harrison, 1994; Loneck, 1994; Fook et al., 1999; Shaw, 1999).

There is also the question of whether practitioner research is that undertaken by practitioners, or whether it can be carried out by non-practitioner researchers, and either focused on practitioners or their practice, or indeed the service users working with practitioners. Is the purpose of practitioner research primarily to focus on the 'what is' rather than the 'how' (Sue White, this volume), and is there enough detail of the 'how' to effectively inform daily practice (Loneck, 1994: 447)? What methods and designs are most appropriate for qualitative practitioner research? The possibilities range from simple statistics to unstructured interviews, to grounded theory analysis, narrative analysis and deconstruction, reflexive methods and ethnographic methods, and debates exist about the combination of methods (Sherman and Reid, 1994b).

I would argue that there is no definitive answer to these questions, as possibilities will vary depending on context and time, and that research practice, like social work practice, is a much more holistic and integrated endeavour than text books would have us believe. In some instances, we may need to know the 'what is' in order to develop new or more critical practice. We may need to 'break the mould' of what we assume we already know to enable this to happen. To some extent our expertise study fits with these goals. In other cases, qualitative research may be needed to directly address perspectives which are lacking, so that practice can be improved. In the case of our expertise study, we also attempted this in that we wished to describe and theorize expert practice from the practitioners' perspectives. I discussed at some length in this chapter the ongoing tensions about whether our expertise study was purely confined to a description of expertise and its development, or whether it should be more geared to changing practice and education for it. Whilst I struggled to ensure that the former was attained, I am well aware that there have been untold changes which have spun off from our work to date. It was therefore both about describing 'what is' and 'what should be', although I think our vision of what should be is more credible because we have claimed to base it on 'what is'.

The type of methods used should also be flexible, and based on an inclusive approach, and to some extent the type of methods used may partly influence the involvement of practitioners. Several writers argue strongly for ethnographic and reflective methods (White, this volume; Harrison, 1994; Bernstein and Epstein, 1994; Shaw, 1996; Fook, 1996) as being pertinent to practice research and indeed to the role of practitioner as researcher. What has been instructive for me in engaging in our expertise study is that whilst it began as a relatively simple qualitative design, perhaps tending towards the more 'positivist' end of qualitative methods, I realized over the course of time, that my own reflexivity was crucial in creating the theory from this process. The research, for me, could not have happened without exercising my reflexive ability, because it was an understanding of these 'tacit' features of my own practice which allowed me to fashion a theory of expertise which could speak across multiple perspectives. As a research practitioner I needed to understand how my own position contributed to my research practice and the material I eventually produced. For social work practitioners the process and concerns are the same. Therefore whilst I would argue that qualitative practitioner research can be carried out by practitioners and non-practitioners, with multiple foci of study, and using different methods, the experience of undertaking our expertise study has convinced me that unless practitioners are involved in some researching of their own practice, the social work profession will lack major material from which to develop critical and responsive practices. Qualitative practitioner research in social work must therefore be inclusive enough to embrace reflexive methods, used by practitioners themselves, focusing on their own practice.

Note

With grateful acknowledgement to Christine Morley for assistance in reviewing literature for this chapter.

Part 3

QUALITATIVE WORK IN SOCIAL WORK

9

Fieldwork Choices in Context

CONTENTS

Ethnography	137
Ethnography and strengths perspectives	138
Applied ethnography	140
Ethnography and researching practice	141
Interviews	142
Focus groups in social work research	146
Simulated interviews	147
Interviewing and sensitivity – the exemplar of children	148
Narrative, life histories and documentary research	150
Documentary sources	154
Conclusion	155
Recommended reading	156

Despite the burgeoning generic literature on qualitative research there is surprisingly little in most of the text books about the relationship between the context of the research and the choice of methodology. More usually, the primary problematic in qualitative research is taken to be the relationship between theory and methodology, with less regard to how this is mediated by the context in which the research is undertaken. Some years ago Brenner et al. (1978) suggested that social research still carries the legacy of the approach to method taken in the natural sciences, that it somehow stands outside the social context:

> The science paradigm of methodology, for a start, does not involve, nor need, any *social*, knowledge about the methodological processes, and here particularly data collection procedures, themselves. The logic of method is, and can be, conceptualised in a socially clean language. (Brenner et al., 1978: 10)

More recent writings on methodology (e.g. Bryman, 1988) see qualitative research as following the logic of *contextualism*, that is showing commitment to understanding beliefs and events within their social context. Bryman argues that this is closely aligned to a commitment to *holism*, an undertaking to examine social entities as wholes to be researched in their entirety (Bryman, 1988: 64).

When presented as abstract ideas discussed without reference to any specific research problem, notions such as contextualism and holism can reasonably seem non-contentious and self-evident. Difficulties come to the fore when we situate them in context, and for the purposes of this discussion we take social work as the specific site or domain of research. As we have argued in Chapter 1, we see social work as constituting a particularly rich and complex network of contexts for making fieldwork choices in qualitative research. Social work has evolved since the nineteenth century as an occupational category which is concerned with the interaction between society and individuals and groups who have been socially defined as problematic (Sheppard, 1995). As soon as we begin to generalize about social work as a context for research then numerous ambiguities emerge which render almost any categorical definition as in need of radical qualification: social work is about negotiation in informal settings such as the home, but informality also sometimes gives way to highly structured formal arenas, such as courts and tribunals; social work nurtures relationships of support and reciprocity within families, groups and communities, but it also enforces social rules, laws and obligations; in the UK social work is largely sanctioned by the state and exists in the interstices between the state and civil society, but increasingly is delivered by non-governmental agencies, and in the USA and many European countries its statutory basis has never been a defining characteristic. The ambiguities and diversities of social work as a form of practice make it formidably difficult to delineate as a bounded field of research. Under these circumstances it is difficult to sustain a view that research problems and methods for tackling them can 'just emerge' from the context. Silverman has called the attitude which seems to underline the presumption that the identification of a topic for research and making methodological choices are apparently self-evident, 'simplistic inductivism' (Silverman, 2000: 61):

> Similarly, sociological ethnographers would identify an activity, institution or subculture and just 'hang out' . . . the idea was to grasp 'reality' in its daily accomplishment. The hope was somehow meaning would 'emerge' by itself from such 'in-depth' exposure to the field. It was believed that any prior definitions of topics or concepts would only stand in the way of the cultural world to which one was being exposed. (Silverman, 2000: 62)

It is ironic that simplistic inductivism parallels some of the assumptions of positivism which qualitative researchers themselves frequently critique, notably its implicit epistemological notion that problems are predetermined and can be discovered without any intervening explicit or implicit theoretical frame (Gould and Harris, 1996). This constitutes what

Silverman again calls a convenient myth of naturalism, the idea that a unified 'reality' exists into which the researcher can immerse herself or himself and from which will emerge through a process of symbiosis a research strategy which explores and describes that reality. One of the risks of holding on to simplistic inductivism – completely atheoretical research which just 'goes with the flow' – is that inadequate attention is paid to the cumulative knowledge from which new studies emerge, and to which they potentially contribute. This is a criticism of qualitative social work research, that it is a collection of idiographic studies which do not build towards an edifice of knowledge (Sheldon, 1978). As Chapter 2 showed, there *is* a significant body of qualitative social work research which as it develops may be dignified as a tradition, and through this literature can be illustrated some of the issues which the social work researcher faces in making methodological choices. The next two chapters then take the six methodological approaches illustrated by Chapters 3 to 8, not as an exhaustive catalogue of the choices which can be made, but to illustrate some of the interplays between context, methodology and the logic of qualitative inquiry.

Ethnography

Tom Hall, in his account in Chapter 3 of doing ethnographic research with young homeless people and staff in an emergency accommodation project, sets out why for him ethnography was the methodology of choice when researching his particular social work context. Thus, it is grounded in the local and particular and makes no over-reaching claims for generalizibility, it produces accounts which move between participation and observation ('the heart of all good ethnography'), and it captures the subtleties of practice behind espoused, formal accounts. Hall's description of producing an ethnographic study vividly exemplifies these features, and in doing so reflects the connection of ethnography to naturalism, the attempt to capture the salient characteristics of a social world without, insofar as possible, interrupting or disturbing it.

Hall's chapter can only illuminate one approach to ethnography, and Atkinson and Hammersley (1994: 257) provide a useful reminder that it is a mistake to view ethnography as a unified paradigm; different positions in social theory give rise to a variety of ethnographies with their own emphases. Instead of an orthodoxy, there are different blendings of theory, research ethics and methodology which underpin a range of schools and sub-types. If there is a commonality between them it is their shared claim to represent the true apostolic spirit of ethnography in opposition to all the rest who have been corrupted from its founding ideals. This is part of what Atkinson and Hammersley describe as one of the 'creation myths' of ethnography (Atkinson and Hammersley, 1994: 249).

Probably, ethnography is more widely-established than ever, but if this is the case then commensurately it is also more disputed at theoretical and methodological levels. Commentaries on research methodology tend to categorize ethnography as part of the social constructionist project, particularly allied to hermeneutics and interpretivism, but as Atkinson and Hammersley remind us, and we discussed in Chapters 1 and 2, ethnography also emerges from an anthropological tradition which was firmly positivist and believed itself to be a scientific endeavour uncovering general laws of social change. More recently, ethnography has become a site within which the wider qualitative arguments about epistemology, method, voice and purpose figure strongly. As we pointed out in Chapter 1, and as demonstrated by the ethnographically oriented contributed chapters in this volume, in social work we find a spectrum between those such as Hall who are tentative about the knowledge claims of ethnography, and those who are firmly committed to applied, action-oriented ethnography (see Edgar and Russell (1998) and below).

What we find is a fairly broad consensus that participant observation is a defining element of the fieldwork approach, although apart from this concept itself being contested, there will also be varying mixes of supplementary methods such as in-depth interviewing and analysis of documentary evidence. Hall (Chapter 3 in this volume) for instance, describes how participant observation of the emergency shelter later was rounded out by analysis of agency documentation, analysis of transcripts of meetings, and selective semi-structured interviews. A further, important distinction in the level of analysis needs to be made between micro-ethnography, based on research into the forms of life of a social sub-group or an organization such as a team in a welfare agency, and macro-ethnography which attempts to capture the culture, behaviour and belief-systems of a whole society. As Fortune (1994) has commented, macro-ethnography, which is hugely labour intensive, is not really and is unlikely to become part of the social work research repertoire. This is not to ignore that macro-ethnographical research is a potential resource, part of the wider body of knowledge which can sensitize social workers to practising in communities to which they are outsiders or newcomers.

Ethnography and strengths perspectives

Ethnographic research in social work has emerged within a range of contexts. Sometimes, as already discussed in Chapter 2, ethnography has been the methodology of choice for social work researchers whose interests are about organizational analysis and the relationship between the agency and professional socialization, culture and the ways in which professional meanings are negotiated and communicated (e.g. Maluccio, 1979; Pithouse, 1998; Satyamurti,1981). But social work researchers have also, like social anthropologists, gone into the 'field', the communities in which social work is practised, to investigate how the rules and beliefs of individuals, groups and communities can be understood in order to sensitize practice. In particular in this respect, ethnography has come to be used by social work researchers to counter deficit models of social functioning of client groups, to show how many people who are supposedly inadequate in fact draw on resources of personal strength and skill to survive their situation. Banks and Wideman (1996), arguing from a Canadian context for an 'engaged ethnography' approach to social work research, argue that twentieth-century social work was characterized by programmes of solutions prescribed in response to the assessed deficits and capacities of people, but that in the twenty-first century it needs to harness processes which work with local identification of community strengths. As an example of this, their empirical work describes the use of ethnography as a method of needs analysis in the community; local volunteers are trained to be ethnographic interviewer-participants. Their research identifies needs which become the focus of further action research programmes, 'Through this experience we have observed how ethnography can transcend the bounds of research to emerge as a strategic motivational vehicle in promoting community praxis' (Banks and Wideman, 1996: 318).

Also working towards developing a 'strengths perspective', Thrasher and Mowbray (1995) used ethnographic methods to research the lives of homeless women and their children showing how their competence was demonstrated through the tasks of seeking shelter, caring for children, and striving to maintain a network of social contacts. Thrasher and Mowbray drew together a sample of 15 homeless female-headed families, living in three shelters in Detroit. The main form of data collection was 'ethnographic interviewing'. The authors distinguish ethnographic from conventional qualitative interviewing as being conducted as a friendly conversation, using general, straightforward questions (How did you become homeless? How do you take care of your children? Who has helped you?), encouraging participants to express their situation in their own language. Themes and continuities between interviews are then built based on the language and terminology employed by the participants, rather than imposed by the researchers:

> Ethnography contextualizes the experiences of these women and elucidates the many challenges they face in their daily lives. By focusing on their perspective through ethnography, we are able to see the strengths these women demonstrated in maintaining and keeping their families together while homeless. (Thrasher and Mowbray, 1995: 99)

Drawing on the women's own analysis of their situation, rather than the discourse of officials and professionals, seeking temporary shelter could be seen as a strategic resourceful action which functioned to maintain the family in the face of potentially overwhelming adversity; it reveals skills of problem-solving, self-management and parenting. From this small but intensive ethnographic study, Thrasher and Mowbray are able to identify both policy implications for supporting access to affordable housing and also for providing individual practitioners with an understanding of the need for respect, sensitivity and practical support to maintain the dignity of families facing homelessness.

Applied ethnography

Hall on the other hand, in his chapter in this volume, is cautious about the contribution which ethnography, with its grounded emphasis and inherently provisional accounts of social worlds, can make to prescriptions for policy and practice. Yet, in the United States of America, and in some developing countries, there is a body of applied ethnography in areas such as health, education and social policy research (Atkinson and Hammersley, 1994: 253). As we have seen, there is also an emergent social work applied ethnographic literature, albeit perhaps not so clearly developed as in those policy areas identified above. Often, applied ethnography involves working within prescribed time constraints, along with other short-cuts in order to produce timely results, and this may be seen as a corruption by the 'pure' ethnographer. As has been noted, there is often concern that ethnography is too labour-intensive and extended over time in order for it to be helpful for the development and evaluation of intervention programmes. However, there has been developed a range of structured, time-limited approaches to ethnography which can be relevant to the pragmatic character of social work programmes and practice development. During the 1980s such approaches included 'rapid assessment procedures', 'rapid rural appraisal', and 'rapid ethnographic assessment' (Grandstaff et al., 1987; Scrimshaw and Hurdato, 1987; Scrimshaw and Gleason, 1992; all cited Pelto, 1994). An example of this family of methods is 'focused ethnographic studies' (FES), developed as a way of supporting 'barefoot' ethnographers who are supervised but may have little prior training, to make rapid ethnographic studies to support programme development.

Pelto, in *The Indian Journal of Social Work*, has described the use of FES in regions of India to study high-risk sexual behaviour in order to inform HIV/AIDS intervention programmes (Pelto, 1994). Although applied in this specific context, FES is based on generic methods transferable to other contexts where the success of intervention is related to close understanding of problem behaviours in their local setting. The first stage involves gathering local vocabulary relevant to the identified behaviours so that subsequent fieldwork employs terminology that will be understood and accepted. The second stage of focused ethnography is to 'densely describe' the target behaviour, taking into account the interpersonal context of risk-taking, and not least to identify care-seeking behaviour. Third, the micro-sites of such behaviour are identified, recognizing in relation to the HIV/AIDS arena that such sites are frequently not in the household but

other meeting locations for casual sex. Next, the local contextual information is gathered which mediates these behaviours; Pelto gives the example
that commercial sex transactions are conducted differently between cities
such as Madras and Bombay. Focused ethnographers go on to gather information on a range of individual determinants (the range of difference
between individuals in managing sexual behaviour) and structural determinants such as economic and situational power and influence of actors.
This range of data is likely to be gathered through methods such as individual and group interviews, and textual data gathered from not only the
target population, but also administrators and practitioners, to gauge
the discrepancies between official constructions of the problem, and that
emerging from the ethnographic street-level data. Emerging hypotheses
identified from the data are developed using probing questions and
iterative analysis of the interview and observational notes so that strategies
for influencing high-risk behaviour and encouraging appropriate help-
seeking behaviour can be supported. Focused ethnography has developed
in the 1990s mainly in the context of health programmes but seems highly
transferable to social work issues and concerns. Usually completed in four
to six weeks, where researchers feel the need to validate findings from FES
research through more conventional surveys, the ethnographically derived
information informs the appropriateness of questionnaire design and the
distribution of relevant populations so that sound sampling frames can
be developed.

Ethnography and researching practice

Ethnography has also become an approach which has been promoted as
having particular relevance to the research of practice and practitioner
research; Goldstein (1991) amongst others has promoted the concept of
the 'ethnographic social worker' because of the perceived synergy between
ethnographic and practice skills. In Chapter 7 Sue White draws out some of
the implications of doing ethnography in the social worker's place of
employment; she makes a positive case for the contribution that detailed
participant observation of routine, taken-for-granted practice can make
to problematizing that practice and rendering it available for reflexive,
systematic analysis.

The case for this has many parallels with the argument reviewed in
Chapter 2 about the relationship between grounded theory and practice.
For instance, Fortune (1994) argues that doing ethnography involves the
suspension of one's own form of knowing, and that this is a disposition
which is integral to the social work injunction to 'start where the client
is', particularly where cross-cultural practice is involved. In terms of skill
development there is a claimed affinity between the development of
acute observational skills in participant observation and the attention to
non-verbal cues and interactive behaviour which are part of making a

social work assessment. The 'ethnographic social worker' is also seen to be practised in the arts of eliciting information by indirect questioning, using differences of nuance in questioning to identify attitudes or beliefs which are consistent or unchanging, particularly where there is a need to communicate with someone who is thought-disordered (Fortune, 1994). Also, as with Gilgun's (1994) claim for grounded theory, there is a view that inductive reasoning, moving from observed phenomena to a conceptualized overview, is characteristic of both ethnography and social work. The problems with this argument that practice and qualitative research are the same are laid out in Chapter 2 and will not be rehearsed again here, but suffice to point out that Fortune, as a protagonist of ethnography in social work does concede that practitioners do not have to give the same kinds of disseminated public account of their findings as researchers (though they may well give other kinds of accounts such as case records or court reports), nor do they have to decide when to stop being a participant observer and change to being an agent of intervention, with all the switching of frames of reference which this involves.

Interviews

> There were questions of course. But they were casual in nature . . . the kind you would ask while having a drink with someone; the kind he would ask you . . . In short, it was conversation. In time the sluice gates of damned up hurts and dreams were opened. (Terkel, *Working*, 1972, cited in Holstein and Gubrium, 1997: 115)

Jonathan Scourfield remarks in Chapter 4 that, 'interviewing is an everyday activity', and it is often seen as something which is inherently unproblematic, provided the interviewer has the social skills to induce the interviewee to open up. Many social work researchers who have made the transition to research from themselves being practitioners may instinctively feel that qualitative research conducted through interviews is more 'do-able' than the full panoply of ethnography. Again, as discussed in Chapter 2, it seems to 'fit like a glove' as a method in which social workers are trained and experienced, particularly where there are issues of sensitivity, for instance interviewing children or survivors of sexual abuse. Despite Studs Terkel's romantic characterization of interviewing, as with ethnography, the methodological literature presents us with rather more complex choices of approach.

Interviewing as a method of data collecting can be undertaken in the full range of social work contexts, but determining the relationship between what the researcher is told in an interview, and the context referred to in that interview, is complex. Not least, there are difficult epistemological problems about whether we can treat the content of an interview as a reliable, 'real' account of external events, or more cautiously whether we should not go beyond interpreting that content as data in itself, a micro-encounter which has no reliability beyond its own reference? In general, social work interviewers seem to follow implicitly, and perhaps for pragmatic reasons, Miller and Glassner's argument for what they call an anti-dualistic treatment of research interviews:

> Research cannot provide the mirror reflection of the social world that positivists strive for, but it might provide access to the meanings people attribute to their experiences and social worlds. While the interview is itself a symbolic interaction, this does not discount the possibility that knowledge of the social world beyond the interaction can be obtained . . . Those of us who aim to understand and document others' understanding choose qualitative interviewing because it provides us with a means for exploring the points of view of our research subjects, while granting these points of view the culturally honoured status of reality. (Miller and Glassner, 1997: 100)

There are a number of approaches in the literature to creating typologies of qualitative interview, but the main dimensions of these tend to be, regardless of context, the amount of structure in the interview, the level of depth the interviewer attempts to achieve, and the extent to which standardization is sought across interviewees and contexts (Punch,1998). As a fairly rough and ready generalization, in social work qualitative research, interviews are usually at some level semi-structured, i.e. they use open-ended questions but are guided by a more or less pre-determined purpose and agenda. Nevertheless, there are numerous sub-types of qualitative interview which might be employed in social work contexts. Flick (1998) writes from a nursing research perspective and has developed a typology of research interviews which transfers helpfully to social work because of its applied emphasis, as follows.

The focused interview. This may be used when researching the views of either professionals or service users, and presents interviewees in the study with pre-determined, standardized material such as a case vignette. This is then used as a basis for exploration through unstructured and semi-structured questions. By asking interviewees to respond to a prompt which is consistent, responses can be compared and distinctions made between broader, general themes and idiosyncratic, individual responses. Originally developed for media research where responses to a film, broadcast, newspaper article, etc. could be compared (Merton and Kendall, 1946), it has been adapted to many other research contexts. In social work we find examples where the stimulus is a case study or vignettes, such as in Fook's expertise study which she discusses in Chapter 8, where social workers' responses to the same material can be compared.

The semi-standardized interview. This approach to interviewing also seeks a compromise between asking very open-ended questions which may produce a free-flowing discussion but little material which can be compared across interviews, and structured closed questioning which produces limited, superficial responses. The interviewer may use a combined or 'layered' approach to combining the format questions so that they alternate between standardized questions which elicit more specific, even codifiable data, and more interrogative follow-up questions which extend and deepen the responses. As with focused interviewing, it is adaptable to many research situations where a deeper understanding of an issue is sought. For instance, Morrow-Kondos et al. (1997) have researched the issues faced by grandparents, who in response to divorce, imprisonment or migration of their sons or daughters, find themselves raising grandchildren, and the social work implications which follow from this. Volunteer respondents were drawn from a support group for grandparents in this situation. In their report of the study the researchers describe using open-ended questions within 'standardized interviewing techniques' (Morrow-Kondos et al., 1997: 37). This approach can produce interviews of varying length as in this study, lasting from one to three hours, being tape recorded, then transcribed and analysed.

The problem-centred interview. This approach is more prominent in the German literature, and may be a variant of the focused interview, but the individual or group is asked to identify and consider a problematic issue, or critical incident, which then is used as a 'peg' or prompt by the interviewer to draw out material relevant to the research. This may be useful as an interview method which elicits lay or professional 'theories-in-use', how a particular problem is construed, and the strategies which follow from these in attempting to problem-solve. It also can be used in researching service users' strengths and capacities for dealing with adversity. Hughes (1998), in a study of young inner-city men, wanted to know what influenced them to give up criminal behaviour. This is in contrast to more positivist research which focuses on the correlates of criminal behaviour. Hughes drew her sample of 20 men, predominantly of African American and Latino-American descent, by 'convenience sampling' from a community programme with which she had contact. Hughes describes in-depth interviews of approximately 90 minutes duration undertaken over a two year period, combining preliminary socio-demographic data collection with open-ended questions seeking explanations of why these individuals felt they had renounced earlier involvement in serious crime. Using a qualitative software program to manage and analyse the transcripts, she built a list of codes to analyse the content. From this she develops a model of the pathway which young men find out of crime involving transitional experiences such as parenting children, the deterrent effect of incarceration or physical harm, and social support. As Shaw argues, drawing on Holstein and Gubrium's (1997) writing on 'active' interviewing, the issues and themes which emerge from the careful analysis of such interviews can also contribute significantly to the evaluation of practice and services (Shaw, 1999a: 174–7).

The expert interview. Flick differentiates this as a specific form of semi-structured interview, where there is a specific focus on the role of the interviewee as representative of expertise in a particular field rather than an attempt to gather wider holistic information about the personal circumstances of the interviewee. Schon's interviews with reflective practitioners, where the accounts of a range of experts are abstracted from the wider context of their lives would be a very direct example, although of course many service users are also expert in their own problem-solving methods and capacities. A useful example of the expert interview is provided by Coady and Wolgien's (1996) study of good therapists' views of how they are helpful. The study is based on interviews with eight therapists (mainly social workers) who were cited by knowledgeable colleagues as being particularly effective. The purpose of Coady and Wolgien's research emerges from interest in the therapeutic research literature which suggests that positive outcomes are not the product of specific theories or techniques of intervention, but are more determined by generic relationship and process factors. Having drawn up a snowball sample of social workers regarded by colleagues as successful, each was interviewed twice. The purpose of the first interview was to explain the research and establish rapport and commitment, the second to ask a range of questions relating to their beliefs about what was helpful and effective in their practice. The interviews were transcribed and transcripts were returned to the therapist for them to amend and annotate. The researchers then read and re-read the transcripts building themes and categories at differing levels of abstraction. Their findings supported the evaluation studies in that their effectiveness was believed to lie in issues such as the quality of relationships, personal qualities of the social worker and client empowerment, rather than formal application of theory and technique.

The ethnographic interview. As described in Scourfield's chapter in this volume, interviews are an important adjunct to participant observation in ethnographic research. Spradley (1979), in his extended discussion of ethnographic interviews, characterizes them as 'a series of friendly conversations' but which contain within them some specific elements, namely: a specific request to hold the conversation; a lay explanation of the purpose of the research and the interview; and the asking of questions which have ethnographic purposes, such as to uncover how interviewees construct meanings attached to their social worlds. Sometimes ethnographic interviewers have stressed the significance of 'race' and ethnicity to draw out what Punch calls, 'the perspectives of the decolonialized, the disadvantaged and the disempowered' (p. 179). Goldstein et al. (1996) used ethnographic interviewing amongst other multiple methods such as observation, document analysis and photo-journalism, to study how ethnically diverse, poor families made use of social services. Sometimes there can be complexities of language and translation where the first language used by the family is not that of the researcher, or the cultural context of the research is not familiar to the interviewer. Goldstein et al. describe using family interviewers from the same ethnic background as the interviewees to work as co-researchers with the academic researchers, and identify some of the benefits of more naturalistic ethnographic-type interviewing without tape recorders, and in the families' own homes.

Focus groups in social work research

A development in interview-based research is the emergence of focus groups. Imported to serious social science research from marketing but informed by Merton's development of the focused interview, the focus group is seen to offer various possibilities as part of the qualitative armoury. Shaw (1996) has previously summarized their advantages as being three-fold: that the interaction in the group is itself the data which enables the researcher to see how perspectives are actively constructed and negotiated in a social setting; the group is a collective corrective to the inherent power imbalance between researcher and subject; and they are helpful in establishing the nature and extent of consensus around an issue. The *focus* comprises the issue/s which are the subject of the research, and although this is likely to be predetermined by the researcher, the focus group is usually regarded as a participatory research method (Kitzinger, 1994). Not surprisingly this apparent contradiction also fuels some debate about the place of the focus group in social work research, at least partially engendered by the marketing pedigree of the method and latter associations with political 'spin-doctoring'. The more sceptical view about the place of focus groups in social work research has been expressed by Dullea and Mullender:

> It is not unknown for so-called participation in social work evaluation to consist of a few representatives of the community being assembled in the ubiquitous focus group, which has no roots in actual community groupings and derives its *modus operandi* from consumerist market research, not from social work practice or values. (Dullea and Mullender 1999: 94)

One example from the social work literature of how focus groups can positively augment other qualitative and quantitative forms of data collection in a community-based study can be found in Gibbs and Bankhead-Greene's (1997) research into the attitudes and experiences of black youths in Los Angeles in the wake of the civil disturbances following the Rodney King police brutality case. The focus group aspect of the study certainly went considerably beyond the merely tokenistic, comprising a sample of 144 youths taking part in group discussions over a 15 month period. The young people were drawn from a broad range of socio-economic backgrounds, neighbourhoods and lifestyles, with diverse experiences in education, the labour market, and the criminal justice system. The groups were semi-structured, lasting 90 minutes to two hours, and addressed a range of issues emerging from the Rodney King case and generalizing to experiences of family and community, the police, crime, gangs and violence, experience of public services and future life plans. The focus groups were taped and transcribed and then coded for content and thematic analysis. Gibbs and Bankhead-Greene comment on the need to establish researcher credibility in the community and they comment that, 'This effort is particularly important in the African-American community with its long history of mistrust and hostility towards researchers who have previously exploited, intimidated and even inflicted harm on the community' (Gibbs and Bankhead-Greene, 1997: 49).

Their work raises some cautionary issues for intending focus group social work researchers. One is that the researchers need to preserve a careful distinction between the purpose of the group for research as opposed to therapeutic or activity-based intervention. This includes paying attention to supporting broad participation, monitoring the dynamics of the group, handling strong emotions such as anger and depression in the group and terminating the discussion appropriately. Young people being expected to disclose sensitive and potentially incriminating material also require clear reassurances about confidentiality and the intended dissemination of the research. By attending to these issues, and by managing wary vigilance on the part of some focus group members and downright hostility from others, Gibbs and Bankhead illustrate that focus groups can make an important contribution to research methods.

Simulated interviews

The focus group is at some levels a contrived setting for conducting research, but it remains naturalistic insofar as members are drawn from the research population and often interviewed within or close to their communities. Taking contrivance much further, there are also research situations in which participants can be simulated or role-played in order to explore the impact of particular variables such as gender or ethnicity on a situation. So far, examples tend to arise from housing or employment research rather than social work, typically where researchers want to examine the influence on selection or allocation decisions of varying the demographic characteristics of applicants (Shaw, 1999a). Using actors or others to simulate clients also has the potential for researching how individual social work practitioners exercise judgement and discretion in interview situations, or comparing between different professions how they respond in an interview situation to a simulated client presenting the same 'story'. Thus, one particular limitation of naturalistic qualitative research, that events cannot be replicated in order to control independent variables, is managed by simulating people or events. There are obstacles to research based on simulated interviews: for instance that they are resource intensive, need extensive preparation such as life scripts and rehearsal of the simulated participants, and may raise ethical objections where entrapment or covert measures are necessary (for instance researching discriminatory responses by professionals to simulated clients). Nevertheless, it has relatively unexplored potential as a research method, particularly where intake or service entry processes to social work services are being researched.

Interviewing and sensitivity – the exemplar of children

That qualitative interview-based research conducted in social work contexts will engage with areas of sensitivity is of course a truism. Given social work's raison d'être as concerned with supporting people to manage their lives within a social context it often, though not always inevitably, addresses personal issues which may be felt to be stigmatizing or deeply personal. Jonathan Scourfield, in Chapter 4, writes about the interplay between his own identity and its impact within interviews with women social workers, either in promoting mutuality and sensitivity (as a parent) or as a barrier to be negotiated (as a man). However, although the qualitative literature frequently gives token acknowledgement to the need to be heedful of the conflicts which can be produced by working in sensitive areas (and for an extended discussion see Lee, 1993), it is worth reminding ourselves that 'sensitivity' is not a given or self-evident commodity. It is located in the dynamics of the interplay between the researcher and the researched; something which may be difficult for one party to broach may be conventional and non-controversial for another, and vice versa. Whether an issue such as sexuality is sensitive is also a matter of context; furthermore it may be something that is dynamic and changing – an initially innocuous research inquiry can later be drawn into more difficult areas or the context may become increasingly sensitized. Given its contingent and negotiated nature, we cannot be prescriptive about managing sensitivity in the context of social work interview research, but it may be helpful to précis Lee's identification of relevant considerations, as follows.

- Giving *informed consent* is something which cannot be regarded as a single event, as disclosures are likely to emerge during the process of an in-depth interview and consent needs to be understood as something which is ongoingly negotiated.
- *Distress* for participants giving interviews is likely to emerge, and researchers need to be able to mobilize sufficient interpersonal skills to manage this, to have in place the support to deal with their own resulting stress, and a reflexive approach to managing the tension between being a researcher and a helper.
- *Power relationships* are also an inalienable characteristic of the research interview. There is now general scepticism that this is obviated by matching interviewer and interviewed on a single demographic variable such as ethnicity or sex. Power inequalities emerge from a constellation of social characteristics which are not neutralized by achieving equivalence on one; power is also a structural characteristic of the research

encounter between one who is researching and another who is being researched. Power remains a contested concept within the social sciences but there is an emergent literature mapping out its many manifestations within the contexts of social work (Gould, 1994).

- *Interviewing conditions* need vigilant attention within the conduct of sensitive interview research. This requires judgements about such matters as whether other family members should be present in interviews, whether interviewees disclosing intimate material are most appropriately dealt with by 'one-off' interviews or by a series of interviews, and whether there will be follow up after termination of interviews.

Many of the methodological issues raised by the notion of sensitivity are inherently also ethical issues. The exemplar which is often used as a peg for discussion of sensitive interview research is that in which the participants are children – clearly a research area which is central in social work. For instance, in a methodological paper on aspects of collecting data from children, Mauthner comments:

> Researching children's lives raises a number of methodological issues to do with consent, access, privacy and confidentiality. *Although these are not unique to children* they do present researchers with specific dilemmas to do with unequal power relationships, mainly age related, that exist between adult researchers and children as participants. (Mauthner, 1997: 17, italics added)

As Shaw (1999a) notes, there has however been a movement away from conceptualizing the problematics of research with children as something located (as implied by Mauthner) within an age-related deficit model of childhood which sees the issues solely in terms of commensurability between developmental stages and capacity to give consent or provide reliable evidence. There is a perceptible shift towards regarding children as autonomous research participants who have similar rights to adults in terms of consenting to give interviews (Greig and Taylor, 1999). Also, there is more understanding that the research interview is not a point of access to an adult-defined understanding of childhood, but is data in its own right about the adult–child encounter:

> One implication for the 'social child' perspective for research is that children's own understanding of their situation may be as valid as any other, and that children are likely to have their own concerns or questions, which may be as important as those brought by the researcher. A similar assumption lies at the heart of much thinking about ethnographic methods, but it has only recently begun to be applied much to social research with children. (Thomas and O'Kane, 1998: 341)

Thomas and O'Kane (1998) describe and review a number of strategies for ethical engagement with children and for their involvement in interviews, focus groups and structured activities as part of researching children's participation in decision making when they are looked after by social services. They reinforce the argument that, 'effective methodology and ethics go hand in hand' (Thomas and O'Kane 1998: 336).

Narrative, life histories and documentary research

Cathy Riessman showed in Chapter 5 how the story told by Asha, of how it was to be a married, childless woman living in Kerala, becomes more than a personal story when the researcher identifies the social positioning of the interviewee: the immediate conversation between Asha and the researchers, the broader cultural discourse about the place of women in contemporary India and the gender politics of the local state, and also in relation to powerful actors in her story such as doctors and influential family members. Life history research is part of a cluster of approaches which includes narrative research, family stories, oral histories, biographical and autobiographical analyses (Martin, 1999). Whether any systematic distinction can be made between these methods is rather doubtful:

> It should be clear that every term carries traces of other terms. Thus, oral histories, personal histories and case histories, like autobiographies and biographies, and self stories and personal experience narratives, define one another only in terms of difference. The meanings of each spill over into the meanings of the other. The attempt to give a fixed meaning is doomed to failure. (Denzin, 1989b: 47)

Between the exponents of life history research in social work there is a general consensus that the perspective finds its intellectual origin in the Chicago School of sociology of the 1920s and 1930s (Martin, 1999; Riessman, 1993). This aspect of the Chicago legacy takes the form of careful and detailed construction of life narratives. Denzin (1989b) has pointed to the later trivialization of the Chicago approach to narrative research after the 1930s, but that it was to become re-energized in his view by later sociological and wider cultural influences: the writing of C. Wright Mills on the sociological imagination; the existential speculations of Jean Paul Sartre on the possibilities of reconstruction and understanding of the life of the other; and the influence of Derrida on the development of deconstruction theory.

In the context of social work research we need to add to Denzin's analysis other significant sociological influences. The theoretical and methodological inheritance of symbolic interactionism is evident, and its subsequent influence on the emergence of grounded theory (Glaser and Strauss, 1967). For instance, Riessman in Chapter 5 explicitly draws on Goffman's method of narrative analysis in her investigation of Indian women's experience of infertility. Second, the development of oral history has found particular synergies both with the methods of interview-based assessment in social work, but also the acknowledgement of work with ethnic groups for whom the oral tradition is more dominant than written histories. Third, in its emergence as a perspective in social work research, particularly in the United States, narrative research and its variants have been significantly transformed from masculine sociology through the influence of feminist theory. Riessman reminds us that the Chicago School in particular was a masculine project; there are no female equivalents of Roller-Jack and the other classic characters of that sociological era (Riessman, 1993: 4). In particular, contemporary narrative and life history research transcends the anecdotal by seeking to connect personal troubles with social issues.

Martin (1999) in discussing narrative and social work research suggests three broad premises which researchers take on when they select a life history or narrative approach to their inquiries: that humans act towards things on the basis of meanings; meaning is derived from interaction with others; and meanings are modified through interpretive processes used in dealing with things encountered. Narrative research also asserts that there is an inherent motivation for people to seek meaning for their own lives through 'storying', or the integrative construction of coherent accounts of sequences of events in their lives through which they create their own identity. Although it is not always explicit, this seems to imply a fairly strong normative theory of human cognition. This finds particular expression in the more 'structural' forms of narrative inquiry which suggest an inherent human tendency under supportive conditions to provide accounts of events which are analytically coded by the researcher into pre-determined sequences such as 'abstract', 'orientation', 'complicating action' and 'resolution' (Bell, 1988, discussed in Riessman, 1993: 34).

Social work operates largely through processes of inquiry which, at least, at an early stage of intervention involve getting people to tell their story; Stenson (1993) for example has investigated the nature of stories told in social work interviews in some detail, noting the 'oral' character and logic of those accounts. Thus, social work interviewing parallels narrative research in terms of technique, but also it has the potential to validate accounts of events told by peoples who, in the historian E.P. Thompson's memorable phrase about the English working class, have suffered the 'condescension of history'. This has had a resonance also in the United States where for three centuries black people were obstructed from writing their own accounts of their lives and events around them. In addition, social work draws on theoretical perspectives, specifically attachment and other psychodynamic theories, which validate reflexive self-accounts by individuals of their histories, as having both diagnostic and therapeutic significance (Fish, 1996).

Reviewing the uses of narrative research in social work we can find four contexts or applications in which narrative has emerged as a fieldwork option: gaining understanding of the perspectives of individuals who belong to socially excluded or marginalized groups; researching therapeutic processes which have an association with narrative or storying methods of intervention; understanding the rebuilding of identity and the positive capacities of people experiencing trauma or loss; and (less developed) evaluation research on policy and practice.

As an example of the first category, giving voice to those who usually are socially excluded, Joyce West Stevens (1997) used narrative methods to research the outlooks of poor African American female adolescents and in particular to describe their aspirations for future achievement and upward social mobility. Conventional views of this social group are that many will become pregnant at an early age, sometimes intentionally, as a result of high-risk sexual behaviour and that the effects of parenting responsibilities fix them in their low-status socio-economic position. Stevens wanted to identify the outlooks of non-pregnant female adolescents who did not conform to this pattern and who showed resilience and future-orientation in their determination to overcome economic disadvantage. For her, narrative research had synergy with social work's traditional concern with the configuration of the individual in their social environment, though for Stevens the narrative approach also went further in enabling a more dynamic appreciation of 'process' as a mediating influence between person and context. An interesting aspect of her research strategy is that narrative research is embedded within a post-positivist research design that compares a group of pregnant with non-pregnant black women, and also compares quantitative data to augment aspects of the narrative data, which in itself is elicited through a semi-structured narrative interview schedule which had been explicitly sensitized to provide an Afrocentric, feminist perspective. This approach reveals that the black non-pregnant young women, although becoming adults in a very deprived, high-risk environment, differ from the pregnant control group in terms of their visionary perspective of future upward social mobility which was related to participation in the institutions of church, education or employment, 'institutional resources that serve as resources that serve as sanctuaries from the dangers of street culture' (Stevens, 1997: 471). Their resilience was shown through discriminating evaluations of their present circumstances whilst having optimistic aspirations towards future possibilities, which led to skilful coping mechanisms in relation to contraception, mate selection and drug use. For Stevens the practice implication of her finding is to confirm the use of strength perspectives, with an emphasis on positive aspects of functioning as a stimulus for changing towards successful coping and survival under adverse circumstances.

Our second context of using narrative methods is to research intervention processes. For instance, Fish (1996) uses narrative as a tool for studying how clients structure and narrate the process of change during clinical social work intervention. This draws on the particular theoretical development that has taken place within attachment theory, perceiving personal narratives as a highly salient method for accessing individuals' development in relation to their personal legacy of attachment and separation from their mother or other primary carers. Thus, the theoretical perspective underpinning this research starts from Bowlby's well-known studies of maternal attachment and separation anxiety, but incorporates later views of writers such as Bruner that, 'the stories individuals tell and the way such stories are told are reflective of and constitutive of the ongoing construction of identity' (Bruner, 1990: 240). Fish discusses the use of a semi-clinical interview schedule developed by Main which encourages clients to tell a narrative which reveals the story of their attachment relations. Main's thesis is that the content and structure of adults' narratives are reflective of their underlying internal model of attachment (Main cited in Fish, 1996: 244). Fish illustrates this through the detailed case study of Mrs B. who was experiencing depression, with feelings of being contagious and 'leprous' following the ending of a special friendship. Her narrative as told early in a therapeutic relationship told the story of being extremely frightened by seeing the film Ben Hur and identifying with the mother and daughter who are confined in a cave with leprosy. As the process of therapy continued Mrs. B. restoried her narrative, including a more realistic and considered evaluation of her identity as a 'leper'. 'Mrs B. had moved from a personal attachment narrative of symptoms, destructive attachment enactments, and the chaos of "the dark cave" and "black hole" to a more fully articulated and complex attachment identity' (Fish, 1996: 250).

This has overlap with the third social work application of this approach, using narrative to understand how people reconstruct their identity in response to change or trauma, and putting this into practice by making available to them positive narratives of reconstruction. Some of these examples relate to women in midlife (Jones, 1994; McQuaide, 1998). McQuaide's hypothesis is that there co-exist two narratives of women's lives in midlife. The culturally dominant one is saturated with medical language and takes as primary points of reference issues such as depression, menopause, emotional instability, hormone deficiency, breast cancer and deals in stereotypes of women struggling to come to terms with forms of abandonment, be it children leaving home, widowhood or loss of social power. McQuaide points to an alternative form of narrative which 'privileges and performs the story of voice', the belief that midlife is an opportunity to make positive life choices, develop deeper and more satisfying relationships with peers, and feelings of life having greater purpose. It is argued that this form of research has two purposes. These narratives, which counter patriarchal dominant narratives, if uncovered and performed, 'contribute to the pool of midlife narratives and meanings that can guide a person's life. Through performing and circulating the alternative, preferred narrative, new images are constructed for the culture' (McQuaide, 1998: 40). McQuaide also provides an illustration of how this positive, counter-intuitive narrative becomes a resource for use in social work practice with women whose preferred story has been of the negative, patriarchal and medicalized kind, through a detailed case study of narrative aspects of work with 'Nancy', a depressed woman with interpersonal difficulties and who tells the story of her life in terms of being used and unloved.

McQuaide shows how the process of long-term intervention can be used to 'open spaces' for Nancy to tell stories of other parts of her life which have been empowered and are demonstrative of positive capacities which could be utilized in her present circumstances, 'Treatment ended with Nancy exchanging a narrative where silence and low self-esteem were privileged to one where voice and self-respect were allowed to be privileged. Space in her original narrative had been opened up for new self-knowledges to be performed' (McQuaide, 1998: 51).

Narrative research in social work is often presented as an idiographic approach to knowledge construction, concerned with the fine grain of individual experience, relayed in the almost confessional confine of an in-depth interview. It has been noted that narratives are also embedded in social structures and relationships. The potential for narrative research to be a vehicle for the purposes of service research and evaluation, the fourth context identified above, has been less developed in the social work literature, but the capability to do this exists through the analysis of commentary on the appropriateness and suitability of services as embedded in the narrative. Mayer and Timms's (1970) classic study of communication between social workers and clients, whilst at one level a sociological analysis of the incommensurability of class-based discourses, is also implicitly evaluative of the casework provided by those workers. This gave rise to a genre of so-called 'client studies' which researched and evaluated social work directly through the voice of service users (Fisher, 1983; Rees, 1979). More recently Hey (1999) has undertaken narrative research with older people in a residential care setting to study how they restory their lives to counter the supposed fragmentation of their later years; but these narratives are also evaluative of the circumstances in which they find themselves and the care and services they receive.

Documentary sources

This discussion so far assumes that the main method of developing narrative is through direct interviews, but a rich source of material is also documentary evidence. Although as yet relatively under-utilized by social work researchers, archives of social work records offer enormous potential for enriching life story research. Client records routinely comprise a variety of sources, including professional reports, assessments and accounts of ongoing practice as well as first-hand materials such as letters and journals (for an extended discussion of the research potential of personal and practice texts found in social work see Shaw 1996: 151–7). Agencies with their origins in nineteenth-century philanthropic institutions, for instance some of the major child welfare voluntary organizations, possess archives which potentially provide a unique context for excavating and reconstructing not only the lives of individuals, but also reflecting the discursive shifts and continuities of social work as a form of practice (Gould,1999b; Parton et al.,

1997). For instance, Parton et al. used records of child protection cases to document the shift towards managerialist preoccupations with risk management, while Gould (1999b) describes using written records from a range of agencies involved in child protection to reconstruct multidisciplinary practice in individual cases. However, a cautionary note often made in relation to the use of official statistics needs to be entered, that social work records, like other written accounts, should not be read as transparent accounts of what happened but rather as data in their own right:

> They (documentary data) are not, however, transparent representations of organizational routines, decision-making processes or professional diagnoses. They construct particular kinds of representations with their own conventions. (Atkinson and Coffey, 1997: 47)

As we have seen, documentary analysis can be used in ethnographic and other multimethod approaches as a supplementary data source. When documents are used as a primary data source they offer advantages and disadvantages (Padgett, 1998b). They are non-reactive insofar as their content remains fixed and impervious to the contingencies associated with face-to-face interviewing which change the data elicited. However, Padgett's argument on this point pays scant regard to the postmodernist argument that texts are not fixed entities, but are actively constructed by the act of reading. Also, her claim that documentary research is less time-consuming is debatable and depends on a range of factors including ease of access, legibility and length of documents. Nevertheless, the availability of new information technology including scanning and machine reading of documents offers the capability to address some of these obstacles. The content analysis of documents presents additional methodological choices. Much of the earlier interest in content analysis, notably in political science, was quantitative in nature, drawing inferences from the frequency of significant words, their degrees of correlation with one another, and so on. More contemporary content analysis is qualitative, and although still attentive to word frequencies, is more holistically oriented and theorized through some form of discourse analysis.

Conclusion

This chapter has reviewed the role of three methods which, whatever the internal conflicts and lacunae between their supporters, are strongly represented within the mainstream qualitative methodological literatures. We have considered how they are deployed, both in the contributed chapters to this volume, but also in the wider social work research literature, to explicate contexts of social work such as the agency, community, intervention programmes, client groups, and interactions between social workers and service users. Some writers on social work would argue, however, that the particular claims to distinctiveness of social work research lie not in relation to these contexts but in its relationship to social work practice itself, and has to be judged by the criterion of 'practice validity', its consistency with the nature and purpose of social work (Sheppard, 1995; Trevillion, 1999). Qualitative practitioner research has been in recent years an important site of innovation in various professional fields, not least in social work, and is closely allied to the development of emancipation as a research purpose. As we have shown, ethnography, interview-based and life story research also contribute significantly to radical, progressive agendas in social work, but in the next chapter we will attend in more detail to the emergence of emancipatory research, qualitative practitioner inquiry, research based on models of reflective learning, and the ways in which these reconfigure the relationship between theory, context and practice.

Recommended reading

The chapter began with a generalization that the methodological literature in qualitative research tends to overlook the relationship between the context of research and choice of method, or regards the relationship as transparent and unproblematic. A significant exception is Miller and Dingwall's edited collection *Context and Method in Qualitative Research* (1997). Several of the contributed chapters are cited in this volume, and Miller and Dingwall's book as a whole is a recommended resource. Ethnography as a method is supremely concerned with context, but too often social work researchers seem to claim that they use ethnographic methods without appreciating the pluralistic, indeed contested, provenance of this field. Atkinson and Hammersley (1994) provide an illuminating introduction to the histories and fault-lines of the development of ethnography, which can help the researcher locate herself within this tradition. Those seeking a critique of some of the more implausible claims of the confessional and reflexive ends of ethnography will find much to enjoy in Seale's (1999) *The Quality of Qualitative Research*.

Most ethnographers of whatever persuasion see an inalienable element of their approach as participant observation. A social work example of a study which draws on extended immersion in the field, and remains a valuable study of social work's ambiguities and incommensurable demands, is Carole Satyamurti's (1981) *Occupational Survival: The Case Of The Local Authority Social Worker*. For an example of action-oriented ethnography, and as a corrective to the Western emphasis of this volume, see Pelto's study of sexual behaviour and AIDs in India (Pelto, 1994). The above chapter contains numerous sketches of interview-based and narrative studies that are relevant to social work. Anything by Cathy Riessman will draw the reader into the rich possibilities of both; her use of narrative techniques

10

Inquiry and Action: Qualitative Research and Professional Practice

CONTENTS

Practising and researching   158
Qualitative practitioner research   159
Practitioner research and mainstream research   160
Is practice a form of inquiry?   162
Practitioner research and empowerment   163
Reflective practice and research   164
Advocacy and qualitative inquiry   168
Advocacy and methodology   169
Insiders, outsiders and standpoints   172
Conclusion   177
Recommended reading   178

The invited chapters that form the core of this book exemplify in practical ways how the setting, culture and audience of qualitative research in social work shape the choice and direction of research methodology. In the previous chapter we drew on the illustrative research of the contributors to show how qualitative inquiry is best taken forward when important practice issues are set in a methodologically aware framework.

Yet we cannot for one moment imagine that this exhausts the relevance of these chapters. For example, several of the contributors reflect on the broader relationship between *inquiry and professional practice*. Hall and – with careful detail – White record how they held both insider and outsider roles in relation to their research participants. Hall 'arrived' as an outsider but became in different ways a partial insider. White started as an insider, yet found herself undergoing a fruitful, if potentially hazardous, process of de-familiarization through which she became in some degree a marginal 'inside "out"' member. Scourfield focuses his chapter on the research and practice relationship through his consideration of what it was like to interview expert professional social work interviewers.

The relationship between research and *identity* is also prominent in the contributed chapters. By way of illustration, both Riessman and Whitmore draw on narrative approaches that place the identity of the participants, including the researcher, centre stage. White's discussion of practitioner research, and Scourfield's consideration of what it meant to be a reflexive researcher, also raise wider questions of what it means to practice reflectively.

Whitmore poses important issues of a different kind. She shows that the research in which she was involved aimed to be at one and the same time rigorous and *emancipatory*. She fruitfully draws on models of inquiry developed in participatory Third World development programmes. Her concerns, and those of the young people with whom she worked, were as much about the moral, political and ethical agenda of the research process, as they were about methodological sophistication. She cautions, in closing her chapter, against the risks of romanticizing the marginalized.

We have referred to these issues in the opening two chapters. In Chapter 1 we noted that much current debate is about the relative weight that should be given to aspects of power, rigour and relativity of meaning, and just how allegiances to more than one of these can be consistently held. For example, how can we hold to both constructed realities and some version of realist positions regarding the existence and nature of reality? Is it possible to hold simultaneously to postmodern relativism and an empowerment vision for research? Can we defend both rigour and some version of advocacy research? In Chapter 2 we traced the unfolding of these concerns in the development of qualitative research in social work. In this chapter we will review these themes and consider ways in which qualitative research is relevant to:

- qualitative practitioner inquiry
- inquiry based on models of reflective learning
- emancipatory practice and research.

Practising and researching

Social workers should be scientific practitioners. Good practice is closely akin to good research, and *vice versa*. Social workers, or at least a significant minority of them, ought to engage in practitioner research. At one level this cluster of deceptively similar assertions is unproblematic. If those who voluntarily or perforce draw on social work intervention are to gain the benefits of best practice, then practice and a broad span of disciplined inquiry ought certainly to be held in close conjunction. However, the relationship between practising and researching represents one of the less satisfactory aspects of current social work practice.

McLeod defines practitioner research as 'research carried out by practitioners for the purpose of advancing their own practice' (McLeod, 1999: 8).

This definition has much going for it. First, it includes a statement of purpose, and hence incorporates an implicit criterion for assessing the quality of research. It is not adequate to define practitioner research simply as research carried out by practitioners, without grounding it on a basis of purpose. Second, it makes explicit a practice rationale, rather than broader policy or academic rationales for research. Finally, it includes an implicit model of how practitioner research can be useful. We pick up the question of qualitative research use in Chapter 11, but we should note here that McLeod seems to assume a fairly direct relationship between research and practice – or, as we may describe it, an 'instrumental' model of information use. On the whole, we agree that the use of practitioner research is usually best pictured in instrumental terms.

The idea that practitioners should be researchers is not a new idea. The clinical research model has honourable precedents in the work of doctors who trailed their vaccination methods on themselves, and in the clinical research of psychotherapists. The advocates of scientific practice in social work also have a history going back two centuries. Charles Loch spent much energy in the late nineteenth century arguing that social work is like science: 'It is science – the science of life – in operation – knowledge doing its perfect work' (quoted Timms, 1968: 59). There is also a substantial literature on the teacher-as-researcher.

There have been diverse arguments in support of practitioner research in social work. It has often been argued that research and practice draw on similar skills. We have referred earlier to McIvor's apt expression of this view when she says,

> The starting point . . . is the twofold belief that practitioners should be encouraged to engage in the evaluation of their own practice and that they possess many of the skills which are necessary to undertake the evaluative task. (McIvor, 1995: 210)

We have said that the relationship between practising and researching represents one of the less satisfactory aspects of current social work practice. Why is this?

Qualitative practitioner research

Two almost polar opposite standpoints have unhelpfully influenced the ways in which the question of the appropriate relationship/s between research and practice has been addressed. On the one hand, practitioner research has been bedevilled by lack of a strategic sense of the overall purpose of such work. For example, the British tradition of practitioner research has often been led by naïve pragmatism about methodology. This leads, among other problems, to an unquestioningly simple view about what counts as evidence. At the other extreme, the question has been partially hijacked by an unduly restrictive agenda about the supposed merits of scientific practice. Paradoxically, this leads to the same problem – an undeveloped, or at least selective, view about the nature of evidence and outcomes in social work.

Qualitative practitioner research is still too often invisible in social work. McLeod describes what is missing as 'knowledge-in-context practitioner research' as against the scientific practitioner model (McLeod, 1999: 13). He identifies the key characteristics of such practitioner research as being 'Born out of personal experience and a "need to know"'. Its aim is to produce knowledge that makes a difference to practice, in which the investigator uses reflexive self-awareness throughout to gain access to implicit meanings. It is hence relatively limited in scope. It 'addresses the moral and ethical issues associated with the combination of researcher and practitioner roles, and with a process of inquiry into the experience of perhaps vulnerable or fragile informants'. The researcher retains ownership of the knowledge that is produced, and 'the findings represent subjective, personal knowing as well as objective, impersonal or "factual" knowledge'. The results are written and disseminated in ways consistent with the above principles (McLeod, 1999: 8, 9).

Practitioner research and mainstream research

The interface between practice and research also is obscured by lack of agreement on the relationship between practitioner research and 'mainstream' research. There is no shortage of arguments in support of seeing practitioner research as either very different from or similar to mainstream research. On the one hand there are those who regard practitioner research as not an imitation of university research but as its own *genre* (Cochran-Smith and Lytle, 1990[1]). We are not convinced. Distinctions between the two, based on methodology or epistemology, are 'tenuous if not untenable' (Smith and Klein, 1986: 55). There are, however, important differences of *purpose* between qualitative research and qualitative practitioner inquiry. Questions of prior research agreements, likely audiences and the utilization of results, all raise distinctive issues for practitioner research.[2]

Differences of purpose will be clarified if the category of 'research' is differentiated. Eisner (1991) helpfully distinguishes qualitative research, qualitative inquiry and qualitative thinking. Such distinctions can helpfully be explored and tested by reflecting on and investigating the inferential processes engaged in by different researchers and professionals. The psychotherapist Erikson contributed valuably to this as part of an early symposium on evidence and inference in the human sciences. He complained that 'clinical workers often fail to make explicit, even to themselves, what inventories of evidential signs they regularly but unwittingly, scan' (Erikson, 1959: 82).

The ways in which the purpose of practitioner inquiry shape practice can be illustrated from practitioner research ethics. For example, the principle of consent includes an assumption of voluntary participation. Practitioner research can make voluntary participation more difficult to ensure. It may be jeopardized if service users fear that refusal to participate will compromise the quality of care they will receive.

Problems arise when the practitioner-researcher role is not well understood by service users. In such cases the service user is likely to see the social worker as primarily a practitioner, and may be less likely to exercise appropriate restrictions on self-disclosure to the practitioner-*researcher* (Archbold, 1986). The relationship between the practitioner-as-researcher and the respondent service user raises further ethical questions. For example, life history interviewing has much to offer social work practitioner research (e.g. Bowen, 1993; Martin, 1999). But 'life history interviewing is invasive, old hurts or traumas may be reopened . . . The truth does not necessarily set one free' (Miller, 2000: 104). In addition, people may agree to take part in life history interviews in the belief that the process may be therapeutic, when in reality it may prove one way.

Finally, ethical issues arise over the relationship between research and advocacy. This has sometimes been discussed in terms of whether 'ethnomethodological indifference' is sometimes necessary. Kayser-Jones and Koenig summarize the dilemma in their consideration of ethical issues in qualitative research with older people.

> The need to document the failure to provide adequate treatment for residents . . . in order to effect policy changes is an important justification for not intervening . . . Investigators have no easy answers when confronted with conflicting values; protecting informants versus improving the care of elderly nursing home residents. (Kayser-Jones and Koenig, 1994: 30)

The views of mainstream ethnographers about practitioner research are as varied as those of social workers. At one extreme, some have implied that the practitioner research movement is something of a circus, based on methodological cop-out and theoretical naïvety (Atkinson and Delamont, 1993). Its practitioners are accused of being anti-intellectual and guilty of lack of scholarship. More temperately, Hammersley is not happy that professional practice should be regarded as isomorphic with inquiry. He also thinks there is a danger of overestimating the benefits to be gained from research, and of an overly optimistic faith in the ability of research to influence policy (Hammersley 1993a, 1993b).

A more positive response can be found from other ethnographers. We have spoken of practitioner research as research *by* practitioners. However, it is also helpful to think about ways in which ethnography may have relevance for practice. Bloor, for example, is not optimistic about the policy impacts from research, but he does believe it has a strong professional practice potential. He argues that 'the real opportunities for sociological influence lie closer to the coalface than they do to the head office, that the real opportunities for sociological influence lie in relations with practitioners, not with the managers of practice' (Bloor, 1997a: 234). He suggests there are two ways in which ethnography might speak to the practitioner. First, it may model a service delivery that can be transferred to service providers. Second, ethnographers may, where appropriate, draw practitioners' attention to practices they think worth dissemination. We consider further this under-developed view of ethnography in Chapter 11.

Is practice a form of inquiry?

We have deliberately given repeated attention to the question of the relationship between forms of practice in research and social work. The question has occurred in the first two chapters and in the previous chapter's review of methodology. Padgett's unequivocal view has been mentioned already. 'Qualitative research is incompatible with the practice mandate when the practitioner is also the researcher. I can see no satisfactory way to blend the two roles' (Padgett, 1998b: 37). This is associated with her scepticism regarding advocacy roles in research. She laments the 'erosion of rigour that comes with the loss of critical distance' (p. 11). We have said sufficient to show that we believe this position is ill founded. We will summarize the main points of our position.

First, we reject straightforward conceptions of knowledge and its relationship to theory and action. This is largely a criticism of assumptions of technical rationality in the relation of research and practice.

Second, we believe that the relationship between the practice of research and the practice of social work should be treated as an empirical matter rather than primarily a theoretical one. It calls for what has been called in a different context, 'a careful and committed empiricism' (Barone, 1992: 145). There is now a growing amount of evidence that sheds light on how practitioners seek to make evaluative sense of their day-to-day practice. Broadly comparable conclusions have been drawn from fieldwork with social workers in American private agencies, the British Probation Service, and practitioners with greatly varying amounts and kinds of professional experience (Elks and Kirkhart, 1993; Humphrey and Pease, 1992; Shaw and Shaw, 1997a, 1997b; Sheppard et al., 2000). Sheppard's recent work highlights the processes of critical appraisal and hypothesis generation in social work practice. There is considerable scope for comparative work on professionals in the human services, health, housing, and education fields. This holds promise for strengthening professional decision-making and improving care management services.

Third, there is what Riessman has called 'a sympathetic connection' between certain kinds of social work and qualitative kinds of data – 'talk, therapeutic conversation, agency records, narratives about experiences with organisations and macro systems' (Riessman, 1994a: ix). The tie is proximate but neither universal, homogeneous nor capable of straightforward transfer from one to the other. It requires methodological work, which Shaw has described as involving 'colonizing' and 'translating' (Shaw, 1996, 1997). Colonizing requires practitioners to act upon research methods rather than simply apply them. Translation raises issues of language and culture, and underscores the interpretative character of the process. Social workers need to develop a dialogic practice, both within social work and with methodologists. For example, Janesick's 'stretching' exercises for qualitative researchers are an example of work based on a learning rationale that provides a fertile basis for professional 'colonizing' and 'translating' (Janesick, 1998). The quality of 'methodological practice' will have an emergent, opportunistic and particularistic character. Whitmore's use of visual methods exemplifies this opportunist quality. To maximize the gains from this process social workers need to avoid remaining too much as insiders. 'The familiar not only breeds contempt, it breeds darkness as well' (Eisner, 1988: xii). Above all, 'methodological practice' will have a participatory and collaborative character.

We have referred to several areas where we believe practitioner social work research has yet to deliver its promise.

- It has been unduly shaped by methodological approaches that treat the nature of evidence too straightforwardly.
- There has been an absence of cross-professional dialogue and development.
- It has a relationship to mainstream social science research methodology that is too subordinate.
- It has failed to develop a qualitative evaluating-in-practice.

In addition to these four points, we need to add that it has:

- tended to adopt a deductive assumption about the relationship between theory and practice;
- been conducted on the unspoken assumption that practitioner expertise need not be challenged by the understandings of service users.

We refer to the first of these points in the closing section of the chapter. We now turn to the criticism regarding the lack of an emancipatory, empowerment agenda in practitioner research.

Practitioner research and empowerment

We started from a definition of practitioner research as research carried out by practitioners for the purpose of advancing their own practice. Despite the strengths of this definition, it is limited by its individualism and the absence of any participation of service users. As a consequence, there is a chronic risk that practitioner research will suffer from institutional capture. Fisher has argued that

> Genuine involvement of service users (cannot) be taken forward if the focus remains on the researcher–practitioner relationship. In a sense, the idea that

problem formulation is/should be resolved through improving the relationship between practitioner and researcher is part of the problem . . . Indeed, there is a clear danger that in focusing on the modes of researcher–practitioner collaboration the voice of the service use is less prominent or simply outnumbered. (Fisher, unpublished)

There is very little literature in social work on ways in which practitioner research might enable the identification of research questions, prioritizing among research topics, or the actual commissioning of research through involvement in the process of reviewing research proposals. More to the point, there is almost no attention given to how service users might be engaged in similar processes through practitioner research.

There are ways in which practitioner research can develop 'critical practice'. Carr and Kemmis developed a case for critical educational practice (Carr and Kemmis, 1986), and direct attention to ways in which the relationship between theory and practice may transcend simplistic notions of theory as something that is 'applied' to practice in an unproblematic fashion. Miller and her colleagues illustrate the potential for such a model, in their accounts of a collaborative project that endured for at least six years (Miller, 1990). Endeavours have also been made to liberate practitioner research from a personalized model that takes academic research and disciplines as given, and limits practitioner inquiry to applying research to practice (Fahl and Markand, 1999). This project seeks to create an identity for practitioner research as *critique* rather than individualized *application*.

Reflective practice and research

Some writers on practitioner research such as Jarvis (1999) locate debates about reflection and reflexivity within wider postmodernist debates about the fragmentation of social structures and the arrival of the 'risk society'. This analysis draws strongly on Beck's (1992) conceptualization of the 'risk society'. Beck would see reflexivity as the dialogue that society has with itself when normal coping mechanisms break down under conditions of rapid change, and risk is generated. Reflection for Beck and Jarvis is an outcome of reflexive modernity, the process of managing risky situations under conditions of such complexity that outcomes cannot be predicted, the breakdown of confidence in the strategies of positivism. Some of this is prefigured in Harré's critique of positivism and the 'myth of certainty'. It also has strong parallels with Giddens's (1991) analysis of the emergence of 'reflexive modernity'. However, reflexivity, Fook has argued, can be viewed not only as a theoretical position, but also as a process which can be integrated within conventional phases of the research process such as *design* (ensuring that the researcher is part of the 'tale'), *data collection* (attending to the effects on the collection of data which are produced by the researcher's identity and behaviour), *interpretation and analysis* (continuous re-interpretation of material to develop complexity) (Fook, 2000b).

Reflection, then, has conventionally been construed as the method by which reflexivity is developed, although as the paragraph above suggests, the distinction between content and process is not without analytical complexities. The concepts of reflection and reflectivity themselves have diffuse intellectual provenances within social theory and, as White has pointed out in her chapter in this volume, they are not without ambiguity. Although sometimes located in the debates outlined above, numerous writers also situate reflection in the American pragmatic tradition associated with writers such as John Dewey (Gould, 1989). In particular they subscribe to the Deweyan notion that reflection is produced when practitioners encounter situations which are problematic and challenge the habits of routine practice. The key impetus in the application of these understandings to researching the development of practice has been the work of Donald Schon and his analysis of 'the death of technical rationality'. Schon rejected the characterization of professional practice as the deductive application of formal knowledge (be it theoretical or empirical) to problems (Schon, 1983). The main propositions of Schon's arguments, particularly as brought forward within the social work literature (Gould 1999a; Gould and Harris, 1996; Gould and Taylor, 1996) are that:

- The *forms of knowledge* which guide practice are often tacit. Many practitioners are unable to articulate the processes which support effective practice, and this is characteristic, even especially so, of expert practitioners (Fook, in this volume; Fook et al., 2000);
- The *context* of practice is formative in generating knowledge. Prescriptions for good practice such as those derived from positivist research fail or have to be modified or interpreted to be usable in the complex, unique contexts within which practice takes place;
- *Problems* are themselves socially constructed and emerge from the interactions between agencies, practitioners and service users. We cannot continue to subscribe, it is argued, to a belief that social problems exist independently of the assumptive frames of reference that actors bring to a situation.

As Fuller and Petch have argued, Schon's work on the epistemology of practice has given a broad impetus to the fields of action and practitioner research. The concept of the reflective practitioner, then, is one in which there is an 'intimate and interactive' (Fuller and Petch, 1995: 6) relationship between thinking and action so that critical analysis of practice by practitioners becomes a form of action research. This might take the form of 'content reflection' (on the descriptive content of a situation), 'process reflection' (analysing strategies employed to tackle a problem) or 'premise reflection' (seeking an understanding of why an issue came to be labelled as a problem) (Mezirow, 1990). Similarly, reflection may be differentiated on a temporal continuum, i.e. it might be anticipatory, reflection in action, or a retrospective analysis. This perspective which promotes practice itself as a form of research, fundamentally reconceptualizes the relationship between theory, practice and research; using the metaphor developed by Usher and Bryant (1989), critical reflection frees practitioners from the 'captive triangle', particularly one which privileges theory and formal research axis as the base of the triangle, with practice as the superstructure. Reflective practitioner research recasts theorizing, researching and practice as all being forms of practice which are interdependent, and often inseparable.

Reflection can give rise to a range of focuses for research (Jarvis, 1999; Schon, 1983):

• frame analysis – the making conscious of the assumptive frameworks that practitioners bring to practice, so that they can also consider alternatives that might lead to more effective reflection on action;
• repertoire building – bringing together examples of good practice that can be used as resource for learning and the development of complex practice (for example, the kind of problem-based or case study learning exemplified by social work educators as part of the Enquiry and Action Learning approach (Burgess, 1992);
• research on methods of inquiry and over-arching theories – such as the use of instances of practice as ways of eliciting established methods of problem-solving, but also to examine alternative strategies – sometimes using structured methods such as critical incident analysis (Fook, 2000; Gould, 1999b);
• research on the process of reflection in action – exploring the process of reflection in order to understand more completely the nature of expertise and how it can be promoted.

Whichever the focus, the reflective research method can be characterized as following four stages in a cyclical process, a cycle closely akin to an experiential learning cycle which may be iterated until no more understanding can be elicited: immersion in experience, reflection-on-action, conceptualization and action (Gould, 1999a). The first stage is of concrete experience, the immersion of the researcher in the situation as it presents itself, be it an agency or the world of the service user. A shared definition is sought with workers or service users of what the problem is, how it has emerged, the context, contributory factors and their effects. This is likely to proceed through a mixture of data collection methods such as participant observation, dialogue and documentary sources. From this engagement develops an initial perspective on the situation, its boundaries and significance. The second stage of inquiry becomes reflection on the emergent picture; this may be in a range of contexts such as with groups of participants, within a supervisory relationship, or as internal mental reflection. Third, a provisional conceptualization of the issues develops, perhaps as a written document but it may be also represented in more unusual or creative media such as video, oral reports, metaphors, visual images, etc. (Gould, 1996; Gould and Taylor, 1996). In the fourth stage the analysis set out in the third stage is translated into prescriptions for action which are then tested and evaluated in practice. This may then lead into further cycles of experience, reflection, conceptualization and action (Baldwin, 2000).

The reflective paradigm has not been without criticism from within the domain of qualitative research as well as from the predictable objections of positivist social scientists. For some commentator's Schon's approach in particular, because of its idiographic nature, tends to overlook relationships of power and oppression (Shaw, 1996), the deconstruction of which of course are central to progressive social work. Similarly, it can be claimed that it lacks a participative dimension by focusing on professionals and their supervisors or mentors, rather than the dialectic between professionals and service users. Despite these weaknesses in Schon's analysis, some social work writers have since taken on these limitations and augmented their approach to incorporate more structural perspectives. Fook (1996) for example is clear in instancing the influence of postmodernism and post-structuralism and their emphasis on contextualizing the subjectivity of research participants, the lessons of femininism in identifying the effects of power in the research relationship, and the legacy of adult educators such as Freire in validating the use of life-experience as a resource in promoting critical autonomy. Others have drawn on Habermas and critical theory to give reflection more radical, political anchorage (e.g. Ixer, 1999; Usher and Bryant, 1989).

The concern that reflective research has so far tended not to be inclusive of service users in the research process needs to be taken seriously, although it is also understandable that its emergence from the domains of adult education and professional development has tended to determine the major preoccupation of reflective research as being with professional learning. Nevertheless, there are examples of how reflective research is engaging with issues of service development. Baldwin (2000) has published a book-length overview of participatory reflective research he initiated with groups of care managers to explore together how community care policies were being implemented at the 'front line'. Baldwin describes a process which changed from a fairly non-productive conventional evaluation study, where practitioners and managers were interviewed and the data analysed by the researcher in linear fashion, towards a participatory model of research in which researcher and practitioners engaged in groups which reflected on issues of policy implementation, sought to incorporate those reflections in practice and met for further self-analysis. Baldwin shows how the research reframed the concept of professional discretion, traditionally construed in the policy implementation literature as something which has a negative impact on intended outcomes, as something which can be embraced as a process which supports empowering practice in the interstices of bureaucratic managerialism. Baldwin has also translated his reflective methodology into working with people with learning difficulties, who were users of local authority services, but with whom he also worked as co-researchers in the evaluation of their services (Baldwin, 1997).

Reflective research rejects the notion that its subjectivity is problematic in qualitative research and needs to be controlled by quasi-positivist strategies such as methodological triangulation. Fook in her chapter in this volume 'celebrates' that subjectivity as both inalienable in qualitative research, but also as a foundation of good practitioner research. Both White and Fook point to reflectivity in research as an engagement with the search for practical solutions in social work practice, much as we earlier said as a part of a pragmatic tradition, and a challenge to the abstracted self-referential relativism of more esoteric forms of deconstructive research. It has already provided the basis for an emergent social work qualitative literature, but there remains a wide range of topics available to qualitative social work researchers to explore through reflective methods, including (adapted from Jarvis, 1999):

- the changing nature of practice
- the relationship between professional education and practice
- how practitioners develop practical knowledge
- the development of expertise
- the development and characteristics of tacit knowledge
- the development of professional identity
- the relationship between practice and continuing professional development.

Advocacy and qualitative inquiry

We noted early in this chapter that most of the contributors raise in different forms the question of whether qualitative inquiry can prove enabling and emancipatory. Research is conventionally viewed as a relatively sophisticated means to a larger end. The problem focus, research design, fieldwork, analysis, reporting and dissemination of results are all seen as the work of experts seeking understanding that will be for the good of some present or future beneficiaries. One of the most far-reaching developments of recent years has been that practitioners within the human services increasingly have been challenged by forms of inquiry that are seen not as means to some external end but also (and for some advocates, solely) as ends in themselves. To borrow an apt phrase from Robert Stake, social workers have become 'reluctant to separate epistemology from ideology, findings from yearnings' (Stake, 1997: 471).

The forms taken by this radical challenge are varied and include feminist research, research within the disability movement, critical theory, justice-based commitments within research, participatory and reflective inquiry of the kinds discussed in the previous section of this chapter, and qualitative

TABLE 10.1 *Foundations of advocacy inquiry*

Foundation	Key words
Political	Power; empowerment; standpoint; structures
Postmodern	Interpretation; meaning; local relevance
Interpersonal learning	Understanding; reciprocity

evaluation as a dimension of direct practice (Reason and Bradbury, 2000). Advocacy positions cover a span of political stances. At one end is located *multi-partisan* and multi-vocal research. This is well established in some American evaluation research, for example in Lee Cronbach and Robert Stake, and also in much interpretive research. More explicit advocacy positions are associated with much British *reformist* policy research, and with some participatory research. House's development of a democratizing position in American evaluation is a prominent example of a reformist position. Radical positions of critical inquiry include the majority of feminist inquiry, research from the disability movement and among mental health 'survivors', and the greater part of research that takes its primary impetus from neo-Marxist critical theory.

These diverse positions stem largely from the different rationales that have been advanced for advocacy research. There are three main rationales, as listed in Table 10.1. It will be apparent that this way of classifying advocacy approaches to qualitative inquiry closely reflects the discussion of paradigms in Chapter 1. Having made that connection, a corresponding comment is necessary. The foundation positions in Table 10.1 are, of course, abstractions. There *are* those who take one main position, perhaps particularly when associated with relatively radical political rationales. We refer to these positions in our subsequent discussion of 'insiders' and 'outsiders'. But it is equally common to encounter those who bridge more than one position – either on practical and opportunistic grounds or on the basis of more general arguments. For example, Reason has been strongly associated with the development of reflective inquiry approaches, but belongs to no single 'camp'. He firmly rejects postmodernism as nihilistic and does not major on any political rationale. However, he distances himself from conventional science. Participatory positions have been used to support conventional arguments for enhanced research rigour, and we briefly examine these positions later in this section. Then again, feminist arguments for postmodern research represent one of the most significant of such 'bridging' positions.

Advocacy and methodology

But before we discuss insider/outsider 'standpoint' arguments, feminist postmodernism and arguments for advocacy as stimuli for research rigour, we need briefly to defend a fundamental but disputed assumption – that qualitative methodology enriches the political, moral and value dimensions of social work research.

Various arguments have been advanced to support scepticism about the value of research methods and methodology. First, there is an understandable resistance to perceived attempts to intellectualize social work. Lorenz traces the emergence of the 'academization' of social work, and notes how it was justified by the argument that if the status of the profession was enhanced through doing respectable research this would in turn benefit service users. This 'fusion of self interest and devotion to best service' (Lorenz, 2000: 1) left criteria for choosing a research methodology in the hands of 'the established regimes of scientific inquiry'. However, with the current crisis of faith in modernity, 'the responsibility for . . . choosing the right criteria . . . falls back into the lap of the professional. The question of the truth of a research method becomes the question of the truth of a practice method and vice versa. And both questions become questions about the accountability to clients and to society at large' (p. 1).

Second, Lorenz's reference to a crisis of faith in modernity links with postmodern mistrust of methods as a modernist search for the key to knowledge. Some interpretivists are suspicious of researchers who are 'too enamoured of procedures or methodology' (Smith, 1992: 104). Eisner is in tune with this position in his remark that 'in qualitative matters cookbooks ensure nothing' (Eisner, 1991: 169). In addition, Lincoln and Guba say that 'The relativism of naturalism suggests that it is impossible (and always will be) to specify any ultimately true methodology for coming to know' (Lincoln and Guba, 1989: 231).

Third, methodological doubts may be one consequence of an appreciation of the theory-laden character of all observation. For example, Garrison infers that only theory can turn phenomena into meaning. Methods 'only provide the syntax, never the semantics' (1988: 25).

However, most important for our present purposes, a diminished concern with methodological cogency has often been associated with an advocacy position on research, where instrumental procedures take second place to wider political issues. Lorenz summarizes the point as follows.

> It is not the choice of a particular research method that determines social work's position socially and politically. Rather it is the ability to engage critically in the political agenda of defining the terms on which knowledge and truth can be established which should form the basis for the search of appropriate research approaches in social work. (Lorenz, 2000: 8)

Oliver has been sceptical of most existing research methodology, although he has acknowledged uncertainty regarding the extent to which research from the disability movement has challenged dominant methodologies. His focus of attention has been on the social relations of research production rather than developing alternatives to interviews, observation and so on (Oliver, 1997: 20–1). Perhaps the main target of dissatisfaction with existing research has been with the alleged claims of conventional researchers to autonomy and independence. Thus Barnes concludes that,

> If disability research is about researching oppression . . . then researchers should not be professing 'mythical independence' to disabled people, but joining with them in their struggles to confront and overcome this oppression. (Barnes, 1996: 110)

In a thoughtful analysis of black research, Stanfield concludes that 'even in the most critical qualitative research methods literature there is a tendency to treat "human subjects" as the passive prisoners of the research process' (Stanfield, 1994: 168).

Others have taken a less distrustful position, and have argued that qualitative methodology is usually the most congenial strategy for advocacy-oriented research, although methodology by itself is never sufficient. Lather takes this position. She refuses to demonize holders of different paradigm positions, and complains about the fuzziness of emancipatory researchers on the need for data credibility checks (Lather, 1986a). She also argues for an empirical stance that is 'open-ended, dialogically reciprocal, grounded in respect for human capacity, and yet profoundly sceptical of appearances and "common sense"' (Lather, 1986b: 269). Starting from a different position, Schwandt argues for seeing evaluation as 'practical hermeneutics' aimed at producing practical-moral knowledge that 'aims to actually move people, not simply to give them good ideas' (1997: 81). He seeks a balance in which 'the special knowledge of the evaluator . . . is not forsworn – but it is no longer definitive. The evaluator retains the critical imperative . . . but relinquishes the belief in the certainty of such judgement' (p. 78).

Others have been still more optimistic regarding the affinity of qualitative methodology with moral or political agenda. Riessman, for example, has written about narrative methods through which 'an individual links disruptive events in a biography to heal discontinuities – what should have been and what was' (1994a: 114). She makes a more general link between qualitative methodology and liberatory positions. 'Because qualitative approaches offer the potential for representing human agency – initiative, language, emotion – they provide support for the liberatory project of social work' (1994b: xv; cf. Barone, 1992).

Dingwall arrives at a similar conclusion, albeit from a very different point. In his consideration of the moral discourse of interactionism, he is impatient with the postmodern repudiation of moral concerns and is concerned with how the moral and empirical plug together. He reaches back to the philosophy of Adam Smith, for viewing sociology as studying the very preconditions for mutual society. 'If we have a mission for our discipline, it may be to show the timeless virtues of compromise and civility, of patient change and human decency, of a community bound by obligations rather than rights' (Dingwall, 1997b: 204). This quotation has been deliberately chosen in contrast to emancipatory models of research, to show that the qualitative analysis 'of what it might take to live a moral life' (p. 204) is neither novel nor the exclusive province of a relatively small cluster of political positions. The position taken in this book is that qualitative research informed by critical concerns 'must neither ignore instrumental issues nor privilege them' (Vanderplaat, 1995: 94).

Insiders, outsiders and standpoints

In arguing for the special relevance of qualitative methods for advocacy research, we have temporarily bracketed consideration of the differences between political and postmodern justifications for such research. We now return to that distinction and briefly consider the methodological characteristics of each position.

Research based on an agenda of radical advocacy is often referred to as based on a 'standpoint' epistemology. A helpful perspective on standpoint positions can be achieved by revisiting in detail a classic paper on the sociology of knowledge by Robert Merton. Merton believed that, as society becomes more polarized, so do contending claims to truth. At its extreme, an active, reciprocal distrust between social groups finds parallel expression in intellectual perspectives that are no longer located in the same universe of discourse. This leads to reciprocal ideological analyses and claims to 'group-based truth' (Merton, 1972: 11). Merton analyses the relative claims of this nature made by those who are epistemological *insiders* or *outsiders* to the group.

The Insider doctrine claims in its strong form that particular groups have monopolistic access to particular kinds of knowledge. In this strong form, the doctrine leads to the position that each group has a monopoly of knowledge about itself. In vernacular terms, 'you have to be one to understand one', because 'the Outsider has a structurally imposed incapacity to comprehend alien groups, statuses, cultures and societies' (p. 15).

Feminist standpoint epistemology exhibits some of the key characteristics of Merton's Insider doctrine. Put simply, in response to the patriarchal assumption that women are *less* able to understand, standpoint theorists argue that women are *more* able to understand. They argue this through two linked assertions – the double vision of the oppressed and the partial vision of the powerful. Women's experience is seen as a more complete[3] and less distorted kind of social experience. Objectivity is rejected for its alleged inherent masculinist bias. Hierarchy within the research relationship is rejected as not simply bad method but bad ethics and bad politics. The research process is typically viewed in advocacy and empowerment terms.

Merton develops several criticisms of strong Insider positions, but his key point for our purposes is that individuals do not have a single organizing status but a complex status set. 'Aggregates of individuals . . . typically confront one another as Insiders and Outsiders' (1972: 22). He enters several caveats that enable a reflective assessment of current standpoint positions in social work. He stresses that he is in no way advocating divisions, nor is he predicting that collectivities cannot unite on single issues. Rather such unity will be difficult and probably not enduring.

Standpoint theory departs from Insider analysis in an important respect. The 'double vision' of the oppressed is in fact an argument for being simultaneously an Insider and an Outsider. This is the idea that 'special perspectives and insights are available to that category of outsiders who have been systematically frustrated by the social system: the disinherited, deprived, disenfranchised, dominated and exploited' (p. 29). The Outsider is a stranger. Quoting from the early sociologist Georg Simmel, Merton concludes that the objectivity of the stranger 'does not simply involve passivity and detachment; it is a particular structure composed of distance and nearness, indifference and involvement' (p. 33).

Social work writers have often failed to distinguish strong and weaker versions of standpoint positions. The weaker form of the doctrine claims that Insiders (and Outsiders) have *privileged* rather than *monopolistic* claims to knowledge. This is a position that avoids the erroneous assumption of some radical advocacy researchers, that social position wholly determines what understanding is possible. We rejected a parallel form of this argument in our discussion of paradigms in Chapter 1. Group identities do significantly influence explanations, but the distinction between tendency and determinism is 'basic, not casual or niggling' (p. 27). Merton concludes that, having accepted that distinction, 'We no longer ask whether it is the Insider or the Outsider who has monopolistic or privileged access to the truth; instead we begin to consider their distinctive and interactive roles in the process of truth seeking' (p. 36). His conclusion has much to recommend it as a starting point for assessing truth claims in advocacy research.

Postmodernism, feminism and qualitative research   Recognition of the weaknesses of strong standpoint positions helped to energize the emergence of alternative feminist approaches to advocacy research in the 1990s, based on a postmodern analysis of society. There are important variations within feminist postmodernism that stem in part from ambiguity about what being postmodern entails. However, there are several recurring themes:

- a movement away from essentializing concepts of women;
- rejection of objectivism in favour of relativism;
- engagement with pluralist and humanist research methodologies;
- a strong claim that all knowledge is contextual and historically specific, often associated with a scepticism regarding cross-cultural explanations;
- rejection of epistemology in exchange for discourse and rhetoric.

To this list feminists add a determination to politicize postmodernism and rescue it from any risk of political complacency. Standard relativist positions usually adopt a 'descriptive' approach to values, and avoid normative judgements. Schwandt concludes that

> The strength of the logic of the descriptive approach is that it recognises that making judgements of values is complex, requires the participation of all those with a stake in an evaluand, and does not rest solely in the pronouncements of the evaluator. Its weakness is that it virtually eliminates a critical voice for evaluators and thus readily plays into the perpetuation of the status quo. (Schwandt, 1997: 82)

Feminists have rejected descriptive approaches to values, and sought a route out of the 'tension between deconstruction and empowerment' (Trinder, 2000: 50). The route has not been clearly mapped. For example, the political prescriptions that emerge from feminist postmodernism some-time seem slightly limp. The solutions are typically in terms of 'temporary agreements and courses of action; and a reminder of the "need to negotiate"' (Fawcett, 2000: 78) – desirable certainly, but scarcely radical. The prescriptions for research also appear to involve a leap of faith. On what grounds, one wonders, can postmodern feminists conclude that research involves 'an acceptance that meanings can be fixed or frozen for a finite period and used as a basis for study'? (Fawcett, 2000: 69). Relativist positions of all kinds have also been troubled by practitioner struggles. Greene is discussing research in education, but her point also holds good for social work:

> Many qualitative practitioners struggle with the dissonance invoked by the mind-dependence of all social knowledge claims in the face of the contextual (as well as personal, ego-related) demands to *'get it right'*, to *'find out what's really going on in this setting'*. (Greene, 1996: 280)

The relativist depiction of experience by itself is insufficient. As Olesen remarks, 'merely taking experience into account does not reflect on how that experience came to be. In short, oppressive systems are replicated rather than criticised in the unquestioning reliance on "experience"' (Olesen, 1994: 167). Feminist postmodern positions are of value when they conclude that feminists should be 'seeking to work with but not romanticise, subjugated voices, searching for moments of social justice' (Trinder, 2000: 81). Riessman has argued to similar effect elsewhere, quoting Ricouer's warning against adopting a 'hermeneutic of suspicion' towards women's narratives (Riessman, 1994b: 130).

Better research? In what sense might advocacy research of the kind exemplified in Whitmore's chapter lead to better research? Can participatory, collaborative research be justified on methodological as well as moral grounds? Should we do it on grounds of citizen and service user rights, or should we (also) do it because it will probably lead to better research 'technically'? The jury is still out on this question.

There is probably a majority of researchers who regard partisan research as intellectually and methodologically compromised. These researchers would agree with Chelimsky when she concludes that 'advocacy is not really an option' (Chelimsky, 1997: 109). A widely held form of this kind of line of reasoning might be stated as follows. In evaluative research where outcome evaluation is central, validity is paramount. In such cases, handing over power and political control to one particular group of stake-holders to frame research questions, design the evaluation and draw evaluative conclusions represents an abdication of responsibility on the part of the evaluator.[4]

In its strongest form, the counter-argument might be expressed as follows. Research with an advocacy agenda will always adopt collaborative, participatory, user-led strategies. Research that does not embrace these strategies will be morally, politically and *methodologically* weaker. This argument goes further than we think safe or justified. It risks leading down the paths of sentimentality and romanticism about which we voiced reservations in the opening chapter. Dingwall believes that romanticism leads to a corrupt sociology. 'What is the value of a scientific enterprise', he asks, 'that is more concerned with being "right on" than with being right?' (Dingwall, 1997a: 64). Furthermore, we cannot dragoon every critical research project into the camp of user-led inquiry. We must retain a major place for those who, while holding unequivocally to a transformative agenda, believe that advocacy need not be direct and explicit, but will often be implicit. In this context, Popkewitz has offered an elegant defence of critical science. He does not believe that the partisan role of science places an obligation on scientists to pursue political commitments through active participation in advocacy movements. Rather, 'social scientists are partisans in the forming of social agendas through the practices of science' (Popkewitz, 1990: 50). Science 'sensitises us to avoid certain possibilities and, at the same time, filters out others. Implicit . . . then are ways in which people are to challenge the world and locate themselves in its ongoing relations' (p. 63).

Popkewitz's argument points us in the direction of exploring ways in which rigour and relevance can be harnessed. Whitmore's chapter embodies that agenda when she says that,

> We assumed that street involved youth were in the best position to evaluate their own services and we were right. They could not have done this alone, however. As much as we want to believe in 'community control', this has to be seen in context, and the reality is that marginalized populations will need our professional support and commitment in working with them. (cf. Whitmore and McKee, 2000)

Assuming, then, that it is desirable, how far is it possible to 'bridge the gap between the activists, on the one hand, and empirically grounded sceptical researchers, on the other' (Bogdan and Taylor, 1994: 295)?

Fisher has recently argued in an unpublished paper that collaborative research service users have a role in problem formulation and the 'technical' aspects of social research. He concludes that:

> User controlled research . . . brings the possibility of technical enhancements to the processes of defining the research 'problem', in ensuring that appropriate data are sought and are accessible, in defining outcome measures and in recognising relevance during analysis. (Fisher, unpublished)

User controlled research will:

1. ensure a problem focus is less reliant on perspectives on social issues held by the dominant group;
2. lead to more representative samples because of lower refusal rates;
3. guarantee better data quality because participants will be less defensive, e.g. in interviews;
4. lead to the development of outcome measures that:

   - pay attention to the *processes* of service delivery
   - understand people within their *social context*
   - reflect the *diversity* of users' views on the quality of life;

5. enable greater theoretical relevance and sensitivity to emerge during data analysis.

He makes this argument from experience as consultant to a user-controlled research project by disabled people in Wiltshire receiving cash payments through the Independent Living Support Service (Evans and Fisher, 1999). Oliver's more extensive work on involving health care consumers in identifying research topics, and prioritizing, commissioning and reporting research, has led her to conclude that consumers tend to highlight issues about patients' views, social contexts, information and support needs, long-term outcomes, and dissemination of research findings to consumers. Her work suggests that these issues are less usually addressed by academic research reviewers, who tend to focus more on technical and economic aspects of research (Oliver, 1999).

There are, of course, several unresolved questions that remain. Fisher's conclusions are based on limited evidence. It is not inevitable that research that is justifiable on moral grounds will also be methodologically sounder. Also, there are ethical questions as to whether research principles concerning informed consent, and confidentiality/privacy are especially at risk in user-controlled research. Finally, even when an alliance of service users and research professionals is accepted as good practice, the role of independent academic judgement is not easily agreed.

Conclusion

The mission for qualitative research in social work has been changed, probably irreversibly, by developments in the areas illustrated in the invited Chapters 6 through 8 of this book, and reviewed in this chapter. Many readers of this book will have been taught social science as either a scientific discipline or even as a critique of morality. Against these traditions, practitioner research, reflective practice and inquiry, and qualitative advocacy research prioritize questions of power, understanding, meaning, justice and 'what it might take to lead a moral life' (Dingwall, 1997b: 204). Merton's warnings against 'social sadism' and 'sociological euphemism' were well made. Social sadism 'is more than a metaphor. The term refers to social structures which are so organized as to systematically inflict pain, humiliation, suffering and deep frustration upon particular groups'. Many sociological concepts 'are altogether bland in the fairly precise sense of being unperturbing, suave, and soothing in effect'. They 'serve to exclude from the attention of the social scientist the intense feelings of pain and suffering' that are the experience of people caught up in what they describe. 'By screening out these profoundly human experiences, they become sociological euphemisms' (Merton, 1972: 38).

In the final chapter we consider a cluster of remaining questions about the consequences of qualitative research in social work. Does qualitative research have anything useful to say about the outcomes of social work? More generally, how might such research prove useful within social work and the wider human services? Do such uses include contributions to developments in theory, practice and method in social work?

Notes

1. The issues are exactly the same in social work and education, and we have drawn on the literature from both fields. This coincidentally enables us to demonstrate the point that social work is the loser whenever it over-emphasizes the distinctiveness of its professional concerns.
2. There is a related question as to whether research and evaluation are similar or different *genres*. Our response is exactly analogous to the position taken here. Differences on grounds of epistemology and methodology are misleading, while distinctions on grounds of purpose are necessary (Shaw, 1999b: 8–11).
3. Trinder helpfully observes that feminist standpoint positions are ambivalent at this point, as to whether it is the privileged position of women in general or that of feminists (Trinder, 2000). Those who hold a classic Marxist acceptance of false consciousness will take the latter position. Trinder (2000) and Shaw (1999a) provide outlines and brief critiques of feminist standpoint theory in social work.
4. This argument has been paraphrased from an interesting exchange between Jane Davidson and David Chavis on the electronic discussion list of the American Evaluation Association in 1999.

Recommended reading

The most comprehensive recent collection of papers on the relationship between action and research is that by Reason and Bradbury (2000).

On practitioner inquiry, McLeod's book was written for counsellors, but it is especially helpful. Jan Fook's book *The Reflective Researcher* (1996) spans some of the issues in practitioner inquiry and reflective practice. One of us has tried to develop a case for 'translating' qualitative methodology for social work practice (Shaw, 1996). We also recommend Bloor's all-too-rare attempt by an ethnographically inclined sociologist to think through the practice implications of their research (Bloor, 1997a).

On reflective practice and research, Schon's account of *The Reflective Practitioner* (1983) has been the starting point for much subsequent discussion, and it is not easy to make sense of subsequent discussions without reading his book first. Perhaps even more helpful as a starting point is the under-rated book by Shakespeare and colleagues (1993). Taylor and White's book (2000) is valuable for its combination of well-informed expression of a broad span of current thinking, and a social work practice agenda.

One aspect of our approach to advocacy and justice-based inquiry has been to urge the need to understand the range of different positions that have been taken. Readers who are seriously interested in this area ought to go back to some of the earlier sources, perhaps starting with Merton (1972), and will also find it useful to read the more strategic discussions such as those in Fawcett et al. (2000), Olesen (2000), and the chapters by Dullea and Mullender, Evans and Fisher, and Humphries in Shaw and Lishman (1999).

11

The Consequences of Qualitative Social Work Research

CONTENTS

Process and outcomes   180
Outcomes   180
Evaluative judgements   180
Qualitative research and outcomes   181
Making use of qualitative research   186
Theorizing research and practice   189
Theory and theorizing   190
Local relevance and general knowledge   194
Theory and practice   199
Recommended reading   201

Throughout this book the writers and contributors have trodden the con-tested borderlands between research and practice. In so doing, they have persistently questioned and challenged commonly-held understandings about both. They have said less about the technical requirements and methods of good qualitative research, and more about the mind-set, values and logics that are essential if qualitative social work research is to prove rigorous and relevant. We have not quite exhausted our agenda. In this final chapter we will confront some conventional positions regarding the contribution of qualitative inquiry to practice.

The following statements probably sound non-contentious. We need:

1. clear evidence regarding the outcomes of social work;
2. instrumental, practical uses from research if social work and human services more generally are to benefit;
3. research that has clear implications that can be applied to social work practice.

We do not disagree. Outcomes evidence, useful research, and theory that entails a practice agenda, are certainly core requirements. But we have qualms about the too-easy tacit connection that is frequently made between these assertions and the role of qualitative research. Proponents of the functional 'horses for courses' approach to research methodology frequently assume that qualitative inquiry is somehow less well equipped to meet these requirements than surveys, longitudinal designs, single-system designs or randomized controlled trials. We noted in the opening chapter that representatives from within quantitative outcome research have accepted that such an approach is narrowing and blinkered. However, we have found no grounds for advocates of qualitative research to be complacent about the merits of their methodologies. We conclude this book with an exploration of the three questions of social work outcomes, the uses of research, and the relations of practice and theory.

Process and outcomes

By way of preamble we should first clarify what we mean by 'outcomes'. Second, we need to rethink the assumptions we make about how evaluative reasoning proceeds.

Outcomes

We need to distinguish between general outcomes, social work outcomes and social work service outcomes (cf. Long, 1994). Research findings, or policy implementation, are examples of outcomes in general. 'Social welfare outcomes' include the effect on social welfare of any type of process, including not only social work services but also informal care, health care, housing, education and so on. 'Social work service outcomes' refers to the effects of social work services. These will be mainly social welfare outcomes, but by no means exclusively so. We should also distinguish between final and intermediate outcomes, and what can be called process-based outcome measures.

There is no implicit valuation of good or bad in the concept of 'outcome', and valuation of outcomes thus becomes a major issue. An outcome is more than a technically measured end point. It involves a valuation of that end point. These points become relevant when we make decisions about the methodology for researching outcomes.

Evaluative judgements

Second, there has been insufficient attention to philosophical contributions to the field of evaluation logic.

> Everyone agrees that information somehow informs decisions, but the relationship is not direct, not simple. Often the more important the decision, the more obscure the relationship seems to be. (House, 1980: 68)

House goes as far as to say that, 'subjected to serious scrutiny, evaluations always appear equivocal' (p. 72). He argues that evaluations can be no more than acts of persuasion. 'Evaluation persuades rather than convinces, argues rather than demonstrates, is credible rather than certain, is variably accepted rather than compelling' (p. 73). Evaluators have too frequently underplayed the role of judgement and hence of argumentation. This has resulted in an unduly technical, methods-oriented analysis, an over-confidence in quantification, and a tendency to represent knowledge in an impersonal, objectified form. Those who fail to accept the 'compelling' conclusions drawn from evaluation are dismissed as irrational. If results are unequivocal then those who fail to accept them are 'wrong'.

There have been several attempts to take a different approach to thinking through the reasoning process involved in constructing justified evaluative arguments. These typically emphasize the complex connection between evidence and conclusions, and commence from the differences between formal and informal reasoning. Whereas formal reasoning assumes a tight fit between the premises and conclusions within an argument, infor-mal logic 'deals with ordinary, everyday language, where rules of inference are less precise and more contextual' (Fournier and Smith, 1993: 317). The key question is whether good but non-deductive reasoning is possible – i.e. reasoning that is not logically valid. 'The consensus among informal logicians is that there can be logically good, but nonvalid reasoning' (Blair, 1995: 73).

This philosophical argument has direct implications for practice because much evaluative reasoning is non-deductive. For example, we may some-times engage in good all-things-considered reasoning, where there are reasons for and against a point of view but where the pros outweigh the cons. The paper by House cited above falls in that category. Also, there has been growing acceptance of the circumstances in which it may be legitimate to reason from factual evidence to evaluative conclusions, where there can be no logical relation of implication for such an argument. Finally, informal logicians have concluded that much reasoning is dialec-tical. Reasons for a claim are seen as a move in an argument – an attempt to persuade, offered as part of an actual or possible exchange between parties who differ.

Qualitative research and outcomes

Following that preliminary ground clearing, we now sketch our views regarding the ways in which qualitative research and evaluation can address outcome questions.

1. There are design solutions analogous to those conventional outcome designs that entail a degree of control.
2. The shift of emphasis from internal validity to questions of external

validity and generalization, has led to a greater sensitivity to the micro-processes of practice and programmes.
3. Developments in symbolic interactionism and ethnomethodology have been applied to outcome questions.
4. The impact of scientific realism has led to a radical rethinking of notions of causality.

Campbell and theory-informing case studies   Qualitative design solutions have been pursued actively by those who have worked on the borders of qualitative and quantitative methodology. For example, Donald Campbell's early position was that 'one-shot' case study designs are uninterpretable with regard to causal attribution. However, through exchanges with Becker and Erikson, he came to the position that the analogy of degrees of freedom provides a major source of discipline for interpreting intensive, cross-cultural case studies. The logic entails testing theories against the predictions or expectations they stimulate, through a general process he describes as pattern matching, based on the premise that 'experimental design can be separated from quantification' (Campbell, 1978: 197). He suggested a paradigm which entails a whole-hearted commitment to both ethnography and comparative studies. Campbell's approach has been developed in Yin's account of case study research (Yin, 1994; cf. Shaw, 1999a, Ch. 7).

Micro-processes   William Reid has been attracted by the potential of 'change-process' research. He does not reject the role of controlled experiments but concludes that 'practical and ethical constraints on experiments necessitate a reliance on the naturalistic study of these relations' (Reid, 1990: 130). This entails a focus on the processes of change during the period of contact between the professional helper and the client system. Rather than relying on aggregated, averaged summary measures of outcomes, this approach returns to the content-analysis tradition in social research, through a greater focus on micro-outcomes.

Reid applies his ideas to social work, although the logic would presumably apply to other forms of change-oriented professional service. A systemic view of intervention is at its root, in which professionals and service users are viewed in a circular, mutually influencing interaction. In this model, 'conventional distinctions between intervention and outcome lose their simplicity' (p. 135). 'It then becomes possible to depict change-process research as a study of strings of intermixed i's and o's' – interventions and outcomes (p. 136). While Reid seeks to defend experiments, he suggests a more naturalistic stance when he says that 'averages of process variables that are devoid of their contexts at best provide weak measures' (p. 137).

Ethnomethodology and symbolic interactionism   Developments in symbolic interactionism and ethnomethodology have enabled qualitative researchers to add a rich, transformative leavening to otherwise flat, two-dimensional depictions of outcomes. Two examples will serve to illustrate this point. First, we saw in Chapter 1 how Miller's work enriches our understanding of the importance of context in qualitative research. He discusses ways in which institutional texts constructed to explain past decisions inevitably gloss over the openness and complexity of the decision-making process (Miller, 1997). He gives the apparently mundane example of evaluation research on a bowel-training programme in a nursing home. The evaluation consisted of counting when and how patients had bowel movements. The programme was judged to have a successful outcome if patients used a toilet or bedpan and ineffective for those who continued soiling beds. One patient had soiled her bed. However, observation methods enabled the researcher to view a nursing aide contesting the definition of this as 'failure' on the grounds that the patient knew what she was doing and had soiled her bed as a protest act against staff favouring another patient. This illustrates how observing the context of text construction illuminates mundane, everyday life. This would not have found a way into the formal outcome record. Text production in institutions is 'micro-politically òrganized', and this includes textual outcome records.

Second, Denzin's interpretive interactionism has had a surprising impact on thinking about service outcomes (Denzin, 1989a; Mohr, 1997). Mohr, for example, extends Denzin's argument to the evaluation of clinical outcomes in health research. She argues that the method leads us to inspect the relationships between personal difficulties, experiences, policies, interventions, and institutions. 'Interpretive interactionism permits intensive scrutiny of the ramifications and outcomes of various interventions' (1997: 284). It can:

1. sort out different ways problems are defined;
2. show how patients experience care. What it is about interventions they find helpful or not, and in what circumstances;
3. identify 'secondary causes' e.g. contexts, culture, and the meanings patients bring.

'Strategic points for intervention can be identified by contrasting and comparing patients' thick descriptions, and these can be used to change, to improve, or to negotiate and renegotiate interventions' (p. 284). It is valuable when 'an outcome may not be readily apparent, and . . . the intervention is something that only the patient and not the professionals can define' (p. 285).

Cause and causal models   The fourth qualitative line of approach to the methodological problems posed by outcome evaluation is rather different. It stems from the stimulus provided by changed thinking regarding the nature of cause, and the corresponding models of causal hypotheses which flow from that thinking. The central idea is of underlying causal mechanisms that cannot be understood by surface workings and measurement. Hence, 'events themselves are not the ultimate focus of scientific analysis . . . Reality consists not only of what we can see but also of the underlying causal entities that are not always discernible' (House, 1991b: 4). The underlying reality produces actual events, of which we have empirical experiences and sense impressions.

This is often described as a *generative* concept of causality.

> When we explain an outcome generatively, we are not coming up with variables or correlates that associate with one another; rather we are trying to explain how the association itself comes about. The generative mechanisms thus actually *constitute* the outcome. (Pawson and Tilley, 1997: 408)

The conventional concept of causation as regularities and associations is dismissed in favour of causal entities which have 'tendencies interacting with other tendencies in such a way that an observable event may or may not be produced' (House, 1991b: 5). House quotes Manicas and Secord saying that, 'For the standard view of science, the world is a determined concatenation of contingent events; for the realist, it is a contingent concatenation of real structures. And this difference is monumental.' Hence, instead of merely documenting the sequence and association of events, the realist seeks to *explain* events.

While this view of cause does not necessarily require a qualitative methodology, it does clearly lend itself to such methods.

> Qualitative studies are not designed to provide definitive answers to causal questions . . . (but) it can still be an appropriately qualified pursuit. (Lofland and Lofland, 1995: 136, 138)

Miles and Huberman are even less reserved. 'The conventional view is that qualitative studies are only good for exploratory forays, for developing hypotheses – and that strong explanations, including causal attributions, can be derived only through quantitative studies.' They describe this view as 'mistaken' (Miles and Huberman, 1994: 147), and insist that qualitative evaluation research

1. can identify causal mechanisms;
2. can deal with complex local networks;
3. can sort out the temporal dimension of events;
4. is well equipped to cycle back and forth between different levels of variables and processes;

They also argue that causal accounts will be local and 'now-oriented' (Lofland and Lofland, 1995: 141) and that analytic induction provides a way of testing and deepening single case explanations. Miles and Huberman develop analytic methods which address causal attribution in both single and multiple case explanations. For example, they advocate the use of field research to map the 'local causal networks' which informants carry in their heads and to make connections with the evaluator's own emerging causal map of the setting. Such maps start from 'causal fragments' which lead on to linked building of logical chains of evidence. Such causal networks

> are not probabilistic, but specific and determinate, grounded in understanding of events over time in the concrete local context – *and* tied to a good conceptualization of each variable. (Miles and Huberman, 1994: 159)

Much of this reasoning was anticipated by Cronbach's arguments regarding causal models. Rejecting the idea of causation as events that can be predicted with a high degree of probability, Cronbach developed twin arguments. First, he argued that causes are contingent on local interactions of clusters of events. More than one cluster may be sufficient, but no one cluster is necessary. Second, he accepted that there are usually missing events or conditions that affect the outcome of a given programme, but about which we know little. He was the first theorist to produce a plausible explanation of contextual factors in evaluation. Hence, he concludes that 'after the experimenter with his artificial constraint leaves the scene, the operating programme is sure to be adapted to local conditions' (Cronbach et al., 1980: 217). Furthermore, 'a programme evaluation is so dependent on its context that replication is only a figure of speech' (p. 222).

Qualitative evaluation cannot resolve the problems of causal conclusions any more than quantitative evaluation, but it can assess causality 'as it actually plays out in a particular setting' (Miles and Huberman, 1994: 10). For example, qualitative evaluation and research share a recognition of the irony of social causes and consequences. Much of the sociology of deviance was based on just this sense of irony, with its exploration of deviant roles as doing necessary 'dirty work'. In evaluative terms, we may ask the question what functions are served by a particular practice that would not be served by its absence? In less functional terms we may ask what are the typical results of this phenomenon in this setting, and what ends are served thereby? Lofland and Lofland make the important observation that causal answers are by and large based on *passivist* conceptions of human nature. Qualitative inquiry has often steered away from causal accounts, not because the methodology is weak in that area but because of a commitment to an *activist* conception of human nature. The Loflands argue that an activist conception will lead to a focus on questions that address both structures and strategies. This will involve 'deciphering and depicting exactly what sort of situation the participants are facing' (Lofland and Lofland, 1995: 146), and understanding the 'incessantly fabricated' strategies people construct to deal with the situation.

Take, for example, Silverman's work on HIV counselling. He is right to conclude that 'it is usually unnecessary to allow our research topics to be

defined in terms of . . . the "causes" of "bad" counselling or the "consequences" of "bad" counselling' (Silverman, 1997: 34), insofar as such
topics reflect the conceptions of social problems as recognized by professional or community groups. Nonetheless, this does not require the abandonment of causal arguments. Inquiry into the ways in which professionals
incessantly fabricate service forms and structures does promise a better way
to understand causes.

Miles and Huberman also develop ways in which ordering and explaining can transcend the level of the individual case through cross-case dis-
plays of data. They are confident of the ability of qualitative inquiry to go
beyond the problems of inferring from association ('the weasel word of
quantitative researchers', p. 222). They summarize the process as follows.

> *Cross-case causal networking* is a comparative analysis of all cases in a sample,
> using variables estimated to be the most influential in accounting for the out-
> come criterion. You look at each outcome measure and examine, for each case,
> the stream of variables leading to or 'determining' that outcome. Streams that
> are similar to or identical across cases, and that differ in some consistent way
> from other streams are extracted and interpreted. (p. 228)

They spell out the steps to accomplishing this analysis, but suggest that it
may not be feasible for either larger or very small samples.

Qualitative research also facilitates the task of *evaluation of outcomes*, and
is opposed to the technicalization of outcome research. This is not exclusively the province of qualitative research, but more conventional, and
strictly evidence-based varieties of outcome research tend to treat such
issues as technical matters. This links to the broader area of value and
political issues.

> Evidence on effectiveness and outcomes and an emphasis on health gain and
> health outcome provide an apparently value-neutral, rational approach and
> means for rationing health and social care. Beneath the range of technical
> issues in assessing outcomes are political and social values that need to be
> explicit. (Long, 1994: 175)

Making use of qualitative research

A focus on outcomes leads fairly directly to the wider question of how
qualitative research might be useful for social work policies, programmes,
projects and practice. At the broadest level, research would be judged
useful if it demonstrably contributed to one or more of the following:

- better policies, services and practice;
- strengthening of the moral purpose of social work;
- promotion of methodological rigour, scope, depth and innovation;

- strengthening of the sense of social work's intellectual nature and location.

We tend to make simple distinctions between research that has a direct, applied purpose and research that is basic and hence where direct use questions are less relevant. This does not work (just as the related sharp distinction between 'research' and 'evaluation' does not work either). Conventional quantitative research on outcomes is linked to a confidence in the instrumental utility of research. The problem with this is that it does not square with evidence on how research is actually used, and it misunderstands the nature of the policy-making process. It is based on a rationalistic model.

> The rationalist model of policy making sees it as a series of discrete events, where each issue to be decided is clearly defined, and decisions are taken by a specific set of actors who choose between well-defined alternatives, after weighing the evidence about the likely outcome of each. (Finch, 1986: 149–50)

The important figure for this question is Carol Weiss, whose work in the 1970s explored how political considerations intrude on evaluation. She addressed three related issues.

First, she delineated the *political context* in which evaluation is located. Although she has been primarily concerned with evaluation and policy research at the federal level, her empirical work with policy and programme staff resonates throughout evaluation theory and practice. This underlines the importance of being clear about the audiences for any inquiry.

Second, she exposed the limitations of conventional instrumental views of the political use of information, through her conceptualization of use as *enlightenment*. With her colleagues she interviewed 155 senior officials in federal, state and local mental health agencies. Officials and staff used research to provide information about service needs, evidence about what works, and to keep up with the field. However, it was also used as a ritualistic overlay, to legitimize positions, and to provide personal assurance that the position held was the correct one. At a broader conceptual level, it helped officials to make sense of the world. For all these purposes, 'It was one source among many, and not usually powerful enough to drive the decision process' (Weiss, 1980: 390). As for direct utilization of research, 'Instrumental use seems in fact to be rare, particularly when the issues are complex, the consequences are uncertain, and a multitude of actors are engaged in the decision-making process' (p. 397).

Research use was also reflected in officials' views of the decision-making process. Decisions were perceived to be fragmented both vertically and horizontally within organizations, and to be the result of a series of gradual and amorphous steps. Therefore, 'a salient reason why they do not report the use of research for specific decisions is that many of them *do not believe that they make decisions*' (p. 398). Hence the title of her paper – 'Knowledge creep and decision accretion'. This provided the basis for her conclusion that enlightenment rather than instrumental action represents the characteristic route for research use.

The enlightenment model 'offers far more space to qualitative research, through its emphasis on understanding and conceptualisation, rather than upon providing objective facts' (Finch, 1986: 154).

Third, Weiss imbued models of use with a realistic view of the *public interest*. More than anything, she has struggled towards a realistic theory of use. Others subsequently have developed such realistic views. For example, Chelimsky suggests that evaluation may have a *deterrence* function. 'In other words, the mere presence of the function, and the likelihood of a persuasive evaluation, can prevent or stop a host of undesirable government practices' (Chelimsky, 1997: 105).

Several cautious remarks are in order. First, we should not become over-pre-occupied with models of research use. Chelimsky believes 'it is often the case that . . . evaluations are undertaken *without any hope of use'*. Expected non-use is characteristic of some of the best evaluations, including 'those that question widespread popular beliefs in a time of ideology, or threaten powerful, entrenched interests at any time' (p. 105). Thus, 'there are some very good reasons why evaluations may be expert, and also unused' (p. 105). Chelimsky's comments are both sane and plausible.

> To justify all evaluations by any single kind of use is a constraining rather than an enabling idea because it pushes evaluators towards excessive preoccupation with the acceptability of their findings to users, and risks turning evaluations into banal reiterations of the status quo. (Chelimsky, 1997: 106)

Second, the enlightenment model should not be adopted as universally appropriate. For example, practitioner research is likely to proceed on a more immediate instrumental view.

Third, the adoption of enlightenment assumptions about research use can easily translate into a defensive posture, arising from the fact that they can readily be used to support an incrementalist approach to social change. The step from an empirical recognition that policy and practice change often proceeds through incremental enlightenment, to a tacit assumption that this is how social change *ought* to proceed, may be logically insupportable, but it is deceptively easy.

Fourth, in counterpoint to the previous point, we should avoid being unduly sanguine about the ability of research to change social work. Hammersley has criticized some professionally driven research approaches on the grounds that they are based on too narrow a concept of research relevance and an overly optimistic faith in the ability of research to influence policy and practice. While he is writing about education, his remarks are relevant to social work. He suggests two grounds for concluding 'there are good reasons to believe that research cannot routinely solve teachers' problems' (Hammersley, 1993a: 430). 'There is no scientific method that guarantees results' (p. 430) and teacher circumstances are diverse and unlikely to be amenable to action in any routine sense. Rather, 'sound practice cannot amount to the straightforward *application* of theoretical knowledge, but is an activity that necessarily involves judgement and draws on experience as much as on . . . scientific knowledge' (p. 430).

Fifth, there is often an important connection between research use and ethics. Consider the ethical and political dilemmas about how research material is used. These issues are sometimes sharper in qualitative research. This arises partly from the greater closeness and consequent trust that may develop between evaluator and participant. In quantitative research the greater distancing may make these issues less agonizing. The risk of betrayal is also increased because of the typical use of smaller samples, the consequent difficulties of protecting the confidentiality of individuals, and the emphasis on the details of how people live their lives. Finch describes from her playgroups research her 'sense that I could potentially betray my informants as a group, not as individuals' (Finch, 1986: 207). 'Where qualitative research is targeted upon social policy issues, there is the special dilemma that findings could be used to *worsen* the situation of the target population in some way' (Finch, 1985: 117).

But none of these caveats reduces the overall value of careful elaboration of what we mean when we speak of research being useful. For instance, everyday social work discussions of evidence-based practice frequently proceed on a misconception at this point. Practice is not and cannot be 'based' on evidence in the straightforward and unproblematic way envisaged by many of its advocates. The discussion of theory and practice in the final pages of this chapter yield further reasons for this conclusion.[1]

Theorizing research and practice

In Chapter 10 we discussed the three practice-related problems of research and professional practice, reflective inquiry and identity, and whether qualitative inquiry can prove enabling and emancipatory. These all have implications for how we think about the relationship between *practice and theory*. Fook's chapter raises a cluster of such issues, both explicitly and implicitly. For example, is it possible to retain the language of 'bias' in qualitative research? Does it make sense to talk about the relationship between theory and fact? Is it possible to generalize from qualitative research? Whitmore is also concerned about generalization. Hall and Scourfield both draw on the logic of grounded, inductive theorizing, which is familiar in much qualitative and ethnographic work. In this part of the final chapter, we will consider ways in which qualitative research contributes to developments in theory, practice and method in social work.

Readers of a book on qualitative *social work* research will need no convincing that research ought to enhance practice. They may need greater persuasion that it ought to enhance theorizing, either by researchers or practitioners. If they consider theory at all, then practitioners are likely to regard it as something developed by social scientists, advocated during training, and available as a rather abstract framework that may be applied to practice. We opened this book by declaring our sympathy for practitioners who flinch at the thought of swallowing the latest dose of expert knowledge. Their misgivings about theories and theorizing are sometimes reinforced by their realization that 'interpretive and social constructionist approaches are . . . ambivalent in regard to the ability of researchers to generate explanations' (Brodie, 2000: 2). This stems from a variety of factors. Qualitative researchers sometimes appear to take a hands-off approach to explaining and making judgements. They favour a descriptive rather than prescriptive approach to values, and prefer that research should be 'oriented to understanding the case more or less as a whole, not for patching its pieces and fixing its problems' (Stake, 1991: 77). This stance goes back to the roots of qualitative research, which provide researchers with 'powerful disincentives to assert responsibility for more than their story. The applicability of the story to other contexts is a judgement left to others' (Greene, 1993: 40–1). Local relevance and the human story are regarded as the primary goals of qualitative research, and not generalizability.

This open-minded stance can give qualitative research in social work 'a *prima donna* image' (Simon, 1986: 52). 'In insisting that ethnographers have the freedom to define problems after they get into the field, ethnography's representatives inadvertently may do more to keep ethnography out of policy research than to keep pretenders out of doing ethnography' (p. 55).

Theory and theorizing

Qualitative researchers have not adopted a unanimous stance of theoretical indifference. Finch, for example, has argued that a concern with theoretically informed empirical research is quite compatible with qualitative research, that a blend of theory and data is the hallmark of good qualitative work, and that 'this particular blend produces precisely the kind of work that is likely to make an impact upon policy because it offers theoretical insights grounded in evidence' (Finch, 1986: 174). Greene (1993) specifies what this might entail. We should

- explicate our own theoretical predispositions;
- describe locally-held theories ('locally meaningful theoretical perspectives in data interpretation' (Greene, 1993: 38));
- attend to emergent theoretical issues;
- integrate substantive theory into research conclusions and recommendations.

'Theory' is, of course, elusive. Once we acknowledge the theory-laden character of all observations, then the distinction between theories and data acquires an inevitable haziness. Even if we accept the need to use the language of theorizing, difficulties continue to occur because 'theory' may refer to formal propositions, worldviews, or working hypotheses. Social work practitioners often use the term in a colloquial sense to refer to models of intervention.

More recently, attention has helpfully moved to recognize the similarities and differences between lay and expert knowledge. The assumption that researchers possess expert knowledge that is different from and inherently superior to 'citizen science' has been widely questioned. The conclusion has been widely reached that 'the products of systematic inquiry will not necessarily be better than the presuppositions built into traditional ways of doing things. It is a modernist fallacy to assume otherwise' (Hammersley, 1993a: 438).

Reflection on the cultural significance of common-sense knowledge, practical knowledge, praxis, tacit knowledge and lay theorizing has substantially reconfigured conventional ideas of the relationship between theory and practice, and served to question the assumptions behind some forms of quantitative inquiry.

Common sense   Campbell gave early expression to some of these ideas. Writing in 1974 when 'many of our ablest and most dedicated graduate students are increasingly opting for the qualitative, humanistic mode' (1979: 49), he expounded his insistence that qualitative, common-sense knowing is the building block and test of quantitative knowing.

Anthropologists, such as Geertz, have suggested several reasons why we should treat common sense as a cultural system – 'a relatively organized body of thought, rather than just what anyone clothed and in his right mind knows' (Geertz, 1983: 75). If it *is* a cultural system and not mere matter-of-fact apprehension of reality, then 'there is an ingenerate order to it, capable of being empirically uncovered and conceptually formulated' (p. 92). It is here, of course, that the argument 'bites' on qualitative research. Pleas to treat common sense seriously must in part include pleas to treat it empirically. Common-sense pictures of the odd, the deviant, the tediously mundane, and the difficult, provide us with out-of-way cases, and are hence of use to us anthropologically, by setting nearby cases in an altered context.

Geertz undertakes this 'disaggregation of a half examined concept' (p. 93). He contends that the uses we gain from common sense are by understanding its 'stylistic features, the marks of attitude that give it its peculiar stamp' (p. 85), rather than its varied content. He identifies properties of 'naturalness', 'practicalness', 'thinness', 'immethodicalness', and 'accessibleness' as those general attributes of common sense found everywhere as a cultural form.

Common sense is, however, not to be seen as a way of sense-making characteristic only of untutored citizens, and explained by the professional or academic expert. Recent reflections on the place of professional practice wisdom owe an indirect debt to this realization. If evaluation is to be relevant, it cannot ignore the common-sense ways in which practitioners endeavour to make evaluative sense of their practical activities (Shaw and Shaw, 1997a, 1997b). In a similar way, recognizing the role of informal logic means that we also need to discover how researchers draw conclusions about evidence.

Tacit knowledge   Common-sense knowledge will often be tacit knowledge. The notion that experts have tacit knowledge was first introduced by Polanyi (1958). The idea has been refined and applied to fields as diverse as medical practice and laser building, social work and the development of nuclear weapons. Tacit knowledge can be defined as knowledge or abilities that can be passed between experts by personal contact but cannot be, or has not been, set out or passed on in formal statements, diagrams, verbal descriptions or instructions for action (Collins, 2000).

The question arises whether tacit, implicit understanding is in tension with more explicit, planned, qualitative research. Stake may seem to suggest as much when he and Trumbull argue that

> For practitioners . . . formal knowledge is not necessarily a stepping stone to improved practice . . . We maintain that practice is guided far more by personal knowings. (Stake and Trumbull, 1982: 5)

Although they do not dismiss formal knowledge, 'the leverage point for change too often neglected is the disciplined collection of experiential knowledge' (pp. 8–9). On this view, good qualitative inquiry will reveal tacit knowledge – 'the largely unarticulated, contextual understanding that is often manifested in nods, silences, humour and naughty nuances' (Altheide and Johnson, 1994: 492). There are actions, judgements and recognitions which we accomplish spontaneously. We do not have to think about them prior to performance. We are often unaware of having learned to do them. While we may remember once being aware of the understanding necessary for action, we typically are now unable to describe the knowings that our actions reveal. It has become 'thinking as usual' knowledge.

> Tacit knowledge exists in that time when action is taken that is not understood, when understanding is offered without articulation, and when conclusions are apprehended without an argument. (Altheide and Johnson, 1994: 492)

The research problem posed by this largely non-discursive knowledge is 'how to talk about what is seldom spoken about' (p. 493). Qualitative researchers in social work often seem ambivalent regarding such knowl-

edge, tending to oscillate between seeing it as potentially liberating or constraining (cf. Scott, 1990). However, there is nothing intrinsically wrong
about an implicit, unarticulated theory. 'Reality is what we choose not to
question at the moment', and 'the better shape science is in, the more
the positions are implicit' (Becker, 1993: 220). A consequence of prioritizing
qualitative work in social work ought to be that different kinds of tacit
knowledge are recognized. The significance of personal contact and practical knowledge sharing between social work practitioners will be brought
out, and sources of trust and mistrust between social workers made clear
(Collins, 2000). This is a big agenda, and one that social work has only
begun to tackle.

Practical knowledge   But this raises a further question. What do we mean
when we refer to 'practical' knowledge? There has been a renewed influence of Aristotelian views of theory and practice on writers in diverse
fields such as ethnography (Hammersley, 1992), constructivism (Schwandt,
1993) and critical evaluation (Carr and Kemmis, 1986). The main effects of
this have been twofold. First, it has led to a welcome reinstatement of the
ethical dimension of reasoning and practice. Second, it has rescued notions
of the practical from its status as second tier, derivative, and derived pre-
scriptively from formal theory. For example, Schwab's influential paper
on understanding curriculum argued for a language of the practical rather
than the theoretical. By practical 'I do *not* mean . . . the easily achieved,
familiar goals which can be reached by familiar means' (Schwab, 1969: 1),
but rather 'a complex discipline . . . concerned with choice and action'
(pp. 1–2).
   Schwandt distinguishes theoretical knowledge ('knowing that'), craft or
skill knowledge ('knowing how'), and practical-moral knowledge ('knowing from'). Ethical reasoning takes place through practical wisdom.
Schwandt wishes to recast evaluative research within this kind of practical
hermeneutics. When we talk about 'application', something more is
intended than the instrumental sense of practicality, but the more fundamental sense of making something relevant to oneself. This involves a
particular kind of knowledge – 'knowing from within or practical-moral
knowledge', which 'requires not cleverness in application but understanding' (Schwandt, 1997: 76). 'Practical-moral knowledge aims to actually
move people, not simply give them good ideas' (p. 81).
   The contributors to this book have no interest in downplaying analytical
knowledge. Reid may be correct when he concludes that 'flawed research
may be better evidence than "low grade" practice wisdom' (Reid, 1994:
476). But we do hope to persuade social workers to abandon the polarized
tensions between 'theory' and 'practice'. To this end, an appreciation of
'practical hermeneutics' will help deliver social workers from seeing good
practice and good qualitative research as the inculcation of hierarchical
knowledge-from-above.

Local relevance and general knowledge

We reminded ourselves at the start of this discussion of theory and practice that qualitative researchers have emphasized the importance of the locally relevant story, and the applicability of the story to other contexts has tended to be a judgement left to others. Miller and Crabtree put it as follows: 'Local context and the human story . . . are the primary goals of qualitative research and not "generalisability"' (1994: 348). There is no way that qualitative researchers should have cold feet about the main thrust of this position, under pressure from advocates of tight evaluation designs, and research funders who talk darkly about 'anecdotalism'. Schwab had in mind the application of curriculum initiatives to schools, but his remarks hold good for analogous applications of intervention initiatives in social work agencies.

> The curriculum will be brought to bear not in some archetypal classroom but in a particular locus in time and space with smells, shadows, seats and conditions outside its walls which may have much to do with what is achieved inside. (Schwab, 1969: 12)

Does this mean, then, that advocates of qualitative work in social work should give up any thought of claiming wider relevance and generality for their work? Indeed, should we go still further and in the name of political and philosophical opposition to modernism reject any act of generalization across social contexts as an act of despotism (Lyotard, in Seale, 1999: 13)? We do not think so. Questions of generalization are closely similar to those regarding outcomes that we discussed earlier in this chapter. They take us immediately back to the basic mind-set that we bring to qualitative inquiry, and to the inadequacies of the functional division-of-labour approach – the horses for courses line of argument – that we have reasoned against through this book. That line of argument could be put in the following way. Qualitative and quantitative method-ologies have their particular strengths. Qualitative research is strong on elucidating process and meaning – quantitative research is the prime vehicle if we need to make inferences regarding causes and outcomes, and if we need to draw conclusions that can be applied more generally. In much social work research, so the reasoning goes, we need to draw exactly the kinds of inference that quantitative research facilitates.

Before we can directly answer the questions, if and how qualitative research can provide a grounding for inferences to other local contexts, we need to heed the implications of our previous consideration of the rela-tionship between scientific and citizen theorizing. If the two are in closer proximity to one another than conventional ideas of science might lead us to assume, then we should also avoid treating ideas of generalization as technical matters constrained within an expert field of discourse.

Processes of drawing judgements about wider application and relevance are not limited to scientists. The process of generalization is present in all learning, and a grasp of generalization in qualitative research will be stronger for an awareness of how we generalize lessons in everyday life. Eisner distinguishes 'generalizing' in the sense of the exact application of what was learned in situation A to situation B, from 'transfer', in which we recognize that all situations are different to some extent. The expression 'transfer of learning' captures exactly his implicit distinction.

> Since no generalization can fit an individual context perfectly, modification is always necessary. This modification requires judgement on the part of intelligent practitioners. (Eisner, 1991: 212)

Pugh has demonstrated the value of reflecting on ideas of categorization, particularization, prototypes and stereotyping for social work practice (Pugh, 1998). Starting from a discussion of generalizing and particularizing in cognitive processing, he develops a critique of unduly simplistic ideas of stereotyping as they have been applied to anti-discriminatory practice. Discussions of this kind are immediately helpful for social work practice, and they are also valuable for the links they point to between everyday, professional and research thinking about those processes. For example, practitioners' understanding of processes of clinical inference will be enriched from a comparison with inferential processes in qualitative research (Erikson, 1959; Geertz, 1973).

Qualitative research contributes to conclusions about wider generality in several ways. First, by questioning an over-optimistic reliance on inferences from internal validity in controlled intervention studies, and by cautioning against the naïve transfer of logics of representativeness and probability from conventional research designs. Second, and more positively, by a productive emphasis on theoretically defensible strategies of generalization, such as naturalistic generalization, analytical generalization and thick description.

Internal and external validity The expression 'internal validity' was coined by Donald Campbell, to describe the confidence with which inferences could be drawn about the relationship between independent and dependent variables within programmes. Of what use, he would argue, is generalizing a relationship if one doubts the relationship itself. His elaboration of threats to internal validity is likely to remain the standard statement.

Lee Cronbach argued in response to the work of Campbell on internal validity and Scriven on the centrality of summative evaluation, that '"external validity" – the validity of inferences that go beyond the data – is the crux of social action, not "internal validity"' (Cronbach et al., 1980: 231). For Campbell, internal validity is about the relations between interventions and outcomes in a given random sample. For Cronbach, experimental designs that rely on rigorous inferences are weak at the very point they claim to be strong – i.e. as context-free statements that will safely gener-alize. 'Campbell's writings make internal validity a property of trivial, past tense, and local statements' (Cronbach, 1982: 137). Cronbach priori-tizes the understanding and explanation of mechanisms operating in a local context, in order that plausible inferences can be drawn regarding other settings, people and interventions that are of interest to policy-makers. It is extrapolation that matters, and validity that goes beyond the data – 'a prediction about what will be observed in a study where the subjects or operations depart in some respect from the original study' (Cronbach, 1986: 94).

Cronbach's arguments are largely unfamiliar within social work, but they have methodologically-radical implications that bear on both qualitative and quantitative research. The issue for him is how we can establish research that will enable us to generalize to people, interventions and set-tings *that were not sampled and are different*. In order to achieve this local, contextualized understanding he rejects the notion of research in which 'the program is to play statue while the evaluator's slow film records its picture' (Cronbach et al., 1980: 56), in favour of case studies that draw primarily though not exclusively on qualitative methods. It is not 'before and after', but 'during-during-during' as he somewhere says, and 'planning inquiry . . . is the art of recognizing tradeoffs and placing bets' (Cronbach, 1986: 103).

We have given space to these arguments partly because they are absent from much routine debate within social work research. We are convinced that this 'tough-minded master of conceptual distinctions' (Scriven, 1986: 15) provides qualitative social work research with a rigorous framework that creates 'truly unique alternatives sensitive to the scholarly need for general knowledge and the practitioner need for local application' (Shadish et al., 1990: 375).[2] There are some problematic aspects and limitations to Cronbach's theory (Shaw, 1999a: Chs 2 and 5), yet these are outweighed by the relevance of his work for debates within qualitative evaluation research about generalization, causal explanations, multi-site case studies, and the policy relevance of research.

Statistical generalization   Qualitative researchers have rightly been wary of the conventional logic of generalization based on probability sampling. However, models of statistical generalization have occasionally been used effectively, for example with multiple case studies. Sinclair reported a large-scale study of hostels for young male offenders that utilized an impressive range of data to draw conclusions regarding the effect of hostel environments on offending (Sinclair, 1970). He went on to argue with others that

> The comparison of a large number of institutions within a single study enables a
> serious weakness of descriptive case studies to be overcome. This is the difficulty

of linking the precise features of the care provided with its immediate and long term effects. (Tizard et al., 1975: 3)

Yet the problems usually outweigh the gains. Conclusions based on probabilities are of limited utility in specific cases. While we might know that 'on average' a particular project, social work intervention, or correctional programme has a given chance of being successful, this does not help us to weigh the particular contingencies for a specific choice. We lose 'case identity', and are left with faceless generalizations. Also, the typical situation facing practitioners, carers or agency managers is not one of exact generalization, but, to repeat Eisner's term, transfer to settings or interventions which are different to some degree.

Analytical generalization Beginning social work researchers often find it hard to envisage an alternative to statistical approaches to generalization. They may tend to revert to analogies with samples and populations, along with assumptions of minimum viable sample sizes. However, using case study designs as an example, when selecting more than one case the logic is not that of sampling but of replication. 'Each case must be selected so that it either (a) predicts similar results (a *literal replication*) or (b) produces contrasting results but for predictable reasons (a *theoretical replication*)' (Yin, 1994: 46).

By way of parenthesis, we should note that Yin's argument should not be confused with the idea that we can extrapolate from particular agencies, families, and other complex unities, on the grounds that the smaller case is a microcosm (literally, a 'little world') of the larger world. This doctrine of a constant analogy between universal nature (the macrocosm) and human nature (the microcosm) is a seductive argument, because it may seem to solve our problems in one move. There certainly are instances where samples of one have intrinsic interest, and we do not need to take the extreme position that cases simply share a common difference. But faith that individual 'cases' are microcosms is a chimera – in Geertz's terms, 'palpable nonsense', and 'an idea which only someone too long in the bush could possibly entertain' (Geertz, 1973: 22)!

A common theoretically-guided approach to generalization is analytic induction. The method proceeds by employing the notion of a 'generic problem', which is applied through explicit and implicit comparisons of instances (Atkinson and Delamont, 1993). The use of this constant comparative method, including the identification of critical and deviant cases, enables the identification of common features between cases. This brief description of analytic approaches illustrates that inferences about generalization are logical ones rather than statistical. Qualitative methods lend themselves more readily to logic of this kind, because 'the place of generalization in social work is closer to the constructivist, naturalistic orientation . . . than to the position of logical positivists' (Reid, 1994: 470).

Vicarious generalization A different approach to generalization is associated with logic that seeks to bridge the experience yielded by the research
and the experience of the research participants and audience. Stake and
Trumbull have evaluative research in mind when they say:

> We believe that program evaluation studies should be planned and carried out in
> such a way as to provide a maximum of vicarious experience to the readers who
> may then intuitively combine this with their previous experience. (Stake and
> Trumbull, 1982: 2)

These are 'self-generated knowings, naturalistic generalisations, that come
when, individually, for each reader, each practitioner, new experience is
added to old' (p. 5). It is the evocation of personal experience that leads,
in their view, to the improvement of practice.

Eisner's ideas of connoisseurship and criticism are based on the same
broad approach to generalization. Eisner poses the interesting question
of the different points of focus for generalization. He wants to include in
this the superficially paradoxical idea of 'retrospective generalization',
which occurs when we see our past in a new light, naming something so
that we can find a new significance in an array of past experience. We
'find a fit between a general statement and our personal histories. New
ideas can reconstruct our past' (Eisner, 1991: 206).

Approaches based on personal experience are difficult to assess, and
are open to the criticism that they diminish the possibility of generalizing
inferences that challenge the wider, structural status quo. They tend to
assume a consensual moral framework, and fit well with Stake's emphasis
on stakeholder case studies. The basic ideas are challenging, but they need
development.

Thick description What defines anthropology is the kind of intellectual
effort it is – an elaborate venture in 'thick description'. So reasoned
Geertz, in what has become a point of reference for subsequent discussion.
It is difficult to read a text on qualitative research without running into the
expression. It is his vision of the relationship between the obscure and the
public, the small and the broadscale, which carries appeal. His argument is
inspirational rather than didactic, and is constructed around a fieldwork
account of Jews, Berbers and French in Morocco in 1912, and an elaborate
story of sheep stealing. He stresses the microscopic character of ethnographic descriptions. 'The anthropologist characteristically approaches . . .
broader interpretations . . . from the direction of exceedingly extended
acquaintances with extremely small matters' (Geertz, 1973: 21). He confronts grand realities of Power, Faith, Oppression, Prestige, Status and
Love, 'but he [sic] confronts them in contexts small enough to take the
capital letters off' (p. 21). Anthropology involves 'looking at the ordinary
in places where it takes unaccustomed forms', so that 'understanding a
people's culture exposes their normalness without reducing their particu-

larity' (p. 14). 'What generality it contrives to achieve grows out of the delicacy of its distinctions, not the sweep of its abstractions' (p. 25).

In his eminently quotable phrase, 'small facts speak to large issues, winks to epistemology, or sheep raids to revolution' (p. 23). Hence, 'The essential task of theory building . . . is not to codify abstract regularities but to make thick description possible, not to generalize across cases, but to generalize within them' (p. 26). The vocation of interpretive anthropology 'is not to answer our deepest questions, but to make available to us answers that others, guarding other sheep in other valleys, have given, and thus to include them in the consultable record of what man has said' (p. 30).

The argument for qualitative research has never been that its claims for generalizability are outstandingly strong. Yet this brief overview demonstrates that qualitative methods should not be avoided because of the fear that their claims for wider relevance are especially weak. This is not the case. Kushner concludes,

> I try always to stay confused by this issue. I believe viscerally in the uniqueness of cases – and this leads me to believe in the necessity to measure quality of . . . processes anew in each context . . . On the other hand my commitment to social justice demands a distributive principle which insists upon comparative measures . . . The tension is irresolvable, I think. But . . . this tension is a rich one. (It) lies at the heart of case study approaches. (Saville Kushner)[3]

Theory and practice

We have engaged in an act of attempted persuasion about the centrality and relevance of concerns about theory and its relationship with practice in qualitative research. First, theory must be reconnected to everyday reasoning by practitioners and service users. Second, qualitative research should not be sidelined on the specious grounds that it is weak at the particular points at which social work most needs a research input. In countering this we opened the chapter with a discussion of the ways in which qualitative social work research challenges and deepens understanding of human service outcomes, and closed it by exploring ways in which we can make plausible claims to wider generalities while sustaining the local and particular.

What conclusions can we draw?   In the first place, we should not be precious about our theories. Too much time spent discussing theory is paralysing. We need to defend social work against attacks, and hence need those people who pursue 'philosophical and methodological worry as a profession' (Becker, 1993: 226). But while we still have to do theoretical work, 'we needn't think we are being especially virtuous when we do it' (p. 221). There are some circumstances where theory has been overemphasized. For example, emancipatory researchers, especially some of those whose work is underpinned by neo-Marxism, should not feel too aggrieved by Lather's vigorous insider warnings against theoretical imperialism – the 'circle where theory is reinforced by experience conditioned by theory' (Lather, 1986b: 261). 'Theory is too often used to protect us from the awesome complexity of the world' and

> In the name of emancipation, researchers impose meanings on situations rather than constructing meaning through negotiation with research participants. (1986b: 265, 267)

Too often, 'one is left with the impression that the research conducted provides empirical specificities for more general, *a priori* theories' (Lather, 1986a: 76).

Lather's remarks point to our second conclusion – that at their worst 'scientific concepts can reinforce a vast array of dangerous or hateful political and moral agendas' (Jacob, 1992: 495).

Third, we should not retreat behind the bunker of the threat of abuse by theory to protect ourselves against the demand that theory and critique must go hand in hand. When theory/practice relationships are viewed as the failure of practitioners to apply the theories developed by those who are engaged in empirical and theoretical pursuits, this distorts reality. To regard theory and practice problems as breakdowns in communication that afflict practitioners is to fail to recognize that practical problems of this kind occur in the course of any theoretical undertaking. To assume that they can somehow be identified and tackled in theory and then 'applied' in practice tends to conceal how they are generated out of practice. As Parton reminds us, practice informs the development of theory as much as, if not more than, *vice versa* (Parton, 2000). To put it more specifically, theoretical problems in social work have in part a social work character. We made this point in our reflections on the limitations of practitioner research in the previous chapter. Fahl and Markand's point about psychology will stand for social science in general when they conclude that 'if *existing* academic psychology and existing professional psychological practice can only be brought together with difficulty, then this "only" says that this type of psychology needs to be criticized and *developed*' (Fahl and Markand, 1999: 75).

Fourth, we should concur with Hall when he questions in his chapter the idea that research is either 'academic' or 'applied'. He remarks that 'one can see what is meant by this distinction . . . but all social research, inasmuch as it is about and results from an engagement with the social world, is "applied"'.

Finally, our vision of the relationship between social work and research must never be utopian – but it must always be radical. It was possibly Einstein who said that 'Things should be as simple as possible, but not any simpler.' Qualitative theory and research should persistently entice us with glimpses of the possibility of seeing the world differently. 'The impact of theory will perhaps be greatest where the ideas have sufficient "fit" with the issues professionals encounter on an everyday basis, while at the same time providing an alternative framework within which to understand these issues' (Brodie, 2000).

In our consideration of generalization in qualitative research we implicitly questioned strong versions of relativism in social research. It is true that 'in effect you have to be a relativist if you are going to study any historical moment in science' (Jacob, 1992: 500). White has drawn on Hacking's work in her contribution to this book, and he expands this stance to argue that relativism can helpfully be adopted as an interesting way of thinking if one is trying to understand a person or another culture (Hacking, 1999). But this willing suspension of belief as an attitude of mind should not be confused with relativism – that combination of 'intuitionism and alchemy' (Geertz, 1973: 30).

> Science can be socially framed, possess political meaning, and also occasionally be sufficiently true, or less false, in such a way that we cherish its findings. The challenge comes in trying to understand how knowledge worth preserving occurs in time, possesses deep social relations, and can also be progressive . . . and seen to be worthy of preservation. (Jacob, 1992: 501)

Notes

1. For a more extended consideration of the uses of qualitative research see Shaw, 1999a.
2. Shaw has described and drawn extensively on aspects of Cronbach's work as applied to qualitative evaluation methodology in the fields of education and human services (Shaw, 1999a).
3. This is extracted from an exchange about case studies of schools, on the American Evaluation Association Discussion List in November 1998.

Recommended reading

For reasons we have discussed in this chapter, qualitative researchers have not written extensively on outcomes issues. Writers who specialize in evaluation research have done some of the main work. A fairly orthodox discussion of outcomes, by a writer sympathetic to qualitative research, has been provided by Weiss (1998). An introduction to outcomes that is more oriented to the claims of qualitative methodology can be read in Shaw (1999a). We have sketched some of the argument from Miles and Huberman (1994), and they devote considerable space to causal issues, and hence by extension to outcome-related questions.

There is no recent book on the uses of qualitative research. The better books were written some time ago, although they are not written in terms of more recent ideas about evidenced-based practice and the debates about reflective learning and justice discussed in Chapter 10. However, the books by writers such as Bulmer (1982) and Finch (1986) are well worth the time spent reading them. The American work of Carol Weiss resonates closely with these books, and will be read with benefit (e.g. Weiss, 1988). Patton writes with a pragmatic and therefore use-oriented approach to qualitative evaluation (Patton, 1997).

The relationship between practice and theory is a wide-ranging problem that needs to be read from different starting points. The chapter shows the writers with whom we share sympathies, and the sources can be followed up. Rather than repeat the sources here, we would recommend following up the ones that interest and challenge you, from the references. But for a stimulating starting point, we recommend the indispensable essay on common-sense knowledge by Geertz (1983).

References

Acker, J. and Esseveld, J. (1983) 'Objectivity and truth: problems in doing feminist research', *Women's Studies International Forum*, 6 (4): 423–35.

Adler, P.A. and Adler, P. (1996) 'Parent-as-researcher: The politics of researching in the personal life', *Qualitative Sociology*, 19 (1): 35–58.

Agar, M. (1980) *The Professional Stranger: An Informal Introduction to Ethnography*. New York: Academic Press.

Altheide, D.L. and Johnson, J.M. (1994) 'Criteria for assessing interpretive validity in qualitative research', in N. Denzin and Y. Lincoln (eds), *Handbook of Qualitative Methods*. Thousand Oaks: Sage.

Altheide, D.L. and Johnson, J.M. (1997) 'Ethnography and justice', in G. Miller and R. Dingwall (eds), *Context and Method in Qualitative Research*. London: Sage.

Archbold, P. (1986) 'Ethical issues in qualitative research', in C.W. Chenitz and J. Swanson (eds), *From Practice the Grounded Theory: Qualitative Research In Nursing*. California: Addison-Wesley.

Argyris, C. and Schon, D. (1974) *Theory in Practice: Increasing Professional Effectiveness*. San Francisco: Jossey-Bass.

Arnold, R., Burke, B., James, C., Martin, D. and Thomas, B. (1991) *Educating for a Change*. Toronto: Between the Lines and the Doris Marshall Institute.

Atkinson, P. (1995a) *Medical Talk and Medical Work*. London: Sage.

Atkinson, P. (1995b) 'Some perils of paradigms', *Qualitative Health Research*, 5: 117–24.

Atkinson, P. (1997) 'Narrative turn or blind alley?', *Qualitative Health Research*, 7 (3): 325–44.

Atkinson, P. and Coffey, A. (1997) 'Analyzing documentary realities', in D. Silverman (ed.), *Qualitative Research*. London: Sage.

Atkinson, P. and Delamont, S. (1993) 'Bread and dreams or bread and circuses? A critique of case study research in evaluation', in M. Hammersley (ed.), *Controversies in the Classroom*. Buckingham: Open University Press.

Atkinson, P., Delamont, S. and Hammersley, M. (1988) 'Qualitative research traditions: A British response to Jacob', *Review of Educational Research*, 58 (2): 231–50.

Atkinson, P. and Hammersley, M. (1994) 'Ethnography and participant observation', in N.K. Denzin and Y.S. Lincoln (eds), *Handbook of Qualitative Research*. Thousand Oaks, CA: Sage.

Atkinson, P. and Silverman, D. (1997) 'Kundera's "immortality": The interview society and the invention of self', *Qualitative Inquiry*, 3: 304–25.

Aull Davies, C. (1999) *Reflexive Ethnography: A Guide to Researching Selves and Others*. London: Routledge.

Avery, M. et al. (1981) 'Techniques for group building', in *Building United Judgement: A Handbook For Consensus Decision-Making*. Madison, WI: Center for Conflict Resolution.

Baldock, J. and Prior, D. (1981) 'Social workers talking to clients', *British Journal of Social Work*, 11: 19–38.

Baldwin, M. (1997) 'Day care on the move: Learning from a participative action research project at a day centre for people with learning difficulties', *British Journal of Social Work*, 27: 951–8.

Baldwin, M. (2000) *Care Management and Community Care: Social Work Discretion and the Construction of Policy*. Aldershot: Ashgate.

Banks, C.K. and Wideman, G. (1996) 'The company of neighbours: Building social support through the use of ethnography', *International Social Work*, 39 (3): 317–28.

Barnes, C. (1996) Disability and the myth of the independent researcher', *Disability and Society*, 11: 107–10.

Barnsley, J. and Ellis, D. (1992) *Research for Change: Participatory Action Research for Community Groups*. Vancouver: Women's Research Centre.

Barone, T.E. (1992) 'Beyond theory and method: a case of critical story telling', *Theory into Practice*, 31 (2): 142–6.

Beck, C.T. (1993) 'Qualitative research: The evaluation of its credibility, fittingness, and auditability', *Western Journal of Nursing Research*, 15 (2): 263–6.

Beck, U. (1992) *The Risk Society*. London: Sage.

Becker, H. (1963) *Outsiders: Studies in the Sociology of Deviance*. London: Sage.

Becker, H. (1993) 'Theory: the necessary evil', in D. Flinders and G. Mills (eds), *Theory and Concepts in Qualitative Research: Perspectives from the Field*. New York: Teachers College, Columbia University Press.

Behar, R. (1993) *Translated Woman: Crossing the Border with Esperanza's Story*. Boston: Beacon.

Bein, A. and Allen, K. (1999) 'Hand in glove? It fits better than you think', *Social Work*, 44 (3): 274–7.

Belcher, J.R. (1991) 'Moving into homelessness after psychiatric hospitalization', *Journal of Social Service Research*, 14 (3–4): 63–77.

Belcher, J.R. (1994) 'Understanding the process of drift among the homeless: a qualitative analysis', in E. Sherman, and W.J. Reid (eds), *Qualitative Research in Social Work*. New York: Columbia University Press.

Belcher, J.R., Scholler-Jaquish, A. and Drummond, M. (1991) 'Stages of homelessness: a conceptual model of social workers in health care', *Health and Social Work*, 1: 87–93.

Bell, S.E. (1988) 'Becoming a political woman: The reconstruction and interpretation of experience through stories', in A.D. Todd and S. Fisher (eds), *Gender and Discourse: The Power of Talk*. Norwood, NJ: Ablex.

Bell, S.E. (1999) 'Narratives and lives: women's health politics and the diagnosis of cancer for DES daughters', *Narrative Inquiry*, 9 (2): 1–43.

Bemak, F. (1996) 'Street researchers: A new paradigm redefining future research with street children', *Childhood*, 3 (2): 147–56.

Benner, P. (1984) *From Novice to Expert: Excellence and Power in Clinical Nursing*. Menlo Park: Addison Wesley.

Bernstein, S.R. and Epstein, I. (1994) 'Grounded theory meets the reflective practitioner', in E. Sherman and W.J. Reid (eds), *Qualitative Research in Social Work*. New York: Columbia University Press.

Besa, D. (1994) 'Evaluating narrative family therapy using single-system research designs', *Research on Social Work Practice*, 4 (3): 309–25.

Best, J. (1989) 'Debates about constructionism', in E. Rubington and M.S. Weinberg (eds), *The Study of Social Problems: Seven Perspectives*. New York: Oxford University Press.

Biestek, F.P. (1961) *The Casework Relationship*. London: Allen & Unwin.

Blair, J.A. (1995) 'Informal logic and reasoning in evaluation', in D.M. Fournier (ed.), *New Directions For Evaluation*, No. 68 *Reasoning in Evaluation: Inferential Links and Leaps*. San Francisco: Jossey-Bass.

Bloom, A.A. (1980) 'Social work and the English language', *Social Casework*, 61: 332–8.

Bloor, M. (1997a) 'Addressing social problems through qualitative research', in D. Silverman, (ed.), *Qualitative Research: Theory, Method and Practice*. London: Sage.

Bloor, M. (1997b) 'Observations of abortive illness behaviour', in M. Bloor (ed.), *Selected Writings in Medical Sociological Research*. Aldershot: Ashgate.

Bogdan, R. and Taylor, S. (1994) 'A positive approach to qualitative evaluation and policy research in social work', in E. Sherman and W. Reid (eds), *Qualitative Research in Social Work*. New York: Columbia University Press.

Boje, D.M. (1991) 'The storytelling organization: A study of story performance in an office-supply firm', *Administrative Science Quarterly*, 36: 106–26.

Borden, W. (1992) 'Narrative perspectives in pychosocial intervention following adverse life events', *Social Work*, 37 (2): 135–41.

Bourdieu, P. (1977a) 'Afterword' to P. Rabinow, *Reflections on Fieldwork in Morocco*. Berkeley: University of California Press.

Bourdieu, P. (1977b) *Outline of a Theory of Practice*. Cambridge: Cambridge University Press.

Bowen, D. (1993) 'The delights of learning to apply the life history method to school non-attenders', in B. Broad and C. Fletcher (eds), *Practitioner Social Work Research in Action*. London: Whiting and Birch.

Brenner, M., Marsh, P. and Brenner, M. (eds) (1978) *The Social Contexts of Method*. London: Croom Helm.

Brodie, I. (2000) 'Theory generation and qualitative research: School exclusion and children looked after', paper from ESRC seminar series 'Theorising social work research', National Institute for Social Work web site <http://www.nisw.org.uk/tswr/brodie.html>

Brun, C. (1997) 'The process and implications of doing qualitative research: An analysis of 54 doctoral dissertations', *Journal of Sociology and Social Welfare*, XXIV (4): 95–112.

Bruner, J. (1986) *Actual Minds, Possible Worlds*. Cambridge, MA: Harvard University Press.

Bruner, J. (1990) *Acts of Meaning*. Cambridge, MA: Harvard University Press.

Bryman, A. (1988) *Quantity and Quality in Social Research*. London: Unwin Hyman.

Bull, R. and Shaw, I. (1992), 'Constructing causal accounts in social work', *Sociology*, 26 (4): 635–49.

Bulmer, M. (1982) *The Uses of Social Research*. London: Allen & Unwin.

Burgess, H. (1992) *Problem-led Learning for Social Work: The Enquiry and Action-Learning Approach*. London: Whiting and Birch.

Burke, B. (1998) 'Evaluating for a change: Reflections on participatory methodology', in E. Whitmore (ed.), *Understanding and Practicing Participatory Evaluation*. New Directions for Evaluation, Vol. 80. San Francisco: Jossey-Bass.

Burman, E. (1994) *Deconstructing Developmental Psychology*. London: Routledge.

Butler, I. (2000) 'A code of ethics for social work and social care research', paper from ESRC seminar series 'Theorising social work research', National Institute for Social Work. http://www.nisw.org.uk/tswr/butler.html.

Campbell, D. (1978) 'Qualitative knowing in action research', in M. Brenner and P. Marsh (eds), *The Social Context of Methods*. London: Croom Helm.

Campbell, D. (1979) 'Degrees of freedom and the case study', in T. Cook and C. Reichardt (eds), *Qualitative and Quantitative Methods in Evaluation Research*. Beverly Hills, CA: Sage.

Capps, L. and Ochs, E. (1995) *Constructing Panic: The Discourse of Agoraphobia*. Cambridge, MA: Harvard University Press.

Carr, D. (1986) *Time, Narrative, and History*. Bloomington: Indiana University Press.

Carr, W. and Kemmis, S. (1986) *Becoming Critical: Education, Knowledge and Action Research.* London: Falmer Press.

Chambers, R. (1997) *Whose Reality Counts? Putting the First Last.* London: Intermediate Technology Publications.

Charon, R. (1986) 'To render the lives of patients', *Literature and Medicine,* 5: 58–74.

Chase, S.E. (1995) *Ambiguous Empowerment: The Work Narratives of Women School Superintendents.* Amherst: University of Massachusetts.

Chelimsky, E. (1997) 'Thoughts for a new evaluation society', *Evaluation,* 3: (1): 97–118.

Clifford, D. (1994) 'Critical life histories', in B. Humphries and C. Truman (eds), *Rethinking Social Research: Anti-Discriminatory Approaches in Research Methodology.* Aldershot: Avebury.

Clifford, J. (1997) *Routes: Travel and Translation in the late Twentieth Century.* Cambridge, MA: Harvard University Press.

Coady, N. and Wolgien, C. (1996) 'Good therapists' views of how they are helpful', *Clinical Social Work Journal,* 24 (3): 311–22.

Cochran-Smith, M. and Lytle, S. (1990) 'Research on teaching and teacher research: the issues that divide', *Educational Researcher,* 19 (2): 2–22.

Cohen-Mitchell, J.B. (2000) 'Disabled women in El Salvador reframing themselves: An economic development program for women', in C. Truman, D. Mertens and B. Humphries (eds), *Research and Inequality.* London: UCL Press. pp. 143–75.

Collins, C., Liken, M., King, S. and Kokinakis, C. (1993) 'Loss and grief among family caregivers of relatives with dementia', *Qualitative Health Research,* 3 (2): 236–53.

Collins, H. (2000) *Tacit Knowledge, Trust and the Q of Sapphire',* Cardiff University School of Social Sciences. Working Paper. <http://www.cf.ac.uk/socsi/>

Collins, P. (1998) 'Negotiating selves: Reflections on "unstructured" interviewing', *Sociological Research Online,* 3 (3): <http://www.socresonline.org.uk/socresonline/3/3/2.html>

Collins, P.H. (1997) 'How much difference is too much? Black feminist thought and the politics of postmodern social theory', *Current Perspectives in Social Theory,* 17: 3–37.

Colquhuon, D. (1996) 'Moving beyond biomedical research in health education', in D. Colquhuon and A. Kellehear (eds), *Health Research and Practice,* Vol. 2. London: Chapman and Hall.

Connell, R.W. (1998) 'Bodies, intellectuals and world society', Plenary address to the British Sociological Association Annual Conference, 'Making Sense of the Body: Theory, Research and Practice', Edinburgh, April.

Cook, J. and Fonow, M. (1986) 'Knowledge and women's interests: Issues in epistemology and methodology in feminist sociology', *Sociological Inquiry,* 56 (winter): 2–29.

Cormican, J.D. (1976) 'Linguistic subcultures and social work practice', *Social Casework,* 57: 589–92.

Critchley, S. (1996) 'Deconstruction and pragmatism – Is Derrida a private ironist or a public liberal', in S. Critchley, J. Derrida, L. Laclau and R. Rorty (ed. C. Mouffe), *Deconstruction and Pragmatism.* London: Routledge.

Cronbach, L. (1982) *Designing Evaluations of Educational and Social Programs.* San Francisco: Jossey-Bass.

Cronbach, L. (1986) 'Social inquiry by and for earthlings', in D. Fiske and R. Shweder (eds), *Metatheory in Social Science: Pluralisms and Subjectivities.* Chicago: University of Chicago Press.

Cronbach, L., Ambron, S., Dornbusch, S., Hess, R., Hornik, R., Phillips, D., Walker, D. and Weiner, S. (1980) *Toward Reform of Program Evaluation.* San Francisco: Jossey-Bass.

Cronon, W. (1992) 'A place for stories: Nature, history, and narrative', *Journal of American History,* 78: 1347–76.

Daly, J. (1998) 'The micropolitics of qualitative health research funding', in J. Daly, A. Kellehear and J. Shoebridge (eds), *Annual Review of Health Social Sciences*, Vol. 8. Palliative Care Unit, La Trobe University, Bundoora.

Davis, L. and Srinivisan, M. (1994) 'Feminist research within a battered women's shelter', in E. Sherman and W.J. Reid (eds), *Qualitative Research in Social Work*. New York: Columbia University Press.

Dean, R.G. (1995) 'Stories of AIDS: The use of narrative as an approach to understanding in an AIDS support group', *Clinical Social Work Journal*, 23 (3): 287–304.

Denzin, N. (1989a) *Interpretive Interactionism*. Englewood Cliffs, NJ: Prentice Hall.

Denzin, N. (1989b) *Interpretive Biography*. Newbury Park, CA: Sage.

Denzin, N. (1989c) *The Research Act in Sociology*. New York: McGraw-Hill.

Denzin, N. and Lincoln, Y. (1994a) 'Entering the field of qualitative research', in N. Denzin and Y. Lincoln (eds), *Handbook of Qualitative Research*. Thousand Oaks, CA: Sage.

Denzin, N. and Lincoln, Y. (1994b) *Handbook of Qualitative Research*. Thousand Oaks, CA: Sage.

Department of Health (1998a) *Modernising Social Services – Promoting Independence, Improving Protection, Raising Standards*. Wetherby: Department of Health.

Department of Health (1998b) *The New NHS, Modern and Dependable: A National Framework for Assessing Performance*. Wetherby: Department of Health.

Derrida, J. (1996) 'Remarks on deconstruction and pragmatism', in S. Critchley, J. Derrida, L. Laclau and R. Rorty (ed. C. Mouffe), *Deconstruction and Pragmatism*. London: Routledge.

DeVault, M.L. (1991) 'Talking and listening from women's standpoint: Feminist strategies for interviewing and analysis', *Social Problems*, 37: 96–116.

Dingwall, R. (1997a) 'Accounts, interviews and observations', in G. Miller and R. Dingwall (eds), *Context and Method in Qualitative Research*. London: Sage.

Dingwall, R. (1997b) 'Conclusion: The moral discourse of interactionism', in G. Miller and R. Dingwall (eds), *Context and Method in Qualitative Research*. London: Sage.

Dingwall, R., Eekelaar, J. and Murray, T. (1983) *The Protection of Children: State Intervention and Family Life*. Oxford: Blackwell.

Dockery, G. (2000) 'Participatory research: Whose roles, whose responsibilities?', in C. Truman, D. Mertens and B. Humphries (eds), *Research and Inequality*. London: UCL Press.

Dreyfus, H. and Dreyfus, S. (1986) *Mind Over Machine: The Power of Human Intuition and Expertise in the Era of the Computer*. Oxford: Basil Blackwell.

Drucker-Brown, S. (1985) 'Participant observation: social anthropologist's view of the label', *Cambridge Anthropology*, 10 (3): 41–73.

Dullea, K. and Mullender, A. (1999) 'Evaluation and empowerment', in I. Shaw and J. Lishman (eds), *Evaluation and Social Work Practice*, London: Sage.

Edgar, I.R. and Russell, A. (eds) (1998) *The Anthropology of Welfare*. London: Routledge.

Eisner, E. (1988) 'Educational connoisseurship and criticism: their form and functions in educational evaluation', in D.M. Fetterman (ed.), *Qualitative Approaches to Evaluation in Education*. New York: Praeger.

Eisner, E. (1991) *The Enlightened Eye: Qualitative Inquiry and the Enhancement of Educational Practice*. New York: Macmillan.

Elks, M. and Kirkhart, K. (1993) 'Evaluating effectiveness from the practitioner's perspective', *Social Work*, 38 (5): 554–63.

Eraut, M. (1994) *Developing Professional Knowledge and Competence*. London: Falmer.

Erikson, E. (1959) 'The nature of clinical inference', in D. Lerner (ed.), *Evidence and Inference*. Illinois: Free Press.

Evans, C. and Fisher, M. (1999) 'Collaborative evaluation with service users: moving towards user-controlled research', in I. Shaw and J. Lishman (eds), *Evaluation and Social Work Practice*. London: Sage.

Everitt, A. (1998) 'Research and development in social work', in R. Adams, L. Dominelli and M. Payne (eds), *Social Work: Themes, Issues and Critical Debates*. London: Macmillan.

Everrit, A., Hardiker, P., Littlewood, J. and Mullender, A. (1992) *Applied Research for Better Practice*. London: Macmillan.

Fahl, R. and Markand, M. (1999) 'The project "Analysis of psychological practice" or: An attempt at connecting psychology critique and practice research', *Outlines*, 1: 73–98.

Farmer, E. and Owen, M. (1998) 'Gender and the child protection process', *British Journal of Social Work*, 28 (4): 545–64.

Fawcett, B. (2000) 'Researching disability: Meanings, interpretations and analysis', in B. Fawcett, B. Featherstone, J. Fook and A. Rossiter (eds), *Practice and Research in Social Work: Postmodern Feminist Perspectives*. London: Routledge.

Fawcett, B., Featherstone, B., Fook, J. and Rossiter, A. (eds) (2000) *Practice and Research in Social Work: Postmodern Feminist Perspectives*. London: Routledge.

Feuerstein, M.-T. (1988) 'Finding the methods to fit the people: Training for participatory evaluation', *Community Development Journal*, 23 (1): 16–25.

Finch, J. (1985) 'Social policy and education: problems and possibilities of using qualitative research', in R. Burgess (ed.), *Issues in Educational Research: Qualitative Methods*. London: Falmer Press.

Finch, J. (1986) *Research and Policy: the Uses of Qualitative Methods in Social and Educational Research*. London: Falmer Press.

Finch, J. and Mason, J. (1990) 'Decision taking in the fieldwork process: theoretical sampling and collaborative working', in R. Burgess (ed.), *Studies in Qualitative Methodology, Vol. 2. Reflections on Field Experience*. Greenwich, CT: JAI.

Fish, B. (1996) 'Clinical implications of attachment narratives', *Clinical Social Work Journal*, 24 (3): 239–53.

Fish, B. and Condon, S. (1994) 'A discussion of current attachment research and its clinical applications', *Child and Adolescent Social Work Journal*, 11 (2): 93–105.

Fisher, M. (1983) *Speaking of Clients*. Sheffield: University of Sheffield.

Fisher, M. (unpublished) 'The role of service users in problem formulation and technical aspects of social research'.

Flanagan, J. (1954) 'The critical incident technique', *Psychology Bulletin*, 51: 327–58.

Flick, U. (1998) *An Introduction To Qualitative Research*. London: Sage.

Fonow, M.M. and Cook, J.A. (eds) (1991) *Beyond Methodology: Feminist Scholarship as Lived Research*. Bloomington: University of Indiana Press.

Fontana, A. and Frey, J.H. (1998) 'Interviewing: the art of science', in D. Denzin and Y. Lincoln (eds), *Collecting and Interpreting Qualitative Materials*. Thousand Oaks, CA: Sage.

Fook, J. (1993) *Radical Casework; A Theory of Practice*. Sydney: Allen & Unwin.

Fook, J. (ed.) (1996) *The Reflective Researcher: Social Workers' Theories of Practice Research*. Sydney: Allen & Unwin.

Fook, J. (1999) 'Reflexivity as method', in J. Daly, A. Kellehear and E. Willis (eds), *Annual Review of Health Social Sciences*. La Trobe University, Bundoora.

Fook, J. (2000a) 'Deconstructing and reconstructing professional expertise', in B. Fawcett, B. Featherstone, J. Fook and A. Rossiter (eds), *Practice and Research in Social Work: Postmodern Feminist Perspectives*. London: Routledge.

Fook, J. (2000b) 'Reflexivity as method', in J. Daly and A. Kellehear, *Annual Review of Health Social Sciences*. Palliative Care Unit, La Trobe University, Bundoora.

Fook, J., Munford, R. and Sanders, J. (1999) 'Evaluation and interviewing', in I. Shaw and J. Lishman (eds), *Evaluation and Social Work Practice*. London: Sage.

Fook, J., Ryan, M. and Hawkins, L. (1996) 'Expertise in social work practice: An exploratory study', *Canadian Social Work Review*, 13 (1): 7–22.

Fook, J., Ryan, M. and Hawkins, L. (1997) 'Towards a theory of social work expertise', *British Journal of Social Work*, 27: 399–417.

Fook, J., Ryan, M. and Hawkins, L. (2000) *Professional Expertise: Practice, Theory and Education for Working in Uncertainty*. London: Whiting and Birch.

Fortune, A. (1994) 'Commentary: Ethnography in social work', in E. Sherman and W. Reid (eds), *Qualitative Research in Social Work*. New York: Columbia University Press.

Foucault, M. (1977) *Discipline and Punish*. Harmondsworth: Penguin.

Foucault, M. (1994) 'An interview with Simon Riggins', in P. Rabinow (ed.), *Michel Foucault: Ethics: The Essential Works*. London: Penguin.

Fournier, D. (ed.) (1995) *Reasoning in Evaluation: Inferential Links and Leaps*. San Francisco: American Evaluation Association/Jossey-Bass.

Fournier, D. and Smith, N. (1993) 'Clarifying the merits of argument in evaluation practice', *Evaluation and Program Planning*, 16 (4): 315–23.

Frank, A.W. (1995) *The Wounded Storyteller: Body, Illness, and Ethics*. Chicago: University of Chicago Press.

Fraser, M.W. (1995) 'Rich, relevant and rigorous: Do qualitative methods measure up?', *Social Work Research*, 19 (1): 25–7.

Freire, P. (1972) *Pedagogy of the Oppressed*. Harmondsworth: Penguin.

Fuller, R. and Petch, A. (1995) *Practitioner Research: The Reflexive Social Worker*. Buckingham: Open University Press.

Furstenberg, A.L. (1989) 'Older people's age self-concept', *Social Casework*, 70 (5): 268–75.

Garfinkel, H. and Sacks, H. (1970) 'On formal structures of practical actions', in J.C. McKinney and E.A. Tirakian (eds), *Theoretical Sociology*. New York: Appleton Century Crofts.

Garrison, J. (1988) 'The impossibility of atheoretical research', *Journal of Educational Thought*, 22 (1): 21–5.

Gaventa, J. (1993) 'The powerful, the powerless and the experts: Knowledge struggles in an information age', in P. Park et al. (eds), *Voices of Change: Participatory Research in the U.S. and Canada*. Toronto: OISE.

Gee, J.P. (1986) 'Units in the production of narrative discourse', *Discourse Processes*, 9: 391–422.

Gee, J.P. (1991) 'A linguistic approach to narrative', *Journal of Narrative and Life History*, 1: 15–39.

Geertz, C. (1973) *The Interpretation of Cultures: Selected Essays*. New York: Basic Books.

Geertz, C. (1979) 'From the native's point of view: on the nature of anthropological understanding', in P. Rabinow and W.M. Sullivan (eds), *Interpretive Social Science: A Reader*. Berkeley: University of California Press. pp. 225–41.

Geertz, C. (1983) *Local Knowledge*. New York: Basic Books.

Geertz, C. (1987) *Works and Lives: The Anthropologist as Author*. Stanford: Stanford University Press.

Gibbs, J.T. and Bankhead-Greene, T. (1997) 'Issues of conducting qualitative research in an inner-city community: A case study of black youth in post-Rodney King Los Angeles', *Journal of Multicultural Social Work*, 6 (1–2): 41–57.

Giddens, A. (1984) *The Constitution of Society: An Outline of a Theory of Structuration*. Cambridge: Polity Press.

Giddens, A. (1987) *Social Theory and Modern Society*. Cambridge: Polity Press.

Giddens, A. (1991) *Modernity and Self-Identity*. Cambridge: Polity Press.

Giddens, A. (1993) *New Rules of Sociological Method*. Stanford: Stanford University Press.

Gilgun, J. (1988) 'Decision-making in interdisciplinary treatment teams', *Child Abuse and Neglect,* 12: 231–9.

Gilgun, J. (1992) 'Hypothesis generation in social work research', *Journal of Social Service Research,* 15 (3–4): 113–35.

Gilgun, J. (1994) 'Hand in glove: The grounded theory approach and social work practice research', in E. Sherman and W.J. Reid (eds), *Qualitative Research in Social Work.* New York: Columbia University Press.

Gilgun, J. and Connor, T.M. (1989) 'How perpetrators view child sexual abuse', *Social Work,* 34: 249–51.

Glaser, B. and Strauss, A. (1967) *The Discovery of Grounded Theory: Strategies for Qualitative Research.* Chicago: Aldine.

Goffman, E. (1961) *Asylums.* New York: Anchor.

Goldstein, A.E., Safarik, L., Reiboldt, W., Albright, L.A. and Kellett, C. (1996) 'An ethnographic approach to understanding service use among ethnically diverse low income families', *Marriage and Family Review,* 24 (3–4): 297–321.

Goldstein, H. (1991) 'Qualitative research and social work practice: Partners in discovery', *Journal of Sociology and Social Welfare,* XVIII (4): 101–19.

Goldstein, H. (1994) 'Ethnography, critical inquiry, and social work practice', in E. Sherman and W.J. Reid (eds), *Qualitative Research in Social Work.* New York: Columbia University Press.

Gordon, L. (1988) *Heroes of Their Own Lives: The Politics and History of Family Violence, Boston 1880–1960.* New York: Viking.

Gould, N. (1989) 'Reflective learning for social work practice', *Social Work Education,* 8 (2): 38–48.

Gould, N. (1994) 'Anti-racist social work: a framework for teaching and action', *Issues in Social Work Education,* 14 (1): 2–17.

Gould, N. (1996) 'Introduction: social work and the crisis of the professions', in N. Gould and I. Taylor (eds), *Reflective Learning for Social Work.* Aldershot: Arena.

Gould, N. (1999a) 'Qualitative practice evaluation', in I. Shaw and J. Lishman (eds), *Evaluation and Social Work Practice.* London: Sage.

Gould, N. (1999b) 'Developing an approach to qualitative audit of inter-disciplinary child protection practice', *Child Abuse Review,* 8: 193–9.

Gould, N. and Harris, A. (1996) 'Student imagery of practice in social work and teacher education: a comparative research approach', *British Journal of Social Work,* 26 (2): 223–38.

Gould, N. and Moultrie, K. (eds) (1997) *Effective Policy, Planning and Implementation: Information Management in Social Services.* Aldershot: Avebury.

Gould, N. and Taylor, I. (eds) (1996) *Reflective Learning For Social Work.* Aldershot: Arena.

Greene, J. (1990) 'Three views on the nature and role of knowledge in social science', in E. Guba (ed.), *The Paradigm Dialog.* Newbury Park, CA: Sage.

Greene, J. (1993) 'The role of theory in qualitative program evaluation', in J. Flinders and G. Mills, *Theory and Concepts in Qualitative Research.* New York: Teachers College Press.

Greene, J. (1994) 'Qualitative program evaluation: practice and promise', in N. Denzin and Y. Lincoln (eds), *Handbook of Qualitative Research.* Thousand Oaks, CA: Sage.

Greene, J. (1996) 'Qualitative evaluation and scientific citizenship', *Evaluation,* 2 (3): 277–89.

Greene, J. and Caracelli, V. (1997) *Advances in Mixed Method Evaluation: The Challenge and Benefits of Integrating Diverse Paradigms.* New Directions For Evaluation, No. 74, San Francisco: Jossey-Bass.

Greenhalgh, T. and Hurwitz, B. (eds) (1998) *Narrative Based Medicine: Dialogue and Discourse in Clinical Practice.* London: BMJ Books.

Greig, A. and Taylor, J. (1999) *Doing Research With Children.* London: Sage.

Greil, A.L. (1991) *Not Yet Pregnant: Infertile Couples in Contemporary America*. New Brunswick, NJ: Rutgers University Press.

Grillo, R.D. (1985) *Ideologies and Institutions in Urban France*. Cambridge: Cambridge University Press.

Guba, E. (ed.) (1990) *The Paradigm Dialog*. Newbury Park, CA: Sage.

Guba, E. and Lincoln, Y. (1988) 'Do inquiry paradigms imply inquiry methodologies?', in D. Fetterman (ed.), *Qualitative Approaches to Evaluation in Education*. New York: Praeger.

Guba, E. and Lincoln, Y. (1994) 'Competing paradigms in qualitative research', in N. Denzin. and Y. Lincoln (eds), *Handbook of Qualitative Research*. Thousand Oaks, CA: Sage.

Gulati, L., Ramalingam, R. and Gulati, I.S. (1996) *Gender Profile: Kerala*. Royal Netherlands Embassy: New Delhi.

Hacking, I. (1999) *The Social Construction of What?* London: Harvard University Press.

Hall, B. (1981) 'Participatory research, popular knowledge and power', *Convergence*, XIV (3): 6–19.

Hall, B. (1992). 'From margins to centre? The development and purpose of participatory research', *American Sociologist*, winter: 15–28.

Hall, C. (1997), *Social Work as Narrative: Storytelling and Persuasion in Professional Texts*. Aldershot: Ashgate.

Hall, C., Sarangi, S. and Slembrook, S. (1997) 'Moral construction and social work discourse', in B.L. Gunnarsson, P. Linell and B. Nordberg (eds), *The Construction of Professional Discourse*. Harlow: Longman.

Hall, C., Sarangi, S. and Slembrook, S. (1999) 'The legitimation of the client and the profession: identities and role on social work discourse', in *Talk, Work and Institutional Order: Discourse in Medical, Mediation and Management Settings*. Berlin: Mouton de Gruyter.

Hall, T. (1997) *Accommodating Inequality*. PhD dissertation, Cambridge University.

Hall, T. (2000) 'At home with the young homeless', *International Journal of Social Research Methodology*, 3 (2): 121–33.

Hall, T. (2001) *No Place Like Home*. London: Pluto Press.

Hammersley, M. (1992) *What's Wrong With Ethnography?* London: Routledge.

Hammersley, M. (1993a) 'On the teacher as researcher', *Educational Action Research*, 1 (3): 425–45.

Hammersley, M. (1993b) 'On practitioner ethnography', in M. Hammersley (ed.), *Controversies in Classroom Research*. Buckingham: Open University Press.

Hammersley, M. (1995) *The Politics of Social Research*. London: Sage.

Hammersley, M. and Atkinson, P. (1995) *Ethnography: Principles in Practice*, 2nd edn. London: Routledge.

Haraway, D. (1992) *Primate Visions*. London: Verso.

Harding, S. (ed.) (1987) *Feminism and Methodology*. Milton Keynes: Open University Press.

Harlow, E. and Hearn, J. (1995) 'Cultural constructions: contrasting theories of organizational culture and gender construction', *Gender, Work and Organisation*, 2 (4): 180–91.

Harré, R. and van Langenhove, L. (eds), (1999) *Positioning Theory*. Malden, MA: Blackwell.

Harrison, B. and ??????, E.S. (1993) 'A note on ethical issues in the use of autobiography in sociological research', *Sociology*, 27(1): 101–9.

Harrison, W.D. (1994) 'The inevitability of integrated methods', in E. Sherman and W.J. Reid (eds), *Qualitative Research in Social Work*. New York: Columbia University Press.

Hastrup, K. (1995) *A Passage to Anthropology*. London: Routledge.

Hawkins, L. (1996) 'Participation of the "researched": Tensions between different paradigms', in J. Fook (ed.), *The Reflective Researcher: Social Workers' Theories of Practice Research.* Sydney: Allen & Unwin.

Heineman Pieper, M. (1994) 'Science not scientism: The robustness of naturalistic clinical research', in E. Sherman and W.J. Reid (eds), *Qualitative Research in Social Work.* New York: Columbia University Press.

Heineman Pieper, M. and Tyson, K. (1999) 'Response to Padgett's "Does the glove really fit?"', *Social Work,* 44 (3): 278–9.

Heron, J. (1996) *Co-operative Inquiry: Research into the Human Condition.* London: Sage.

Hey, V. (1999) 'Frail elderly people: difficult questions and awkward answers', in S. Hood, B. Mayall and S. Oliver (eds), *Critical Issues In Social Research: Power and Prejudice.* Buckingham: Open University Press.

Hick, S. (1997) 'Participatory research: An approach for structural social workers', *Journal of Progressive Human Services,* 8 (2): 63–78.

Holbrook, T.L. (1995) 'Finding subjugated knowledge: personal document research', *Social Work,* 40 (6): 746–51.

Holland, S. (2000) 'The assessment relationship: interactions between social workers and parents in child protection assessments', *British Journal of Social Work,* (30): 149–63.

Holstein, J.A. and Gubrium, J.F. (1997) 'Active interviewing', in D. Silverman (ed.), *Qualitative Research: Theory, Method and Practice.* London: Sage.

Holstein, J.A. and Gubrium, J.F. (2000) *The Self We Live By: Narrative Identity in a Postmodern World.* New York: Oxford University Press.

hooks, b. (1984) *Feminist Theory: From Margin to Centre.* Boston: South End Press.

House, E. (1980) *Evaluating With Validity.* Beverly Hills, CA: Sage.

House, E. (1991a) 'Evaluation and social justice: where are we now?', in M. McLaughlin and D. Phillips (eds), *Evaluation and Education: At Quarter Century.* Chicago: Chicago University Press.

House, E. (1991b) 'Realism in research', *Educational Researcher,* 20 (6): 2–9.

Housley, W, (1999) 'Role as an interactional device and resource in multidisciplinary team meetings', *Sociological Research Online* <http://www.socresonline.org.uk/socresonline/4/3/housley.html>

Housley, W. (2000) 'Stories, narrative and teamwork', *Sociological Review* 48 (3): 425–43.

Howe, D. (1996) 'Surface and depth in social work practice', in N. Parton (ed.), *Social Theory, Social Change and Social Work.* London: Routledge.

Howe, K.R. (1988) 'Against the quantitative-qualitative incompatibility thesis', *Educational Researcher,* 17 (8): 10–16.

Hughes, M. (1998) 'Turning points in the lives of young inner-city men forgoing destructive criminal behaviours: A qualitative study', *Social Work Research,* 22 (3): 143–51.

Humphrey, C. and Pease, K. (1992) 'Effectiveness measurement in the Probation Service: a view from the troops', *Howard Journal,* 31 (2): 31–52.

Hunter, K.M. (1991) *Doctor's Stories: The Narrative Structure of Medical Knowledge.* Princeton, NJ: Princeton University Press.

Hutson, S. and Liddiard, M. (1994) *Youth Homelessness.* London: Macmillan.

Hyde, C. (1994) 'Reflections on a journey: A research story', in C.K. Riessman (ed.), *Qualitative Studies in Social Work Research.* Thousand Oaks, CA: Sage.

Hyde, C. (1998) 'Multicultural development in human service agencies: Meeting the challenges of implementation', Society for the Study of Social Problems (association paper).

Hyden, L.C. (1997) 'Illness and narrative', *Sociology of Health and Illness,* 19: 48–69.

Ixer, G. (1999) 'There is no such thing as reflection', *British Journal of Social Work,* 29 (4): 513–28.

Jacob, E. (1987) 'Qualitative research traditions: a review', in *Review of Educational Research*, 57 (1): 1–50.

Jacob, M.C. (1992) 'Science and politics in the late twentieth century', *Social Research*, 59 (3): 487–503.

Janesick, V.J. (1998) *'Stretching' Exercises for Qualitative Researchers*. Thousand Oaks, CA: Sage.

Jarvis, P. (1999) *The Practitioner-Researcher*. San Francisco: Jossey-Bass.

Jeffery, P., Jeffrey, R. and Lyon, A. (1989) *Labour Pains and Labour Power: Women and Childbearing in India*. London: Zed.

Jeffrey, R. (1993) *Politics, Women and Well Being: How Kerala Became 'a Model'*. Delhi: Oxford University Press.

Jewell, M.L. (1993) *'It Don't Make No Sense': An Ethnography of a Homeless Shelter*. Dissertation, Bryn Mawr.

Jindal, U.N. and Gupta, A. (1989) 'Social problems of infertile women in India', *International Journal of Fertility*, 34: 30–3.

John, I.D. (1990) 'Discursive style and psychological practice', *Australian Psychologist*, 25 (2): 115–32.

Johnson, J. (1995) 'In dispraise of justice', *Symbolic Interaction*, 18 (2): 191–205.

Jokinen, A., Juhila, K. and Pösö, T. (1999) *Constructing Social Work Practices*. Aldershot: Ashgate.

Jones, J. (1994) 'Embodies meaning: Menopause and the change of life', *Social Work in Health Care*, 19 (3–4): 43–65.

Kadushin, A. (1972) *The Social Work Interview*. New York: Columbia University Press.

Kayser-Jones, J. and Koenig, B. (1994) 'Ethical issues', in J.F. Gubrium and A. Sankar (eds), *Qualitative Methodology in Aging Research*. Thousand Oaks, CA: Sage.

Kazi, M.A.F. (1996) 'The Centre for Evaluation Studies at the University of Huddersfield: A profile', *Research on Social Work Practice*, 6 (1): 104–16.

Kazi, M.A.F and Wilson, J. (1996) 'Applying single-case evaluation methodology in a British social work agency', *Research on Social Work Practice*, 6 (1): 5–26.

Kellehear, A. (1993) *The Unobtrusive Researcher: A Guide to Methods*. Sydney: Allen & Unwin.

Kellehear, A. (1998) 'Ethical issues for the qualitative researcher: Some critical reflections', in J. Daly, A. Kellehear and J. Shoebridge (eds), *Annual Review of Health Social Sciences*, 8: 14–18.

Kelley, P. and Clifford, P. (1997) 'Coping with chronic pain: assessing narrative approaches', *Social Work*, 42 (3): 266–77.

Kent, J. (2000) 'Group inquiry: A democratic dialogue?', in C. Truman, D. Mertens and B. Humphries (eds), *Research and Inequality*. London: UCL Press.

Kerslake, A. and Gould, N. (eds) (1996) *Information Management For Social Services*. Aldershot: Ashgate.

Kirby, S. and McKenna, K. (1989) *Experience, Action, Research: Methods from the Margins*. Toronto: Garamond.

Kitzinger, J. (1994) 'Focus groups: Method or madness?', in M. Bolton (ed.), *Challenge and Innovation: Methodological Advances in Social Research on HIV/AIDS*. London: Taylor and Francis.

Kleinman, A. (1988) *The Illness Narratives: Suffering, Healing, and the Human Condition*. New York: Basic Books.

Krumer-Nevo, M. (1998) 'What's your story? Listening to the stories of mothers from multi-problem families', *Journal of Clinical Social Work*, 26 (2): 177–94.

Labov, W. (1982) 'Speech actions and reactions in personal narrative', in D. Tannen (ed.), *Analyzing Discourse: Text and Talk*. Washington, DC: Georgetown University Press.

Laird, J. (1984) 'Sorcerers, shamans and social workers: the use of ritual in family-centered practice', *Social Work*, 29: 123–29.

Laird, J. (1988). 'Women and stories: Restorying women's self-constructions', in M. McGoldrick, C. Anderson and F. Walsh (eds), *Women in Families: A Framework for Family Therapy*. New York: Norton.

Lang, N. (1994) 'Integrating the data processing of qualitative research and social work practice to advance the practitioner as knowledge builder: tools for knowing and doing', in E. Sherman and W. Reid (eds), *Qualitative Research in Social Work*. New York: Columbia University Press.

Langellier, K. (2001) '"You're marked": Breast cancer, tattoo and the narrative performance of identity', in J. Brockmeier and D. Carbaugh (eds), *Narrative and Identity: Studies in Autobiography, Self, and Culture*. Amsterdam and Philadelphia: John Benjamins.

Lather, P. (1986a) 'Issues of validity in openly ideological research', *Interchange*, 17 (4): 63–84.

Lather, P. (1986b) 'Research as praxis', *Harvard Educational Review*, 56 (3): 257–77.

Latimer, J. (1997) 'Figuring identities: older people, medicine and time', in A. Jamieson, S. Harper and C. Victor (eds), *Critical Approaches to Ageing and Later Life*. Buckingham: Open University Press.

Latour, B. (1988) 'The politics of explanation: an alternative', in S. Woolgar, *New Frontiers in the Sociology of Knowledge*. London: Sage.

Latour, B. (1999) *Pandora's Hope: Essays on the Reality of Science Studies*. London: Harvard University Press.

Law, J. (1994) *Organizing Modernity*. Oxford: Blackwell.

Lazar, B. (1998) 'The lull of tradition: A grounded theory study of television violence, children and social work', *Journal of Child and Adolescent Social Work*, 15 (2): 117–31.

Lazzari, M., Ford, H. and Haughey, K. (1996) 'Making a difference: Women of action in the community', *Social Work*, 41 (2): 197–205.

Lee, R. (1993) *Doing Research on Sensitive Topics*. London: Sage.

'Legal Storytelling' (1989) [Special issue]. *Michigan Law Review*, 87 (8).

Letters: 'The Kerala Difference' (1991) *New York Review of Books*. 24 October.

Lever, J. (1981) 'Multiple methods of data collection: a note on divergence', *Urban Life*, 10 (2): 199–213.

Lewis, J. and Glennerster, H. (1996) *Implementing the New Community Care*. Buckingham: Open University Press.

Liebow, E. (1967) *Talley's Corner: A Study of Negro Streetcorner Men*. Boston: Little, Brown.

Lincoln, Y. (1990) 'The making of a constructivist: a remembrance of transformations past', in E. Guba (ed.), *The Paradigm Dialog*. Newbury Park, CA: Sage.

Lincoln, Y. and Guba, E. (1989) 'Ethics: the failure of positivist science', *Review of Higher Education*, 12 (3): 221–40.

Lincoln, Y. and Guba, E. (1985) *Naturalistic Inquiry*. Newbury Park, CA: Sage.

Linde, C. (1993). *Life Stories: The Creation of Coherence*. New York: Oxford University Press.

Lishman, J. (1999). 'Introduction', in I. Shaw and J. Lishman (eds), *Evaluation and Social Work Practice*. London: Sage.

Lofland, J. and Lofland, L. (1995) *Analysing Social Settings*. Belmont: Wadsworth.

Loneck, B. (1994) 'Commentary: Practitioner researcher perspective on the integration of qualitative and quantitative research methods', in E. Sherman and W.J. Reid (eds), *Qualitative Research in Social Work*. New York: Columbia University Press.

Long, A. (1994) 'Assessing health and social outcomes', in J. Popay and G. Williams (eds), *Researching the People's Health*. London: Routledge.

Longres, J.F. (1994) 'Self-neglect and social control: A modest test of an issue', *Journal of Gerontological Social Work*, 22 (3–4): 3–20.

Lorenz, W. (2000) 'Contentious Identities – social work research and the search for professional and personal identities', paper from ESRC seminar series 'Theorising social work research', National Institute for Social Work web site <http://www.nisw.org.uk/tswr/lorenz.html>

Lukes, S. (1974). *Power: A Radical View*. London: Macmillan.

Macdonald, G. (1999) 'Social work and its evaluation', in F. Williams, J. Popay and A. Oakley (eds), *Welfare Research: A Critical Review*. London: UCL Press.

Maguire, P. (1987) *Participatory Research: A Feminist Perspective*. Amherst, MA: Center for International Education.

Majone, G. (1989) *Evidence, Argument and Persuasion in the Policy Process*. New Haven, CT: Yale University Press.

Maluccio, A.N. (1979) 'The influence of the agency environment on clinical practice', *Journal of Sociology and Social Welfare*, 6: 734–55.

Marks, D. (1995) 'Gendered "care" and the structuring of group relations: child-professional-parent-researcher', in E. Burman, P. Alldred, C. Bewley, B. Goldberg, C. Heenan, D. Marks, J. Marshall, K. Taylor, R. Ullah and S. Warner, *Challenging Women: Psychology's Exclusions, Feminist Possibilities*. Buckingham: Open University Press.

Martin, M. (2000) 'Critical education for participatory research', in C. Truman, D. Mertens and B. Humphries (eds), *Research and Inequality*. London: UCL Press.

Martin R.R. (1987) 'Oral history in social work education: chronicling the black experience', *Journal of Social Work Education*, 23 (3): 5–10.

Martin, R. (1994) 'Life forces of African-American elderly illustrated through oral history narratives', in E. Sherman and W. Reid (eds), *Qualitative Research in Social Work*. New York: Columbia University Press.

Martin, R. (1999) 'Histories in social work', in I. Shaw and J. Lishman (eds), *Evaluation and Social Work Practice*. London: Sage.

Mattingly, C. (1998) *Healing Dramas and Clinical Plots: The Narrative Structure of Experience*. New York: Cambridge University Press.

Mattingly, C. and Garro, L.C. (eds) (2000) *Narrative and Cultural Construction of Illness and Healing*. Berkeley: University of California Press.

Mauthner, M. (1997) 'Methodological aspects of collecting data from children: Lessons from three research projects', *Children and Society*, 11: 16–28.

May, T. and Williams, M. (eds) (1998) *Knowing the Social World*. Buckingham: Open University Press.

Mayer, T. and Timms, N. (1970) *The Client Speaks: Working Class Impressions of Casework*, New York: Atherton Press.

McGrath, M. (1991) *Multi-Disciplinary Teamwork*. Aldershot: Avebury.

McIvor, G. (1995) 'Practitioner research in probation', in J. McGuire (ed.), *What Works? Reducing Offending*. New York: Wiley.

McKay, D. (1988) 'Value free knowledge: myth or norm?', in D. McKay, *The Open Mind and Other Essays*. Leicester: Inter-Varsity Press.

McKeganey, N. and Bloor, M. (1991) 'Spotting the invisible man: the influence of male gender on fieldwork relations', *British Journal of Sociology*, (42) 2: 195–210.

McKeganey, N., MacPherson, I. and Hunter, D. (1988) 'How "they" decide: exploring professional decision making', *Research, Policy and Planning*, 6 (1): 15–19.

McLennan, G. (1995) 'Feminism, epistemology and postmodernism: reflections on current ambivalence', *Sociology*, 29 (2): 391–409.

McLeod, J. (1999) *Practitioner Research in Counselling*. London: Sage.

McQuaide, S. (1998) 'Opening space for alternative images and narratives of midlife women', *Journal of Clinical Social Work*, 26 (1): 39–53.

Mertens, D.M. (1998) *Research Methods in Education and Psychology: Integrating Diversity with Quantitative and Qualitative Approaches*. Thousand Oaks, CA: Sage.

Mertens, D.M. (1999) 'Inclusive evaluation: Implications of transformative theory for evaluation', *American Journal of Evaluation,* 20 (1): 1–14.

Merton, R.K. (1972) 'Insiders and outsiders: A chapter in the sociology of knowledge', *American Journal of Sociology,* 78 (1): 9–47.

Merton, R.K. and Kendall, P.L. (1946) 'The focused interview', *American Journal of Sociology,* 51: 541–7.

Mezirow, J. (1990) 'How critical reflection triggers transformative learning', in J. Mezirow and Associates (eds), *A Guide To Transformative and Emancipatory Learning.* San Francisco: Jossey-Bass.

Mies, M. (1983) 'Towards a methodology for feminist research', in G. Bowles and R. Duelli Klein (eds), *Theories of Women's Studies.* London: Routledge and Kegan Paul.

Miles, M. and Huberman, A. (1994) *Qualitative Data Analysis: An Expanded Sourcebook.* Thousand Oaks, CA: Sage.

Miller, G. (1997) 'Contextualizing texts: Studying organisational texts', in G. Miller and R. Dingwall (eds), *Context and Method in Qualitative Research.* London: Sage.

Miller, G. and Dingwall, R. (eds) (1997) *Context and Method in Qualitative Research.* London: Sage.

Miller, J. (1990) *Creating Spaces and Finding Voices: Teachers Collaborating for Empowerment.* New York: State University of New York Press.

Miller J. (1994) 'A family's sense of power in their community: Theoretical and research issues', *Smith College Studies in Social Work,* 64 (3): 221–41.

Miller, J. and Glassner, B. (1997) 'The "inside" and the "outside": finding realities in interviews', in D. Silverman (ed.), *Qualitative Research. Theory, Method and Practice.* London: Sage.

Miller, R. (2000) *Researching Life Stories and Family Histories.* London: Sage.

Miller, W. and Crabtree, B. (1994) 'Clinical research', in N. Denzin and Y. Lincoln (eds), *Handbook of Qualitative Methods.* Thousand Oaks, CA: Sage.

Mills, C.W. (1959) *The Sociological Imagination.* New York: Oxford University Press.

Mishler, E.G. (1986) *Research Interviewing: Context and Narrative.* Cambridge, MA: Harvard University Press.

Mishler, E. G. (1995) 'Models of narrative analysis: A typology', *Journal of Narrative and Life History,* 5 (2): 87–123.

Mishler, E.G. (1999) *Storylines: Craftartists' Narratives of Identity.* Cambridge, MA: Harvard University Press.

'MIT Theory: Behaviours which contribute to productivity of a group' (1975) Unpublished. Handout at Group Process Lab, Atlantic Christian Training Centre, Tatamagouche, Nova Scotia.

Mizrahi, T. and Abramson, J. (1985) 'Sources of strain between physicians and social workers: Implications for social workers in health care settings', *Social Work in Health Care,* 10 (3): 33–51.

Mohr, W.K. (1997) 'Interpretive interactionism: Denzin's potential contribution to intervention and outcomes research', *Qualitative Health Research,* 7 (2): 270–86.

Monaghan, J. and Just, P. (2000) *Social and Cultural Anthropology: A Very Short Introduction.* Oxford: Oxford University Press.

Moran-Ellis, J. (1996) 'Close to home: the experience of researching child sexual abuse', in M. Hester, L. Kelly and J. Radford (eds), *Women, Violence and Male Power.* Buckingham: Open University Press.

Morgan, D. (1981) 'Men, masculinity and the process of sociological enquiry', in H. Roberts (ed.), *Doing Feminist Research.* London: Routledge and Kegan Paul.

Morrow-Kondos, D.S., Weber, J., Cooper, K. and Hesser, J. (1997) 'Becoming parents again: Grandparents raising grandchildren', *Journal of Gerontological Social Work,* 28 (1–2): 35–46.

Mullen, E.J. (1995) 'Pursuing knowledge through qualitative research', *Social Work Research,* 19 (1): 29–32.

Mulroy, E. (1997) 'Building a neighbourhood network: Interorganizational collaboration to prevent child abuse and neglect', *Social Work,* 42 (3): 255–64.

Nag, M. (1988) 'The Kerala formula', *World Health Forum,* 9 (2). Geneva: World.

Nelson, C., Treichler, P.A. and Grossberg, L. (1992) 'Cultural studies', in L. Grossberg, C. Nelson and P.A. Treicher (eds), *Cultural Studies.* New York: Routledge.

Nichols-Casebolt, A. and Spakes, P. (1995) 'Policy research and the voices of
women', *Social Work Research,* 19 (1): 49–55.

Oakley, A. (1998) 'Science, gender and women's liberation: an argument against
postmodernism', *Women's Studies International Forum,* 21 (2): 133–46.

Ochs, E., Smith, R. and Taylor, C. (1989). 'Dinner narratives as detective stories',
Cultural Dynamics, 2: 238–57.

O'Hagan, K. and Dillenburger, K. (1995) *The Abuse of Women in Childcare Work.*
Buckingham: Open University Press.

Okely, J. (1987) 'Fieldwork up the M1: Policy and political aspects', in A. Jackson,
Anthropology at Home. London: Tavistock.

Olesen, V. (1994) 'Feminisms and models of qualitative research', in N. Denzin and
Y.S. Lincoln (eds), *Handbook of Qualitative Research.* London: Sage.

Olesen, V. (2000) 'Feminisms and qualitative research at and into the millennium',
in N. Denzin and Y. Lincoln (eds), *Handbook of Qualitative Research* (2nd edn).
Thousand Oaks, CA: Sage.

Oliver, M. (1990) *The Politics Of Disablement.* Basingstoke: Macmillan.

Oliver, M. (1997) in C. Barnes and G. Mercer (eds), *Doing Disability Research.* Leeds:
The Disability Press.

Oliver, S. (1999) 'Users of health services: following their agenda', in S. Hood,
B. Mayall and S. Oliver (eds), *Critical Issues in Social Research: Power and Prejudice.*
Buckingham: Open University Press.

Padfield, M. and Proctor, I. (1996) 'The effect of interviewer's gender on the interviewing process: a comparative enquiry', *Sociology,* 30 (3): 355–66.

Padgett, D. (1998a) 'Does the glove really fit? Qualitative research and clinical social
work practice', *Social Work,* 43 (4): 373–81.

Padgett, D. (1998b) *Qualitative Methods in Social Work Research.* Thousand Oaks,
CA: Sage.

Padgett, D.K. (1999) 'The research–practice debate in a qualitative research context',
Social Work, 44 (3): 280–2.

Parton, N. (1991) *Governing the Family,* Basingstoke: Macmillan.

Parton, N. (1999) 'Some thoughts on the relationship between theory and practice
in and for social work', paper from ESRC seminar series 'Theorising social work
research', National Institute for Social Work website. <http://www.nisw/org/uk/
+swr/parton.htr>

Parton, N. (2000) 'Some thoughts on the relationship between theory and practice
in social work', *British Journal of Social Work,* 30 (4): 449–63.

Parton, N., Thorpe, D. and Wattam, C. (1997) *Child Protection: Risk and the Moral
Order.* Basingstoke: Macmillan.

Patton, M. Q. (1990) *Qualitative Evaluation.* Newbury Park, CA: Sage.

Patton, M.Q. (1997) *Utilization Focussed Evaluation.* Thousand Oaks, CA: Sage.

Patton, M.Q. (1999) 'Some framing questions about racism and evaluation:
Thoughts stimulated by Professor Stanfield's "Slipping through the front door"',
American Journal of Evaluation, 20 (3): 437–44.

Pawson, R. and Tilley, N. (1997) 'An introduction to scientific realist evaluation', in
E. Chelimsky and W. Shadish (eds), *Evaluation for the 21st Century.* Thousand
Oaks, CA: Sage.

Pease, B. and Fook, J. (eds) (1999) *Transforming Social Work Practice: Postmodern
Critical Perspectives.* Sydney: Allen & Unwin.

Pelto P.J. (1994) 'Focused ethnographic studies on sexual behaviour and AIDs
STDs', *The Indian Journal of Social Work,* 55 (4): 689–91.

Pelto, P.J. and Pelto, G.H. (1978) 'Ethnography: the fieldwork enterprise', in J.J. Honigmann (ed.), *Handbook of Social and Cultural Anthropology*. Chicago: Rand McNally.

Phillips, D. (1987) *Philosophy, Science and Social Inquiry*. New York: Pergamon.

Phillips, D. (1990) 'Postpositivistic science: myths and realities', in E. Guba (ed.), *The Paradigm Dialog*. Newbury Park, CA: Sage.

Philp, M. (1979) 'Notes on the form of knowledge in social work', *The Sociological Review*, 27 (1): 83–111.

Pinch, T. and Pinch, T. (1988) 'Reservations about reflexivity and new literary forms or why let the devil have all the good tunes', in S. Woolgar, *Knowledge and Reflexivity: New Frontiers in the Sociology of Knowledge*. London: Sage. pp. 178–97.

Pithouse, A. (1998) *Social Work as an Invisible Trade*. Aldershot: Avebury.

Pithouse, A. and Atkinson, P. (1988) 'Telling the case. Occupational narrative in a social work office', in N. Coupland (ed.), *Styles of Discourse*. London: Croom Helm.

Plummer, K. (1995) *Telling Sexual Stories: Power, Change and Social Worlds*. New York: Routledge.

Polanyi, L. (1985). 'Conversational storytelling', in T.A. Van Dijk (ed.), *Handbook of Discourse Analysis*. London: Academic Press.

Polanyi, M. (1958) *Personal Knowledge*. London: Routledge and Kegan Paul.

Polkinghorne, D.E. (1988) *Narrative Knowing and the Human Sciences*. Albany: State University of NY Press.

Pollard, A. (1985) 'Opportunities and difficulties of a teacher ethnographer: a personal account', in R.G. Burgess, *Field Methods in the Study of Education*. Lewes: Falmer. pp. 217–33.

Polsky, H.W. (1962) *Cottage Six: The Social System of Delinquent Boys in Residential Treatment*. New York: Wiley.

Pomerantz, A.M. (1978) 'Attributions of responsibility: Blamings', *Sociology*, 12: 115–21.

Popay, J. and Williams, G. (1998) 'Qualitative research and evidence-based health-care', *Journal of the Royal Society of Medicine*, Supplement 35, Vol. 91, 32–7.

Popkewitz, T. (1990) 'Whose future? Whose past?', in E. Guba (ed.), *The Paradigm Dialog*. Newbury Park, CA: Sage.

Pugh, R. (1998) 'Attitudes, stereotypes and anti-discriminatory education: developing themes from Sullivan', *British Journal of Social Work*, 28: 939–59.

Punch, K. (1998) *Introduction To Social Research: Quantitative and Qualitative Approaches*. London: Sage.

Punch, M. (1994) 'Politics and ethics in qualitative research', in D. Denzin and Y.S. Lincoln (eds), *Handbook of Qualitative Research*. London: Sage.

Ragin, C. (1992) 'Cases of "what is a case?"', in C. Ragin and H. Becker (eds), *What is a Case? Exploring the Foundations of Social Inquiry*. Cambridge: Cambridge University Press.

Ragin, C. and Becker, H. (eds) (1992) *What is a Case? Exploring the Foundations of Social Inquiry*. Cambridge: Cambridge University Press.

Reason, P. (ed.) (1994a) *Participation in Human Inquiry*. London: Sage.

Reason, P. (1994b) 'Three approaches to participative inquiry', in D. Denzin and Y.S. Lincoln (eds), *Handbook of Qualitative Research*. London: Sage.

Reason, P. and Bradbury, H. (2000) *Handbook of Action Research: Participative Inquiry and Practice*. Thousand Oaks, CA: Sage.

Rees, Stuart (1979) *Social Work Face To Face*. New York: Columbia University Press.

Reid, W. (1990) 'Change-process research: A new paradigm?', in L. Videka-Sherman and W. Reid (eds), *Advances in Clinical Social Work Research*. Silver Spring, MD: NASW Press.

Reid, W. (1994) 'Reframing the epistemological debate', in E. Sherman and W. Reid (eds), *Qualitative Research in Social Work*. New York: Columbia University Press.

Reid, W. (1995) 'Research overview', in R.L. Edwards and J.G. Hopps (eds), *Encyclopedia of Social Work*, 19th edn, Vol. III. Washington, DC: NASW Press.

Reinharz, S. (1992) *Feminist Methods in Social Research*. New York: Oxford University Press.

Riessman, C.K. (1987) 'When gender is not enough: Women interviewing women', *Gender and Society*, 1 (2): 172–207.

Riessman, C.K. (1990a) *Divorce Talk: Women and Men Make Sense of Personal Relationships*. New Brunswick, NJ: Rutgers University Press.

Riessman, C.K. (1990b) 'Strategic uses of narrative in the presentation of self and illness: A research note', *Social Science and Medicine*, 30 (11): 1195–1200.

Riessman, C.K. (1991) 'Beyond reductionism: Narrative genres in divorce accounts', *Journal of Narrative and Life History*, 1 (1): 41–68.

Riessman, C.K. (1993) *Narrative Analysis*. Newbury Park, CA: Sage.

Riessman, C.K. (1994a) 'Making sense of marital violence', in C.K. Riessman (ed.), *Qualitative Studies in Social Work Research*. Thousand Oaks, CA: Sage.

Riessman, C.K. (1994b) 'Preface: Making room for diversity in social work research', in C.K. Riessman (ed.), *Qualitative Studies in Social Work Research*. Thousand Oaks, CA: Sage.

Riessman, C.K. (ed.) (1994c) *Qualitative Studies in Social Work Research*. Thousand Oaks, CA: Sage.

Riessman, C.K. (2000a) '"Even if we don't have children [we] can live": Stigma and infertility in South India', in C. Mattingly and L.C. Garro (eds), *Narrative and Cultural Construction of Illness and Healing*. Berkeley: University of California Press.

Riessman, C.K. (2000b) 'Stigma and everyday resistance practices: Childless women in South India', *Gender and Society*, 14 (1): 111–35.

Riessman, C.K. (2001a) 'Analysis of personal narratives', in J.F. Gubrium and J.A. Holstein (eds), *Handbook of Interviewing*. Newbury Park, CA: Sage.

Riessman, C.K. (2001b) 'Positioning gender identity in narratives of infertility: South Indian women's lives in context', in M.C. Inhorn and F. van Balen (eds), *Interpreting Infertility: Childlessness, Gender, and the New Reproductive Technologies in Global Perspective*. Berkeley: University of California Press.

Rorty, R. (1991) 'Feminism and pragmatism', *Radical Philosophy*, 59: 3–14.

Rorty, R. (1996) 'Response to Simon Critchley', in S. Critchley, J. Derrida, L. Laclau and R. Rorty (ed. C. Mouffe), *Deconstruction and Pragmatism*. London: Routledge.

Rosaldo, R. (1989) *Culture and Truth: The Remaking of Social Analysis*. Boston: Beacon Press.

Rose, N. (1989) *Governing the Soul: The Shaping of the Private Self*. London: Routledge.

Rose, N. (1998) *Inventing Our Selves: Psychology, Power and Personhood*. Cambridge: Cambridge University Press.

Rosenwald, G. and Ochberg, R. (eds) (1992) *Storied Lives: Cultural Conditions of Self Understanding*. New Haven, CT: Yale University Press.

Rubin, L.B. (1981) 'Sociological research: the subjective dimension', *Symbolic Interactionism*, 4 (1): 42–57.

Ruckdeschel, R., Earnshaw, P. and Firrek, A. (1994) 'The qualitative case study and evaluation: Issues, methods and examples', in E. Sherman and W. Reid (eds), *Qualitative Research in Social Work*. New York: Columbia University Press.

Ryan, M. (1996) 'Doing longitudinal research: A personal reflection', in J. Fook (ed.), *The Reflective Researcher: Social Workers' Theories of Practice Research*. Sydney: Allen & Unwin.

Saari, C. (1994) 'An exploraton of meaning and causation in clinical social work', *Clinical Social Work Journal*, 22 (3): 251–61.

Sandelowski, M. (1991) 'Telling stories: Narrative approaches in qualitative research', *Image: Journal of Nursing Scholarship*, 23 (3): 161–6.

Sands, R. (1995) 'The elusiveness of identity in social work practice with women: A postmodern feminist perspective', *Clinical Social Work Journal*, 24 (2): 167–86.

Sands, R.G. (1988) 'Sociolinguistic analysis of a mental health interview', *Social Work,* 33 (2): 149–54.

Sands, R.G. (1989) 'The social worker joins the team: A look at the socialization process', *Social Work in Health Care,* 14: 1–15.

Sands, R.G. (1990) 'Ethnographic research: A qualitative research approach to the study of the interdisciplinary team', *Social Work in Health Care,* 15: 115–29.

Sarbin, T.R. (ed.) (1986) *Narrative Psychology: The Storied Nature of Human Conduct.* New York: Praeger.

Satyamurti, C. (1981) *Occupational Survival: The Case Of The Local Authority Social Worker.* Oxford: Basil Blackwell.

Scheff, T. (1997) 'Part/whole morphology: Unifying single case and comparative methods', *Sociological Research Online* 2.3.1 <http://www.socresonline.org.uk/socresonline/2/3/1/html>

Schon, D. (1983) *The Reflective Practitioner: How Professionals Think in Action.* New York: Basic Books.

Schwab, J. (1969) 'The practical: A language for curriculum', in *School Review.* November, pp. 1–23.

Schwandt, T. (1993) 'Theory for the social sciences: crisis of identity and purpose', in D. Flinders and G. Mills (eds), *Theory and Concepts in Qualitative Research: Perspectives from the Field.* New York: Teachers College Press.

Schwandt, T. (1997) 'Evaluation as practical hermeneutics', *Evaluation,* 3 (1): 69–83.

Scott, D. (1989) 'Meaning construction and social work practice', *Social Service Review,* 63: 39–51.

Scott, D. (1990) 'Practice wisdom: the neglected source of practice research', *Social Work,* 35 (6): 564–8.

Scott, S. (1998) 'Here be dragons: researching the unbelievable, hearing the unthinkable. A feminist sociologist in uncharted territory', *Sociological Research Online,* 3 (3): <http://www.socresonline.org.uk/socresonline/3/3/1.html>

Scriven, M. (1986) 'New frontiers of evaluation', *Evaluation Practice,* 7 (1): 7–44.

Seabury, B.A. (1980) 'Communication problems in social work', *Social Work,* 25: 40–4.

Seale, C. (1999) *The Quality of Qualitative Research.* London: Sage.

Sen, A. (1999) *Development as Freedom.* New York: Knopf.

Shadish, W., Cook, T. and Leviton, L. (1990) *Foundations of Program Evaluation: Theories of Practice.* Newbury Park, CA: Sage.

Shakespeare, P., Atkinson, D. and French, S. (eds) (1993) *Reflecting on Research Practice.* Buckingham: Open University Press.

'Shared leadership and membership functions' (1975) Handout at a Group Process Lab, Atlantic Christian Training Centre, Tatamagouche, Nova Scotia.

Shaw, I. (1996) *Evaluating in Practice.* Aldershot: Ashgate.

Shaw, I. (1997) *Be Your Own Evaluator: a Guide to Reflective and Enabling Evaluating.* Wrexham: Prospects Publishing.

Shaw, I. (1998) 'Practice and research for housing the socially excluded', in I. Shaw, S. Lambert and D. Clapham (eds), *Social Care and Housing.* London: Jessica Kingsley.

Shaw, I. (1999a) *Qualitative Evaluation.* London: Sage.

Shaw, I. (1999b) 'Seeing the trees for the wood: the politics of evaluating in practice', in B. Broad (ed.), *The Politics of Research and Evaluation.* Birmingham: Venture Press.

Shaw, I. (2000a) 'Just inquiry? Research and evaluation for service users', in H. Kemshall and R. Littlechild (eds), *Participation in Social Care: Researching for Practice.* London, Jessica Kingsley.

Shaw, I. (2000b) 'Research and social work', in M. Davies (ed.), *Encyclopedia of Social Work.* Oxford: Blackwell.

Shaw, I. and Lishman, J. (eds) (1999) *Evaluation and Social Work Practice*. London: Sage.

Shaw, I. and Shaw, A. (1997a) 'Keeping social work honest: evaluating as profession and practice', *British Journal of Social Work*, 27 (6): 847–69.

Shaw, I. and Shaw, A. (1997b) 'Game plans, buzzes and sheer luck: doing well in social work', *Social Work Research*, 21 (2): 69–79.

Sheldon, B. (1978) 'Theory and practice in social work: a re-examination of a tenuous relationship', *British Journal of Social Work*, 8 (1): 1–22.

Sheppard, M. (1995) 'Social work, social science and practice wisdom', *British Journal of Social Work*, 25 (3): 265–93.

Sheppard, M., Newstead, S., Di Caccavo, A. and Ryan, K. (2000) 'Reflexivity and the development of process knowledge in social work: a classification and empirical study', *British Journal of Social Work*, 30(4), 465–88.

Sherman, E. and Reid, W. (1994a) 'Coming of age in social work – The emergence of qualitative research', in E. Sherman and W. Reid (eds), *Qualitative Research in Social Work*. New York: Columbia University Press.

Sherman, E. and Reid, J. (eds), (1994b) *Qualitative Research in Social Work*. New York: Columbia University Press,.

Shokeid (Minkovitz) M. (1970) 'Fieldwork as predicament rather than spectacle', *Archives of European Sociology*, XI: 111–22.

Silverman, D. (1993) *Interpreting Qualitative Data*, London: Sage.

Silverman, D. (1997) *Discourses of Counselling: HIV Counselling as Social Interaction*. London: Sage.

Silverman, D. (2000) *Doing Qualitative Research: A Practical Handbook*. London: Sage.

Simon, E.L. (1986) 'Theory in education evaluation, or, what's wrong with generic-brand anthropology?', in D. Fetterman and M. Pitman (eds), *Educational Evaluation – Ethnography in Theory, Practice and Politics*. Newbury Park, CA: Sage.

Sinclair, I. (1970) *Hostels for Probationers*. London: HMSO.

Sinclair, I. (2000) 'Methods and measurement in evaluative social work', paper from ESRC seminar series Theorising Social Work Research. National Institute for Social Work web site, available at: www.nisw.org.uk/tsivr/sinclair.html

Smith, D. (2000) 'The limits of positivism revisited', paper from ESRC seminar series 'Theorising social work research', National Institute for Social Work web site <http://www.nisw.org.uk/tswr/smith.html>

Smith, J. (1992) 'Interpretive inquiry: A practical and moral activity', *Theory into Practice*, 31 (2): 100–6.

Smith, L. and Klein, P. (1986) 'Qualitative research and evaluation: triangulation and multi-methods reconsidered', in D.D. Williams (ed.), *Naturalistic Evaluation*. New Directions in Program Evaluation, No. 30. San Francisco: Jossey-Bass.

Spradley, J.P. (1979) *The Ethnographic Interview*. Orlando, FL: Harcourt Brace Jovanovich.

Stacey, J. (1988) 'Can there be a feminist ethnography?', *Women's Studies International Forum*, 11 (1): 21–7.

Stainton Rogers, R. and Stainton Rogers, W. (1992) *Stories of Childhood: Shifting Agendas of Child Concern*. Hemel Hempstead: Harvester Wheatsheaf.

Stake, R. (1991) 'Retrospective on "The Countenance of Educational Evaluation"', in M. McLaughlin and D. Phillips (eds), *Evaluation and Education at Quarter Century*. Chicago: University of Chicago Press.

Stake, R. (1997) 'Advocacy in evaluation: a necessary evil?', in E. Chelimsky and W. Shadish (eds), *Evaluation for the 21st Century*. Thousand Oaks, CA: Sage.

Stake, R. and Trumbull, D. (1982) 'Naturalistic generalizations', *Review Journal of Philosophy and Social Science*, 7: 1–12.

Stancombe, J. and White, S. (1997) 'Notes on the tenacity of therapeutic presuppositions in process research: examining the artfulness of blamings in family therapy', *Journal of Family Therapy*, 19 (1): 21–41.

Stanfield, J. (1994) 'Empowering the culturally diversified sociological voice', in A. Gitlin (ed.), *Power and Method: Political Activism and Educational Research.* New York: Routledge.

Stanfield, J.H. II (1999) 'Slipping through the front door: Relevant social scientific evaluation in the people-of-color century', *American Journal of Evaluation,* 20 (3): 415–32.

Stanley, L. and Wise, S. (1993) *Breaking Out Again.* London: Routledge.

Steier, F. (1991) *Reflexivity and Research.* London: Sage.

Stenson, K. (1993) 'Social work discourse and the social work interview', *Economy and Society,* 22 (1): 42–76.

Stevens, J. W. (1997) 'Opportunity, outlook and coping in poor urban African American late-age female adolescent contraceptors', *Smith College Studies in Social Work,* 67 (3): 456–75.

Strathern, M. (1987) 'The limits of auto-anthropology', in A. Jackson (ed.), *Anthropology at Home.* London: Tavistock.

Strauss, A. (1987) *Qualitative Analysis for Social Scientists.* Cambridge: Cambridge University Press.

Strauss, A. and Corbin, J. (1990) *Basics of Qualitative Research: Grounded Theory Procedures and Techniques.* Newbury Park, CA: Sage.

Strong, P. and Dingwall, R. (1989) 'Romantics and stoics', in J. Gubrium and D. Silverman (eds), *The Politics of Field Research: Sociology Beyond Enlightenment.* London: Sage.

Sullivan, N. (1995) 'Who owns the group? The role of worker control in the development of a group', *Social Work With Groups,* 18 (2–3): 15–32.

Sullivan, W. (1991) 'Technical assistance in community mental health: A model for social work consultants', *Research on Social Work Practice,* 1 (3): 289–315.

Swift, K. (1995) *Manufacturing 'Bad Mothers'. A Critical Perspective on Child Neglect.* Toronto: University of Toronto Press.

Swigonski, M. (1993) 'Feminist standpoint theory and questions of social work research', *Affilia,* 8 (2): 171–83.

Tandon, R. (1981) 'Participatory research in the empowerment of people', *Convergence,* XIV (3): 20–9.

Tanner, K. and Le Riche, P. (1999) 'Work in progress: the contribution of observation to the development of good practice and evaluation', in I. Shaw and J. Lishman (eds), *Evaluation and Social Work Practice.* London: Sage.

Taylor, C. and White, S. (2000) *Practising Reflexivity in Health and Welfare; Making Knowledge.* Buckingham: Open University Press.

Thomas, N. and O'Kane, C. (1998) 'The ethics of participatory research with children', *Children and Society,* 12: 336–48.

Thornton, S. and Garret, K.J. (1995) 'Ethnography as a bridge to multicultural practice', *Journal of Social Work Education,* 31 (1): 67–74.

Thrasher, P. and Mowbray, C.T. (1995) 'A strengths perspective: An ethnographic study of homeless women with children', *Health and Social Work,* 20 (2): 93–101.

Thyer, B. (1989) 'First principles of practice research', *British Journal of Social Work,* 19 (4): 309–23.

Thyer, B. (2000) Review of I. Shaw and J. Lishman (eds) (1999) 'Evaluation and Social Work Practice', *British Journal of Social Work,* 30 (3): 401–2.

Timms, N. (1968) *The Language of Social Casework.* London: Routledge

Tizard, J., Sinclair, I. and Clarke, R. (eds) (1975) *Varieties of Residential Experience.* London: Routledge and Kegan Paul.

Trend, M.G. (1979) 'On the reconciliation of qualitative and quantitative analyses', in T. Cook and C. Reichardt (eds), *Qualitative and Quantitative Methods in Evaluation Research.* Beverly Hills, CA: Sage.

Trethewey, A. (1997) 'Resistance, identity and empowerment: A postmodern feminist analysis of clients in a human service organization', *Communication Monographs*, 64 (4): 281–301.

Trevillion, S. (1999) 'Social work, social networks and network knowledge', paper from ESRC seminar series 'Theorising social work research', National Institute for Social Work web site. <http://www.nisw.org.uk/tswr/trevil.html>

Trinder, L. (2000) 'Reading the texts: Postmodern feminism and the "doing" of research', in B. Fawcett, B. Featherstone, J. Fook and A. Rossiter (eds), *Practice and Research in Social Work: Postmodern Feminist Perspectives*. London: Routledge.

Truman, C. (2000) 'New social movements and social research', in C. Truman, D. Mertens and B. Humphries (eds), *Research and Inequality*. London: UCL Press.

Truman, C., Mertens, D. and Humphries, B. (eds) (2000) *Research and Inequality*. London: UCL Press.

Uberoi, P. (ed.) (1993) *Family, Kinship and Marriage in India*. New Delhi: Oxford University Press.

Usher, R. and Bryant, I. (1989) *Adult Education as Theory, Practice and Research: The Captive Triangle*. London: Routledge.

Vanderplaat, M. (1995) 'Beyond technique: issues in evaluating for empowerment', *Evaluation*, 1 (1): 81–96.

Wadsworth, Y. (1984) *Do it Yourself Research*. Collingwood: VCOSS.

Walden, T., Wolock, I. and Demone, H. (1990) 'Ethical decision-making in human services: A comparative study', *Families in Society: The Journal of Contemporary Human Services*, 71 (2): 67–75.

Ward, T., Connolly, M., McCormack, J. and Hudson, S. (1996) 'Social workers' attributions for sexual offending against children', *Journal of Child Sexual Abuse*, 5 (3): 39–56.

Warren, L. (1998) 'Considering the culture of community care: anthropological accounts of the experiences of frontline carers, older people and a researcher', in I.R. Edgar and A. Russell (eds), *The Anthropology of Welfare*. London: Routledge.

Webb, C. (1992) 'The use of the first person in academic writing: objectivity, language and gatekeeping', *Journal of Advanced Nursing*, 17: 747–52.

Weedon, C. (1987) *Feminist Practice and Poststructuralist Theory*. Oxford: Blackwell.

Weiss, C. (1980) 'Knowledge creep and decision accretion', *Knowledge, Creation, Diffusion, Utilisation*, 1 (3): 381–404.

Weiss, C. (1988) 'If programme decisions hinged only on information', *Evaluation Practice*, 9 (1): 15–28.

Weiss, C. (1998) *Evaluation: Methods for Studying Policies and Programs*. New York: Prentice-Hall.

Wells, K. (1995) 'The strategy of grounded theory: Possibilities and problems', *Social Work Research*, 19 (1): 33–6.

West, C. (1996) 'Ethnography and orthography: a modest methodological proposal', *Journal of Contemporary Ethnography*, 25 (3): 327–52.

White, H. (1987) *The Content of the Form: Narrative Discourse and Historical Representation*. Baltimore: Johns Hopkins University Press.

White, S. (1997a) 'Beyond retroduction? Hermeneutics, reflexivity and social work practice', *British Journal of Social Work*, 27 (9): 739–53.

White, S. (1997b) *Performing Social Work: An Ethnographic Study of Talk and Text in a Metropolitan Social Services Department*, unpublished PhD thesis, University of Salford.

White, S. (1998a) 'Time, temporality and child welfare: Notes on the materiality and malleability of time(s)', *Time and Society*, 7 (1): 55–74.

White, S. (1998b) 'Interdiscursivity and child welfare: the ascent and durability of psycholegalism', *Sociological Review*, 46 (2): 264–92.

White, S. (1999a) 'Examining the artfulness of risk talk', in A. Jokinen, K. Juhila and T. Pösö, *Constructing Social Work Practices*. Aldershot: Ashgate.

White, S. (1999b) 'Performing rationality: The limits of management in a social services department', in M. Dent and M. O'Neill, *Dilemmas for European Health, Education and Social Services*. Staffordshire University Press.

Whitmore, E. (1991) 'Evaluation and empowerment: It's the process that counts', *Empowerment and Family Support Networking Bulletin*, 2 (2): 1–7. Ithaca, NY: Cornell University Empowerment Project.

Whitmore, E. (1994a) 'Empowerment in program evaluation: a case example', *Canadian Social Work Review*, 7 (2): 215–29.

Whitmore, E. (1994b) 'To tell the truth: Working with oppressed groups in participatory approaches to inquiry', in P. Reason (ed.), *Participation in Human Inquiry*. London: Sage.

Whitmore, E. (ed.) (1998) *Understanding and Practicing Participatory Evaluation*. New Directions for Evaluation, Vol. 80. San Francisco: Jossey-Bass.

Whitmore, E. and McKee, C. (2000) 'Six street youth who could', in P. Reason and H. Bradbury (eds), *Handbook of Action Research: Participative Inquiry and Practice*. Thousand Oaks, CA: Sage.

Whyte, W.F. (1981) *Street Corner Society: The Social Structure of an Italian Slum*. Chicago: University of Chicago Press.

Williams, G. (1984) 'The genesis of chronic illness: Narrative re-construction', *Sociology of Health & Illness*, 6 (2): 175–200.

Willis, P. (1976) 'The man in the iron cage: notes on method', *Working Papers in Cultural Studies*, 9: 135–43.

Witkin, S. and Gottschalk, S. (1988) 'Alternative criteria for theory evaluation', *Social Service Review*, 62 (2): 211–24.

Wolcott, H. (1990) 'On seeking – and rejecting – validity in qualitative research', in E.E. Eisner and A. Peshkin (eds), *Qualitative Inquiry and Education*. New York: Teachers College Press, Columbia University.

Woolgar, S. (1988) *New Frontiers in the Sociology of Knowledge*. London: Sage.

Woolgar, S. and Pawluch, D. (1985) 'Ontological gerrymandering: the anatomy of social problems explanations', *Social Problems*, 32 (3): 214–27.

Wuest, J. (1995) 'Feminist grounded theory: An exploration of the congruency and tensions between two traditions in knowledge discovery', *Qualitative Health Research*, 5 (1): 125–37.

Yin, R.K. (1994) *Case Study Research*. Thousand Oaks, CA: Sage.

Young, K.G. (1987) *Taleworlds and Storyrealms: The Phenomenology of Narrative*. Boston: Martins Nijhoff.

Subject Index

abuse 68–71
access 52–3, 61
actors perspective 7, 9, 18 *see also* knowledge
advocacy research *see* justice
analysis 8, 64, 77–82, 88–9, 130, 147
anthropology 7, 11, 53, 58, 103, 138, 191, 198

case studies 16, 17, 20, 34–5, 182, 197
cause 70, 74, 107–8, 112, 183–6
children 63, 64, 65, 75–81, 100–1, 108–12, 148–50, 154–5
common sense *see* knowledge
constructionism 4, 7, 18, 66, 111–4, 138, 190
context 8, 9, 14, 15, 17–23, 56–7, 58, 63, 65, 66, 135–6, 142, 156, 160, 165, 192, 194
conversation analysis 19

development 87–8
disability 100–1

emancipatory research *see* justice
empirical practice 44
empowerment *see* justice
ethics 8, 21–3, 31, 43, 96, 114, 118, 120, 147–8, 149, 160–1, 189, 193
ethnocentrism 4

ethnography 5, 11, 13, 16, 18, 49–59, 63, 101, 104, 137–42, 1 45–6, 156
ethnomethodology 9, 182–3
evaluation 18, 65, 84–7, 144, 175, 177, 180–1, 192, 193, 198
evidence 159–60, 163, 187
evidence based practice 15, 25, 28, 44
expertise 117–9, 120–1, 128, 163

feminism 11, 37, 67, 93, 151, 172, 173–4, 177
fieldwork 53–4
focus groups 146–7

gender 61–4, 67–72, 73, 74, 125, 148, 152, 153
generalization 5, 7, 8, 14–5, 16, 125–6, 194–9
grounded theory 36, 42, 64, 141–2
groupwork 86

histories
    life histories 8, 150, 161
    oral histories 37, 150–1
homelessness 36, 50–59, 139

induction 7, 11, 17, 124, 136–7, 142, 197
infertility 75–81

insiders 101, 103–12, 157, 172–3
interpretive sociology 19
interviewing 10, 18, 30, 53, 60,
  63–6, 74, 142–50

justice based research 4, 73, 97–8,
  113, 168–76
  advocacy research 11
  emancipatory research 11, 15,
    83–99, 158
  empowerment research 85, 90,
    94–6, 97, 163–4
  user-led research 6

keyworking 55, 56, 57
knowledge
  common sense 191–2
  lay theory 8, 30
  practical knowledge 193
  tacit knowledge 192–3
  see also actors perspective and
    theory

language 19, 71
lay theory see knowledge
life history see histories
marxism 35–6, 39
masculinity see gender

narrative 8, 11, 15, 37–8, 73–82,
  150–4, 156

objectivity 9, 19, 38, 59, 112, 126–7,
  173
organization research 19–20, 40,
  41, 66
oral history see histories
outcomes 3, 5, 26–8, 97–8, 180,
  181–6

paradigms 23–6, 29–30, 31, 43
participatory research 15, 39, 84,
  86, 118, 121–2 see justice
participant observation 20, 21, 30,
  41, 51, 53–4, 101, 107, 138
positivism 66, 117, 123–7, 128
postmodernism 17, 38, 39, 66, 128,
  155, 170, 173–4
power 19, 85, 93–6, 148–9
practical knowledge see knowledge
practitioner research 10, 11, 104–8,
  119–23, 129–31, 158–64, 165
pragmatism 5, 14, 25, 26, 34,
  165
process 3, 10, 28, 97

qualitative research
  characteristics 6–8, 17–18
  development in social work
    32–46
quality issues 15, 26, 28, 115,
  125–7, 156, 195–6
quantitative research 26–31, 38, 40,
  170–2, 180, 194

realism 39, 66
reflection 101–2, 164–8
reflexivity 7, 11, 15, 61–2, 100–15,
  127–9, 164–5
relativism 25, 114, 174, 201
reliability see quality issues
representation 34, 38
risk 84, 101, 108, 164
Romanticism see Sentimentalism

self 38, 40, 91–93
sentimentalism 4, 175
simulated interviews see
  interviewing
social exclusion 6, 50, 84, 92
social policy 42, 69

social work practice 10, 11, 14–5, 31, 151, 195 *See* abuse, children, gender, homelessness, keyworking and youth social work

social work practice and research 3, 12, 15–7, 42–4, 64, 66–7, 130, 141, 158, 162–3

standpoint epistemology 172–3, 177

story telling *see* narrative

structuration 19

structures 15, 19, 71, 124

symbolic interactionism 8, 13, 17, 183

tacit knowledge *see* knowledge

text 19, 28, 101, 107–8, 154–5

theory 7, 15, 17, 40, 105–6, 128, 129, 189–93, 193, 197, 199–201. *See* actors perspective and knowledge

thick description 6, 42, 198–9

trust 97

trustworthiness *see* quality issues

user-led research *see* justice

uses of research 11, 58, 86, 118, 140–1, 159, 161–2, 186–9, 190

validity *see* quality issues

vignettes 125, 143

voice 102

what works? *See* evidence based practice

writing 89–90 *see* text

youth social work 83–99

Name Index

Abramson, J. 36, 41
Acker, J. 22
Adler, P. 101, 107
Adler, P. A. 101, 107
Agar, M. 7, 103
Allen, K. 130
Altheide, D. 22, 39, 192
Archbold, P. 22, 161
Arnold, R. 86
Atkinson, P. 5, 21, 25, 34, 45, 65, 75, 105, 107, 113, 137, 140, 155, 156, 161, 197
Aull Davies, C. 104
Avery, M. 86

Baldwin, M. 39, 41, 120, 122, 167
Bankhead-Greene, T. 146
Banks, C. 139
Barnes, M. 171
Barnsley, J. 87
Barone, T. 162, 171
Beck, C. 126
Beck, U. 164
Becker, H. 15, 26, 35, 193, 199
Behar, R. 73
Bein, A. 130
Belcher, J. 36, 41
Bell, S. 73, 74, 151
Bemak, F. 39
Benner, P. 119
Bernstein, S. 118, 131
Besa, D. 37
Best, J. 66
Biestek, F. 123
Blair, J. 181

Bloor, M. 53, 62, 161, 178
Bogdan, R. 175
Boje, B. 73
Borden, W. 38
Bourdieu, P. 55, 104
Bowen, D. 89, 161
Bradbury, H. 169, 178
Brenner, M. 135
Brodie, I. 190, 201
Brun, C. 33
Bruner, J. 73, 153
Bryant, I. 166, 167
Bryman, A. 27, 135, 136
Bull, R. 18, 108
Bulmer, M. 202
Burgess, H. 166
Burke, B. 86
Burman, E. 109
Butler, I. 31

Campbell, D. 182, 191
Capps, L. 73
Caracelli, V. 27, 29, 30, 31
Carr, D. 73
Carr, W. 164, 193
Chambers, R. 85, 87
Charon, R. 74
Chase, S. 73
Chelimsky, E. 27, 175, 188
Clifford, D. 81
Coady, N. 145
Cochran-Smith, M. 160
Coffey, A. 155
Cohen-Mitchell, J. 98
Collins, H. 192, 193

Collins, P. 63, 81
Colquhoun, D. 117
Condon, S. 37
Connell, R. 72
Connor, T. 41
Cook, J. 93, 97
Crabtree, B. 194
Critchley, S. 114
Cronbach, L. 185, 195, 196
Cronon, W. 73

Daly, J. 117
Davis, L. 37
Dean, R. 74
Delamont, S. 21, 105, 161, 197
Denzin, N. 13, 17, 33, 34, 45, 122, 15, 183
Derrida, J. 113
DeVault, M. 73
Dillenburger, K. 61
Dingwall, R. 16, 18, 21, 26, 31, 41, 156, 172, 175, 177
Dockery, G. 94
Dreyfus, H. 124
Drucker-Brown, S. 53
Dullea, K. 84, 95, 146

Edgar, I. 58, 138
Eisner, E. 8, 22, 33, 160, 163, 170, 195, 198
Elks, M. 162
Ellis, D. 87
Epstein, I. 118, 131
Eraut, M. 120
Eriksen, E. 160, 195
Evans, C. 40, 85, 86, 96, 176
Everitt, A. 91, 117, 118

Fahl, R. 164, 200
Farmer, E. 69, 70
Fawcett, B. 17, 26, 174, 178
Feuerstein, M-T. 95

Finch, J. 5, 22, 125, 187, 188, 189, 190, 202
Fish, B. 37, 151, 152, 153
Fisher, M. 26, 35, 40, 85, 96, 154, 164, 176
Flanagan, J. 119
Flick, U. 8, 9, 34, 36, 37, 38, 45, 143
Fontana, A. 63
Fook, J. 10, 116, 118, 121, 123, 126, 127, 128, 130, 131, 165, 166, 167, 178
Fonow, J. 93, 97
Fortune, A. 16, 138, 141, 142
Foucault, M. 71, 114
Fournier, D. 181
Frank, A. 73
Freire, P. 128
Frey, J. 63
Fuller, R. 10, 165

Garfinkel, H. 110
Garrison, J. 170
Garro, L. 73
Gaventa, J. 93
Gee, J. 73
Geertz, C. 6, 7, 38, 102, 104, 191, 195, 197, 198, 201, 202
Giddens, A. 19, 24, 30, 59, 111, 164
Gibbs, J. 146
Gilgun, J. 41, 42, 46, 118, 124, 130, 142
Glaser, B. 36, 150
Glassner, B. 66, 143
Glennerster, H. 42
Goldstein, H. 16, 32, 118, 141, 145
Gordon, L. 70
Gottman, E. 35
Gottschalk, S. 23
Gould, N. 16, 42, 46, 120, 136, 149, 154, 155, 165, 166, 167
Greene, J. 7, 25, 27, 29, 30, 31, 174, 190
Greenhalgh, T. 74
Greig, A. 149

Greil, A. 79
Grillo, R. 52
Guba, E. 22, 23, 24, 31, 126, 128, 129, 170
Gubrium, J. 73, 142, 144
Gulati, L. 78, 79, 82
Gupta, A. 78

Hacking, I. 107, 112, 201
Hall, B. 93
Hall, C. 19, 102, 108
Hall, T. 50, 54
Hammersley, M. 13, 25, 26, 65, 105, 115, 137, 140, 156, 161, 188, 191, 193
Haraway, D. 72
Harding, S. 93
Harlow, E. 66
Harré, R. 76
Harris, A. 136, 165
Harrisa, W. 130, 131
Harrison, B. 22
Hastrup, K. 59
Hawkins, L. 118, 121
Hearn, J. 66
Heron, J. 6, 39, 122
Heineman-Pieper, M. 42, 43
Hey, V. 154
Hick, S. 94
Holland, S. 64
Holstein, J. 73, 142, 144
hooks, b. 85
Housley, W. 19
Howe, D. 69, 70
Howe, K. 26
Huberman, A. 6, 7, 8, 34, 36, 184, 185, 186, 201
Hughes, M. 144
Humphrey, C. 162
Hunter, K. 74
Hurwitz, B. 74
Hutson, S. D. 52
Hyde, C. 37, 120, 124
Hyden, L. 74

Ixer, G. 102, 167

Jacob, E. 5
Jacob, M. 200, 201
Janesick, V. 6, 13, 163
Jarvis, P. 164, 166, 168
Jeffrey, P. 80
Jeffrey, R. 79, 82
Jindal, V. 76
Johnson, J. 22, 39, 192
Jokinen, A. 10, 17
Jones, J. 153
Juhila, K. 10
Just, P. 59

Kadushin, A. 64, 65
Kayser-Jones, J. 22, 161
Kellahear, A. 118, 120, 123
Kemmis, S. 164, 193
Kendall, P. 143
Kent, J. 97
Kirby, S. 87
Kitzinger, J. 146
Kirkhart, K. 162
Klein, P. 160
Kleinman, A. 74
Koenig, B. 22, 161
Krumer-Nevo, M. 37
Kushner, S. 199

Labov, B. 102, 114, 115
Laird, J. 74
Lang, N. 17, 31
Langellier, K. 76
Lather, P. 171, 200
Latimer, J. 113
Latour, B. 102, 114, 115
Law, J. 102, 106, 115
Lazar, B. 37
Lazzari, M. 36
Lee, R. 148
Le Riche, P. 21

Lever, J. 65
Lewis, J. 42
Liddiard, M. 52
Lincoln, Y. 13, 22, 24, 33, 34, 45, 122, 126, 128, 129, 170
Linde, C. 73
Lishman, J. 18, 23, 94, 118, 178
Lofland, J. 184, 185
Lofland, L. 184, 185
Loneck, B. 130
Long, A. 180, 186
Lorenz, W. 170
Lukes, S. 9
Lyon, E. 22
Lytle, S. 160

Macdonald, G. 5, 27
Maguire, P. 93
Majone, G. 42
Maluccio, A. 35, 41, 138
Markand, M. 164, 200
Marks, D. 109, 113
Martin, M. 93
Martin, R. 150, 151, 161
Mason, J. 125
Mattingley, C. 73, 74
Mauthner, M. 149
May, T. 23
Mayer, J. 35, 41, 154
McKay, D. 26
McKee, C. 94, 96, 175
McKeganey, N. 21, 30, 62
McKennah, K. 87
McIvor, G. 16, 159
McLennan, G. 26
McLeod, J. 158, 160, 178
McQuaide, S. 153, 154
Mertens, D. 85, 95
Merton, R. 14, 172, 173, 177, 178
Mezirow, J. 165
Miles, M. 6, 7, 8, 34, 36, 184, 185, 186, 201
Miller, G. 19, 20, 31, 156, 183
Miller, J. 66, 143, 164

Miller, R. 161
Miller, W. 194
Mishler, E. 73, 76, 82
Mizrahi, T. 36, 41
Mohr, W. 183
Monagahn, J. 59
Moran-Ellis, J. 63
Morgan, D. 62
Morrow-Kondos, D. 144
Mowbray, C. 139
Mullen, E. 125
Mullender, A. 84, 95, 146

Nag, M. 82
Nelson, C. 122

Oakley, J. 66
Ochberg, R. 73
Ochs, E. 73, 82
O'Hagan, K. 61
O'Kane, C. 148
Okely, J. 104
Olesen, V. 126, 174, 178
Oliver, M. 94, 95, 171
Oliver, S. 26, 176
Owen, M. 69, 70

Padfield, M. 62
Padgett, D. 10, 16, 31, 32, 37, 43, 46, 65, 130, 155, 162
Parton, N. 41, 69, 154, 200
Patton, M. Q. 26, 85, 202
Pawluch, D. 26
Pawson, R. 184
Pease, B. 128
Pease, K. 162
Pelto, G. 103
Pelto, P. 103, 140, 156
Petch, A. 10, 165
Philp, M. 70
Phillips, D. 23, 26
Pithouse, A. 13, 17, 18, 36, 138

Plummer, K. 74
Polanyi, M. 82, 192
Polkinghorne, D. 73
Pollard, A. 107
Polsky, H. 35
Pomerantz, A. 108
Popay, J. 40
Popkewitz, T. 26, 175
Poso, T. 10
Proctor, I. 62
Pugh, R. 195
Punch, K. 143, 145
Punch, M. 117

Ragin, C. 21
Reason, P. 39, 121, 169, 178
Rees, S. 35, 154
Reid, W. 3, 10, 13, 18, 25, 26, 27, 32, 35, 36, 44, 46, 130, 182, 193, 197
Reinharz, S. 93
Riessman, C. K. 8, 10, 32, 37, 38, 74, 75, 76, 79, 80, 81, 82, 85, 150, 151, 156, 162, 171, 174
Rorty, R. 26, 113
Rosaldo, R. 73
Rose, N. 109
Rosenwald, G. 73
Rubin, L. 65
Ruckdeschel, R. 17
Russell, A. 58, 138
Ryan, M. 117

Sacks, H. 110
Sandelowski, M. 74
Sands, R. 38
Sarbin, T. 73
Satyamurti, C. 35, 41, 138, 156
Scheff, T. 19
Schon, D. 3, 128, 165, 166, 178
Schwab, J. 193, 194
Schwandt, T. 26, 174, 193
Scott, D. 193
Scott, S. 63

Scriven, M. 196
Seale, C. 23, 25, 38, 40, 156, 194
Sen, A. 81, 82
Shaddish, W. 196
Shakespeare, P. 178
Shaw, A. 162, 192
Shaw, I. 6, 10, 13, 16, 18, 21, 22, 23, 25, 26, 28, 30, 39, 42, 115, 118, 125, 126, 130, 131, 144, 146, 147, 149, 154, 162, 167, 177, 178, 182, 192, 196, 201
Sheldon, B. 137
Sherman, E. 10, 13, 17, 32, 35, 36, 130
Sheppard, M. 60, 136, 156, 162
Shokeid, M. 106
Silverman, D. 19, 60, 75, 136, 186
Simon, H. 190
Sinclair, I. 27, 196
Smith, D. 21
Smith, J. 170
Smith, L. 160
Smith, N. 181
Spradley, J. 64, 145
Srinivison, M. 37
Stacey, J. 22
Stainton-Rogers, R. 109
Stake, R. 168, 190, 192, 198
Stancombe, J. 105, 113
Stanfield, J. 85, 171
Stanley, E. 91
Steier, F. 126, 129
Stenson, K. 19, 41, 70, 151
Stevens, J. 38, 152
Strathern, M. 104, 106
Strauss, A. 36, 64, 123, 150
Strong, P. 26
Swift, K. 67, 68, 70
Swigonski, M. 24

Tanner, K. 21
Tandon, R. 93
Taylor, C. 101, 113, 167, 178
Taylor, J. 149, 165
Taylor, S. 175

Thomas, N. 149
Thrasher, P. 139
Thyer, B. 5, 26
Tilley, N. 197
Timms, N. 35, 41, 154, 159
Tizard, J. 197
Trend, M. 28
Trethewey, A. 38
Trevillion, S. 156
Trinder, E. 174, 177
Trumball, D. 192, 198
Truman, C. 85, 92, 93, 97
Tyson, K. 43
Uberoi, P. 80

Vanderplaat, M. 80
Van Langenhove, L. 76

Wadsworth, Y. 121
Walden, T. 119
Ward, T. 36
Warren, L. 58

Weedon, C. 71
Weiss, C. 187, 201, 202
Wells, K. 117
West, C. 108, 152
White, H. 73
White, S. 60, 105, 109, 113, 115, 178
Whitmore, E. 39, 84, 89, 92, 93, 94, 96, 175
Whyte, W. 35
Wideman, G. 139
Williams, G. 40, 73
Williams, M. 23
Willis, P. 58
Wise, S. 91, 101, 107
Witkin, S. 23
Wolcott, H. 9
Wolgien, C. 145
Woolgar, S. 26, 101, 102
Wuest, J. 122

Yin, R. 182, 197
Young, K. 73